Our National Park System

Our National Park System

CARING FOR AMERICA'S GREATEST NATURAL
AND HISTORIC TREASURES

Dwight F. Rettie

FOREWORD BY STEWART L. UDALL

University of Illinois Press   URBANA AND CHICAGO

© 1995 by the Board of Trustees of the University of Illinois
Manufactured in the United States of America
C 5 4 3 2 1

This book is printed on acid-free paper.

Library of Congress Cataloging-in-Publication Data

Rettie, Dwight Fay, 1930–
      Our national park system : caring for America's greatest natural
  and historic treasures / Dwight F. Rettie : foreword by Stewart L.
  Udall.
         p.   cm.
  Includes bibliographical references (p.   ) and index.
  ISBN 0-252-02148-7 (cloth : acid-free paper)
      1. United States. National Park Service—History. 2. National
  parks and reserves—United States—History. I. Title.
  SB482.A4R48   1995
  333.78'3'0973—dc20   94-22632
                                                                 CIP

In memory of James C. Rettie

Contents

Illustrations follow page 122

Foreword

Stewart L. Udall

As a long-time friend of America's national parks, I am pleased to report that according to recent public opinion surveys National Park Service employees rank among the most trusted people in our society. But who, exactly, are these friendly men and women? And what is the nature of their challenging work? Such questions are rarely posed, much less answered.

The typical book about America's national parks is a lavishly illustrated travelogue: in essence, it provides the reader with a scenic tour from the Everglades to Yosemite, with other stops along the way. In these pages, however, my longtime friend Dwight Rettie takes us on a less well-trod and in many ways much more interesting path. His book offers an insider's tour, not of the parks themselves, but of the national park system and the National Park Service, the agency responsible for its care.

One could not find a better guide. As a Park Service and Department of the Interior employee, Rettie's career spanned momentous years; by his retirement in 1986, he had served under six presidents and nine Interior secretaries. During the sixties and seventies, he witnessed the addition of more than sixty new units to the national park system. In 1980, he saw its gross acreage double overnight with President Carter's signing of the Alaska Lands Bill. And during the decade that followed, he saw the system under siege as Interior Secretaries James Watt and Donald Hodel unsuccessfully tried to turn back the clock on conservation.

This book reflects the devotion of someone whose adult life has been inextricably intertwined with conservation and parks. It is obvious that Dwight has thought long and hard about the national park system over many years. He is intimately familiar with its tremen-

dous strengths, as he is with its troubling shortcomings. He under-
stands the challenges of the future as well as he does the lessons of
the past.

When Yellowstone, America's first national park, was established
122 years ago it was in many ways a fluke. Those who first articulated the national park idea did not understand its full implications.
In particular, they did not understand that the park concept would,
in time, come to be a crucible in which Americans began to forge a
more tender relationship with the land.

Today, however, it is abundantly clear that the national park idea
has indeed been a wonderful contribution to humankind. America's
parks are living reminders of the ultimate power and ordered beauty
of the natural world. Tens of millions of people travel endless miles
to see them. Our park system has inspired 125 other nations to set
aside parks of their own; about 3 percent of the Earth is now in parks,
nature reserves, and other conservation areas. Dwell on that, for it
is a miracle of sorts and becoming more so each day.

One of the great ironies of the American park system is that it was
assembled without benefit of a blueprint. What we enjoy today has
been stitched together over more than a century like a giant quilt—
park by park—by the loving hands of thousands of people who wanted to save something precious for their children and grandchildren.
In the words of former Park Service Director Russell Dickenson, "It
is hard to imagine how even a conscious plan could have achieved
so much so well." If each park is, as someone once said, an "island
of hope," then the American archipelago stretches from northern
Alaska to the Virgin Islands in the Caribbean to Guam in the Pacific,
half a world away.

Fortunately, Rettie's love for the parks does not blind him to the
challenges they now face. Certainly, no one is better qualified to di-
agnose the park system's troubles and prescribe a cure. Lacking an ideological ax to grind, he discusses, in meticulously balanced fashion, the
highly politicized (and often bizarre) process by which new parks and
monuments are established; the monumental intricacies of park planning and budgeting; the dramatic evolution of the ranger corps; the
dangerous belief held by some Park Service administrators that more
roads, visitors, and campgrounds are always better; the troubling deterioration of park system infrastructure; looming environmental
threats; and the difficulties posed by skyrocketing visitation.

The concluding chapter is a précis describing how to make the
agency more effective. In Dwight's view, "the greatest shortcoming
of the national park system is that for all its majesty, for all the irre-

placeable wonders it contains . . . for all the love that is bestowed upon it . . . it is not yet a real system." A unified mission and better management could help make the park system immune to assault from any quarter—a laudable goal all park lovers can embrace.

Dwight's book is a clarion call to action, a message that our park system is a living legacy, entrusted to the care of the National Park Service. Now, perhaps more than at any time in its history, the agency needs strong leadership and adequate funding to meet the challenges it faces. But even more than that, the system needs the vociferous and steadfast support of conservationists and other lovers of history and wild places and wild things.

So read this book, and then bring, if you haven't already, the national parks into your life. Seize every opportunity to visit them. If experience is any guide, they will enrich you beyond measure, for they are a great gift, one of our nation's most inspired and enduring creations.

Acknowledgments

Inspiration for writing this book came in major part from the late Dr. Albert Lepawsky of the Department of Political Science, University of California at Berkeley. His wise insights and warm enthusiasm helped shape and periodically renew my commitment for public service through a collegial friendship that spanned almost forty years.

I would like to express my gratitude to former colleagues in the National Park Service for their support during the writing of this book. I am especially indebted to the former director, Russ Dickenson, who was responsible for the career change that drew me to the Park Service and who contributed directly to this effort. Barry Mackintosh, NPS bureau historian, never failed to answer obscure questions and locate old data. Special thanks to Carol Aten, Warren Brown, Richard Curry, Tom DuRant, Brian Feeney, Boyd Finch, Mike Finley, Mario Fraire, Denis Galvin, Ross Holland, Reed Jarvis, Mike Lambe, Rick Lewis, Joan Mitchell, Duncan Morrow, Chuck Odegaard, Jerry Rogers, Bruce Sheaffer, Gloria Sullivan, Bob Utley, Dottie Whitehead, and Bryce Workman, and others cited in the notes. I am also grateful to former directors Gary Everhardt, Bill Whalen, the late Connie Wirth, and to the late Bill Mott.

I extend thanks and appreciation to Tim Frank of the Palm Beach Landmarks Commission and Jim Griffin for helpful information and insights on Mar-A-Lago; to Babbie and Dick Joyce aboard *Pharaon*, who helped in a special way; to Delores and John Parker on *Windsong II*; and to National Park Service associates Joan and Jim Stewart on *Gannet*. Advice and encouragement I received from Martin Duberman, from Sydelle Kramer, and from Randy Brock helped at important times during my writing. Thanks also to the librarians on the fifth floor of the main Broward County (Fla.) Public Library in Ft. Lauderdale and those in the Interior Department library in Washington, D.C. I am also grateful to Judith McCulloh, Elizabeth G. Dulany, and Theresa L. Sears of the University of Illinois Press for helping to guide the manuscript along toward publication. My special thanks to my editor, Rita Darlene Disroe, whose skills every reader will unknowingly appreciate at least as much as I.

Finally, I am most of all indebted to my wife, Karen, who gave up three years' world cruising and worked so that I might write the book that could not be written at sea.

For errors of fact or judgment, I share no credit; they are mine alone.

Abbreviations

F.Y.	Fiscal Year
NB	National Battlefield
NBP	National Battlefield Park
NHL	National Historic Landmark
NHP	National Historical Park
NHRes	National Historical Reserve
NHS	National Historic Site
NHT	National Historic Trail
NL	National Lakeshore
NM	National Monument
NMem	National Memorial
NMP	National Military Park
NP	National Park
NPres	National Preserve
NPS	National Park Service
NRes	National Reserve
NR	National River
NRA	National Recreation Area
NS	National Seashore
NSR	National Scenic River
NST	National Scenic Trail
OMB	Office of Management and Budget
OPM	Office of Personnel Management
WSR	Wild and Scenic River

Note: The word "park" with a small "p" is used broadly and may apply to *any* unit of the national park system. "Park" with a capital "P" always means a National Park. The National Park Service is also referred to as NPS, the Park Service, or just the Service.

Introduction

Few features of the American landscape and culture have the name recognition of the National Parks. They are visited by millions of people every year and revered by countless others who may never visit. For many people the parks are more than merely beautiful places, more than history and heritage, touching instead something deep in the human spirit, reminding us that we are part of a great cosmic enterprise in which the mysteries that surround its workings are cause for thought, reflection, and reverence. The parks kindle the wish to discover the world in which we live and to sample the world of our forebears and the places and things that bridge the gulf of time that separates us from our past. The parks are something about which poets write and into which philosophers delve. They are things to capture on film, canvas, and by the printed word. Our National Parks are places to be experienced with all one's senses.

The first National Park, Yellowstone, was created in 1872. Since that year, more than 365 other areas that collectively make up what is now called the *national park system* have joined Yellowstone. The modern system includes historic sites, battlefields, recreation areas, and other units across a wide geographic expanse. Since 1916 the national park system has been in the care of the National Park Service, a bureau in the U.S. Department of the Interior.

The existence and permanence of the national park system are largely taken for granted. However, during the years of its growth the national park system has lost some five dozen areas. The second National Park, Mackinac National Park in Michigan, created only three years after Yellowstone, was abolished in 1895. Some parks were transferred to other federal, state, or local governments. Other parks were returned to private ownership. One park was never given any form of on-site protection, and after thirty years looters had stripped it of all reason for existence.

Proposals have been advanced from time to time to divest other areas, on grounds Congress or a president made a mistake in adding an area to the system. Tastes may change or the facts on which earlier decisions were based may now be believed to be untrue. Some park "hit lists" have even been drawn up by professionals in the National Park Service. As recently as mid-1992 the then secretary of the Interior endorsed carving off a seventy-four-acre tract at Petroglyph National Monument in New Mexico for the private development of a golf course. Is it possible a consensus could be forged at some time in the future to execute someone's hit list?

About a dozen park areas have been authorized by Congress but never acquired or, if acquired, never developed for public visitation or use. How much discretion ought the National Park Service have to ignore new or authorized areas? For what reasons and for how long? At what cost to the resource? Some new parks were contingent on donations of land that have never materialized. Should the national park system depend on voluntary donations of nationally significant resources?

The modern creation of new park system areas by Congress has become what has been widely called a "park barrel," in which previously existing high standards of park selection have been compromised in the interest of local economic development or to honor someone unimportant. There were, however, no agreed-upon standards or guidelines to shape the growth of the national park system. It just grew site by site in response to the pleading of a constituency or the foresight or ambition of one or more members of Congress. New units were only rarely first proposed by the National Park Service.

The absence of agreed-upon standards for site selection and the lack of any national plan or strategy by which the merits of individual proposals may be weighed is a principal cause of today's park barrel. The political agendas of recent presidents to avoid enlargement of the federal estate have left the National Park Service without its own agenda, thereby leaving the initiative for all new park areas to the whim of Congress and interest groups.

The National Park Service has often been a reluctant bride in the wedding of new sites and areas to the system, especially those that cross new frontiers of representation or move into a new environment. In the early days much of the Service was uncomfortable managing historic sites; and in later times large parts of the Service only reluctantly took on responsibilities for the urban National Recreation Areas.[1]

The National Parks and Conservation Association, a strong park system support group, has argued in times past that the National Park Service should be removed from the Department of the Interior and given the status of an independent agency. Others have suggested transfer of the parks or selected park management functions (such as visitor accommodations and food services) to a nonfederal or quasi-governmental institution. It is argued the parks would then be better insulated from pressures that favor over-development or excessive visitation.

Just how permanent is the national park system? How well shielded is it from interests that would shrink its size or manipulate permitted uses? How can the processes by which units are added to the system gain the integrity necessary to make every new unit secure for all time? Is absolute permanence an essential characteristic of the national park system? Or should the national park system be reviewed from time to time and units eliminated or altered to reflect contemporary thought and values?

Once secured, how can decision making and programming of capital investments and maintenance adequately deal with a long-term commitment to preservation? The resources of the national park system are often fragile. Sometimes they have been badly abused. Natural healing processes will take several generations of investment and care. All this must be accomplished, however, in a governmental structure whose longest time-line is the six-year term of a United States senator.

The National Park Service as well as its supporters perceive that the national park system is in trouble. Discussions focus on the need for large-scale reinvestment in the park system infrastructure, such as roads, bridges, water and sewer systems, and visitor facilities. The system also needs additional staff and new types of skills to upgrade resource protection or improve the quality of services to park visitors. In addition, the parks are the object of often serious threats from external forces: air and water pollution, urban encroachments, blight and decay, the spread of exotic animal or plant species, and other adversities. There is also need to eliminate the large land acquisition backlog—rounding out existing parks—to save money in the long run and prevent possible incompatible or damaging developments in the short term.

The National Park Service recently issued a report characterizing the bureau as "beset by controversy, concern, weakened morale, and declining effectiveness."[2] The report details a myriad of internal staffing, management, and organizational problems requiring the attention of the agency's top leadership and that of the administration and Congress.

In this book, I assert that important policy issues—including those mentioned above and others detailed in the chapters to follow—affect the existence, permanence, and condition of the national park system. Those problems need to be addressed by a broad spectrum of the interested public and by the president and the Congress. The time to do that is now, while supporters are concerned for the parks and while the National Park Service is sensitized to the need for change.

Today's circumstances are the consequence of a long history of concern for the best of America's natural and historic places. A complete history of the National Park idea and of the growth and development of the National Park Service as a bureau are beyond the scope of this book. Readers are encouraged to refer to sources cited in the bibliography, especially the books by former directors Albright, Hartzog, and Wirth and the scholarly studies by Ise, Rothman, and Runte. The following historical overview sets the stage for the issues discussed in later chapters.

Yellowstone National Park existed for forty-four years before there was a National Park Service to care for it. The first National Park did not, however, come about because of any organized movement or articulate national objective.[3] It came into being because a small group of men experienced it first hand and agreed among themselves that it ought to be set aside as a public park.[4] In those years the public domain—lands owned by the federal government as a consequence of the nation's westward expansion—was the object of purchase and claim, from homesteads to gold mines. Without a law to withdraw the lands from public entry, the wonders that Yellowstone holds would have surely transferred to private ownership. At the urging of the men who had experienced Yellowstone in person, the support of several writers and publishers and a small group in Congress, the act creating Yellowstone National Park passed the Congress and was signed by President Ulysses S. Grant on March 1, 1872.[5] In the early days funds and staff to care for the park were meager to nonexistent. Poaching and trespass were common. The pattern would continue for over thirty years.

In 1906, in response to concerns about the destruction and looting by pot hunters of Indian cliff dwellings and other Native American ruins in the Southwest, Congress passed the Antiquities Act that gave broad new protection for historic and prehistoric artifacts on the public domain through fines for looting and injuring them. The

law also gave the president authority to "declare by public proclamation historic landmarks, historic and prehistoric structures, and
other objects of historic or scientific interest situated upon lands
owned or controlled by the Government of the United States to be
national monuments."[6] The law was used by President Theodore
Roosevelt to create Petrified Forest, Devils Tower, El Morro, and Mon-
tezuma Castle National Monuments and to begin a long process of
saving parts of the Grand Canyon of the Colorado. The Antiquities
Act has been used by more than a dozen presidents to create national monuments.

Between 1872 and 1916 thirty-six areas were set aside by Congress
and the president in units that would become part of the domain
administered by the National Park Service upon its creation in 1916.
The bureau was created to care for the parks and monuments then
administered by the U.S. Department of the Interior. At the time other
units were administered by the General Land Office, the Department
of Agriculture, the War Department, and an office in the District of
Columbia.[7] Between creation of the National Park Service and a major reorganization in 1933 some eighty-four new areas were set aside
that would one day be part of the system. Of that number thirty-six
were assigned to offices other than the Park Service and two were
authorized but never established by the Park Service.

In 1933 President Franklin D. Roosevelt enlarged the domain under NPS jurisdiction by transferring to it fifty-six parks, national monuments, battlefields, national cemeteries, and Washington, D.C., sites.
The move was prompted by the pleading of Director Horace Albright,
who saw the move as one that would make the National Park Service truly a national agency and give it a broadened constituency that
would assure more attention (and money) from Congress.

The early years of the National Park Service were times of struggle
for its leadership to gain the funds and people necessary to care for
the parks.[8] Collateral work to develop a cadre of park professionals
to carry out the day-to-day responsibilities in the parks was no less
important. No such line of work—combining resource-related skills
and services for a growing number of visitors—previously existed.

The early units managed by NPS were largely natural area parks and
national monuments in the West. It was not until the reorganization
of 1933 that the Service's agenda took on major responsibilities for
historic areas and resources. The years of the New Deal also saw NPS
overseeing the operations of as many as 600 camps of the Civilian
Conservation Corps that provided Depression era employment for
more than 120,000 men. A total of 118 CCC camps were in units of

the national park system, where enrollees constructed roads, bridges, buildings, and hundreds of recreation facilities, many of which are still in use today.[9] CCC funding also paid for the first sizable group of biologists working in the parks, numbering as many as 27.

During the 1920s and 1930s the Park Service played a leading part in the development of park systems at the state level. The Service helped in the formation of the National Conference on State Parks that sparked the growth of new state systems and helped professionalize agencies rampant with political patronage. NPS also took on the actual development of areas that were later turned over to the states. A group of parks dubbed "National Recreation Demonstration Areas" was put together through the federal purchase of submarginal agricultural lands that were converted into parks. Almost all of them still serve public park needs in either state or federal jurisdiction.

With the addition of new historic sites by the reorganization of 1933, new legislation broadened the NPS sphere of influence in historic preservation, such as happened with passage of the Historic Sites Act of August 21, 1935. This law authorized the Park Service to engage in surveys and other assistance under a national policy to "preserve for public use historic sites, buildings and objects of national significance for the inspiration and benefit of the people of the United States."[10]

The law inaugurated the national historic landmarks program, under which the secretary of the Interior could designate sites and structures not in federal ownership, thereby giving them the prestige associated with a "national" designation and at least some color of protection.[11] The law also authorized new areas for addition to the National Park Service but only if no federal funds were involved. The first area added under the law was Jefferson National Expansion Memorial in St. Louis, Missouri.

As long as the National Park Service has been associated with the field of historic preservation, the Service has struggled with the limits for its engagement with historic areas. The nominal standard for such involvement begins with the notion that any area must have national significance to qualify for NPS management. As will be explained in a later chapter on park system nomenclature, national significance has very much to do with the eye of the beholder. Sometimes disagreements over whether a site is nationally significant take the form of esoteric disputes between differing historical perspectives. In other instances, such differences boil down to the politics of management by a federal agency versus administration by a state or local government or by a private body.

During World War II the parks and the Service retrenched in a major way. Appropriations to NPS dropped from $21.1 million in 1940 to $4.6 million in 1944. Recovery came back quickly, however, and by 1947 funding was back up to $26 million. Visitation was also growing and the backlog of needs and deferred maintenance was getting out of hand. By the time Conrad L. Wirth became director in late 1951, the Service was plagued by decrepit facilities of all types and inadequate facilities to meet growing visitation levels. Wirth's answer was to invent MISSION 66, a ten-year reinvestment and development program, which he presented to President Dwight D. Eisenhower in January 1956. The president gave the program his support and so did Congress, which appropriated more than $1 billion for MISSION 66 projects over the next ten years.

The year 1966, which saw the end of the MISSION 66 effort, also saw the beginning of a new and wider range of NPS responsibilities in the field of historic preservation. In that year Congress passed the Historic Preservation Act, which defined major new departures for the entire preservation movement at all levels of government and in private efforts. NPS would oversee a National Register of Historic Places, keeping tabs on sites, structures, and objects of not only national significance, but also those associated with state and local interest. NPS also administered a program of grants-in-aid to the states for historic preservation purposes. The new law also created the Advisory Council on Historic Preservation with responsibilities for coordinating federal actions in the field and with the unique authority to "comment" on federal actions that it believed could adversely affect historic resources.[12]

These "exterior" programs in historic preservation suffered from the outset, being regarded by many NPS professionals as something in which the Service simply should not be engaged. The Service has usually found new departures difficult to assimilate into its perceived mission. In part for that reason, the external programs in historic preservation were reorganized early in the Carter administration. The secretary of the Interior consolidated them with the recreation grant-in-aid functions of the Bureau of Outdoor Recreation into a new bureau, the Heritage Conservation and Recreation Service (HCRS). The new bureau was, however, short-lived. In 1981 the external programs were returned to the National Park Service when HCRS was abolished by Secretary of the Interior James Watt.

The 1960s also saw a new environmental ethic emerging in public policy and in public support for new conservation initiatives under the leadership of Presidents Kennedy and Johnson and Secretary of the Interior Stewart L. Udall. In those years a "last chance" effort succeeded in saving irreplaceable beaches and waterside resources at seashore and lakeshore parks on the Atlantic, Gulf of Mexico, and Pacific Coasts and Great Lakes.

Other national legislation during the 1960s and 1970s was also having an impact on management of areas by the National Park Service. The Wilderness Act of 1964,[13] which gave statutory sanction to road-free areas, set in motion a process for studying and subsequently designating such areas on lands administered by the Park Service and other federal land management agencies. In 1970 the National Environmental Policy Act[14] caused major changes in the way in which federal project planning would be accomplished. This new law required levels of public disclosure unknown before, compelled public involvement in federal project planning, and forced all agencies to consider and assess the environmental impacts of proposed actions. After the Park Service organic act, no single law has probably ever had such profound and enduring influence on the work of NPS. Also in 1970 Congress gave its first official recognition to the idea and concept of a *national park system*. This law and its consequences are discussed in detail in the following chapter.

In 1971 Congress passed the Alaska Native Claims Settlement Act (ANCSA)[15] to reconcile the land claims of Alaska's Native Americans and the often competing claims arising out of Alaska having become a state in 1959. ANCSA also contained provisions permitting the president to withdraw from the operation of the public land laws (homesteading, mining, and so forth) up to 80 million acres in Alaska "suitable for addition to or creation as units of the National Park, Forest, Wildlife Refuge, and Wild and Scenic Rivers Systems." The law and withdrawals would remain in effect for five years or until Congress acted. Following two years of study, Secretary of the Interior Rogers C. B. Morton, recommended the addition of some 32.3 million acres to the national park system.

When the Senate bogged down in considering the complicated and controversial proposals for the Alaska lands, President Jimmy Carter took the proverbial bull by the horns and a scant seventeen days before the withdrawals were due to expire he used the Antiquities Act authority to proclaim fifteen new national monuments and two expansions of existing monuments. In 1980 the lands were sorted out in new legislation, the Alaska National Interest Lands Conservation Act (ANILCA).[16] That law added more than 47 million acres to the national park system—far more than was proposed originally by the previous administration.

Since the end of World War II the national park system has grown from 180 to some 367 units and has doubled in acreage. Visitation has increased from about 20 million to over 364 million.[17] Appropriations have increased from about $5.5 million ($36.8 million in constant 1990 dollars) to well over $1 billion in 1994. The Service's tasks have become more complicated in the wake of revised understandings of the effects of actions and developments on the environment. Other laws relating to endangered species, toxic and hazardous materials, workplace safety, accessibility for the disabled, relocation assistance, and the government-wide impact of nondiscrimination laws and policies have greatly complicated and expanded the responsibilities of NPS managers and staff. These corollary duties have often been placed upon the system without the coincident addition of funds or staff.

The National Park Service now manages areas, sites, buildings, artifacts, and works of art of inestimable value. Whether the numbers associated with growth and other realities, particularly in recent years, spell adequacy or disaster (or something in between) is the subject of later chapters.

The modern national park system is a complicated array of natural and historic resources, managed by an equally complicated system of people and financial assets. In the following chapters, I hope to sort through the complications and discover threads and meanings that can shape the future of the system.

NOTES

1. In the early days Directors Mather and Albright sought to add various historic sites to the domain of the Park Service. Both men had an interest in things historic, but, more particularly, they saw such additions as an expedient means for enlarging the political constituency of the bureau east of the Mississippi.

2. *National Parks for the 21st Century,* 4.

3. The year 1872 is traditionally associated with the beginning of the national park system, but nineteen areas now included in the system had their origins earlier than Yellowstone. Some people claim that Yosemite was really the first National Park inasmuch as Congress undertook to create that park in 1864 through transfer of land to the state of California for "public use, resort, and recreation . . . inalienable for all time." The federal park was established in 1890 and in 1906 the lands ceded to the state were returned to become part of modern Yosemite NP. It is also possible to argue that Hot Springs NP (Ark.) was the beginning. It was reserved from the public domain in 1832, though it did not garner the title National Park until 1921. The other early units included parks in Washington, D.C. (1790); Ford's Theatre (1866);

and twelve National Cemeteries (1863 to 1870), all of which are now part of the national park system.

4. In 1870 a well-appointed expedition visited Yellowstone under the leadership of Henry D. Washburn, a former congressman and Civil War general. Washburn and others wrote glowing articles about the wonders they had seen, sparking others to visit the area, including the U.S. Geological Survey, photographer William Jackson, and painter Thomas Moran. Moran's large canvas "Grand Canyon of the Yellowstone" was hung in the Capitol, and can be credited with "speaking louder than a thousand words" on behalf of the park.

5. 17 STAT. 32.

6. 34 STAT. 225. It is interesting to note that scenery or natural area values were not included in the list of reasons for creating national monuments. Needless to say the words "historic or scientific interest" have served as adequate. For an account of the passage of the Antiquities Act, see Rothman, *Preserving Different Pasts*, 34–51.

7. The National Capital Parks, the National Mall, and the White House were part of the original L'Enfant plan to establish a permanent national capital, beginning with seventeen public reservations purchased in the early years, and now made up of some three hundred sites. The National Capital Parks were managed by the Office of Public Buildings and Public Parks of the National Capital until 1933, when they were transferred to the National Park Service.

8. See Appendix 5 and figure 1. For an account of the early years, see Albright, *Birth of the National Park Service*.

9. For a firsthand account of the Park Service role in the Civilian Conservation Corps, see Wirth, *Parks, Politics, and the People*. Wirth was the NPS official primarily responsible for the program. He later served as NPS director from 1951 to 1964.

10. 49 STAT. 666.

11. National Historic Landmarks have no legally enforceable protection solely by virtue of that designation. The mere declaration, however, affords a modicum of nonlegal protection that has had a surprisingly durable record of success. The landmark program is regarded by many people, especially within the Service, as a useful means to relieve the pressure of adding less than suitable sites to the system.

12. Although the Advisory Council on Historic Preservation has no authority to veto federal (or local) actions that might adversely affect a historic property, in practice its power to "comment" on such actions has caused many proposed actions to be modified and some to be abandoned entirely. The council, made up of private citizens and representatives of federal agencies, has a distinguished record of successes against a collection of formidable economic and political forces.

13. 78 STAT. 890.

14. 83 STAT. 852.

15. 85 STAT. 688.

16. 94 STAT. 2371.

17. NPS is in 1994 engaged in a massive revision of its visitation statistics—largely downward. Official estimates have dropped from about 350 million (1991) to 267 million (1991, calculated in 1994.) See note t at Appendix 5.

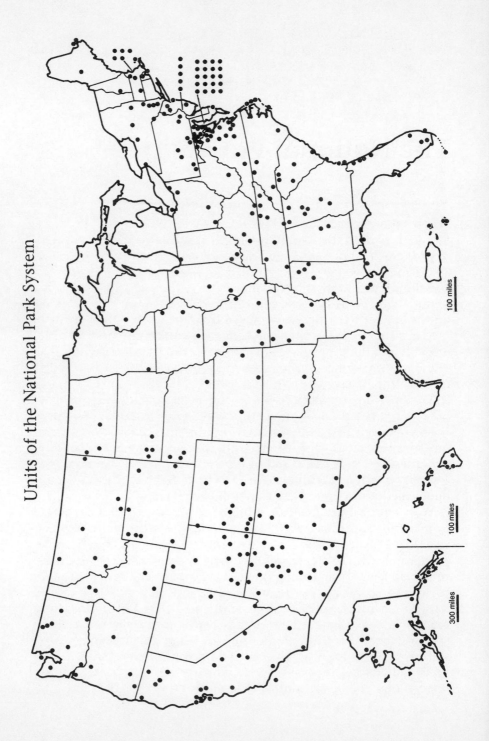

Units of the National Park System

ONE

The National Park System

When Yellowstone National Park was set aside on March 1, 1872, the first such park in the world, no one then foresaw that it would one day become part of a uniquely American conglomerate of more than 365 sites—the *national park system*.

Before creation of the National Park Service in 1916 the parks, monuments, battlefields, and historic sites that would one day make up the system were loosely managed by staffs in the Department of the Interior, the Department of Agriculture, the Army, and an office of parks and buildings serving facilities in the District of Columbia. There was no connection between the agencies involved or the sites for which they were responsible.

The first time the word "system" was used in describing parks we have today was probably in 1918, by the man who would become the second director of the National Park Service, Horace M. Albright. Albright is credited with having written the first statement containing criteria for new parks, and in it he referred to the "national park system" collectively.[1] However, in 1918 three National Parks were not under the jurisdiction of the National Park Service.[2]

Years later former Director Albright wrote about what he meant by a "national park *system*."[3] "When we had organized the Park Service in 1917, each of the fifteen existing national parks was an independent entity. Gradually we hired new superintendents, enunciated our policies for managing the parks, added to the field staffs, and begun to make them feel they were part of a National Park Service rather than just employees at an individual park." Two years later Albright added insight into those early perceptions about the national park system:[4] "It is a lofty but erroneous belief that Stephen Mather and I were great idealists, that we indulged in philosophical discussions and charted the ways we would carry out our dreams for the reservations under our control. There wasn't any magnificent master plan, only a series of problems that had to be solved as they arose. We improvised as we went along."

Though books written about the National Park Service and system abound with lofty descriptors of their significance—of the great contributions that their existence has made to the quality of both personal lives and the life of the nation, and of their importance for the future—little exists to define the nature and substance of the system. For all of its history, the national park system has been essentially an improvisation.

The first congressional recognition of the resources administered by the National Park Service as a "system" did not come until 1970, when Congress sought to legislatively include everything then under NPS jurisdiction in a single coherent system. Congress declared that

> these areas, though distinct in character, are united through their interrelated purposes and resources into one national park system as cumulative expressions of a single national heritage; that individually and collectively, these areas derive increased national dignity and recognition of their superb environmental quality through their inclusion jointly with each other in one national park system preserved and managed for the benefit and inspiration of all the people . . .; and that it is the purpose of this Act to include all such areas in the System.[5]

Congress clearly recognized that the national park system is something more than the sum of its parts. Taken together it is a statement about our national patrimony and a reflection of "high public value[s]." The system includes "any area of land and water now or hereafter administered . . . through the National Park Service."[6]

However, there never has existed any substantive definition of such a system. If anything managed by the Park Service is part of the system, what is or ought to be managed by NPS? What is a concept or plan against which elements of the system might be described or valued? In the famous 1918 policy letter that Horace Albright wrote for the signature of Secretary of the Interior Franklin K. Lane the focus of new parks was to be on "scenery of supreme and distinctive quality or some natural feature so extraordinary or unique as to be of national interest and importance . . . [through] areas which express in . . . the highest terms the particular class or kind of exhibit which they represent."

Albright's language suggests that the system was something intended to "represent" different scenery and natural features. To the extent such a description captured his grand design for a system, its emphasis was on securing that which was unique and of the highest quality, rather than defining the scope or limits of things to be represented. At the same time that Albright wrote this policy letter, he and Mather were seeking to enlarge the system to include lands east of the Mississippi, the most notable successes being Great Smoky Mountains (Tenn., N.C.), Mammoth Cave (Ky.), and Shenandoah (Va.) National Parks.

Directors of the National Park Service have not generally had much to say about a grand design for the system. The director in the Bush administration, James M. Ridenour, suggested that the national park system might already or soon be completed, at least with respect to natural areas. He also said that

> we can't continue to expand the system indefinitely. There are limits. As far as I'm aware, no one has ever run the 100-yard dash in nothing flat. In the same way, we can't transform the whole of the United States into a national park . . . I would not want to see our "crown jewels" suffer further deterioration at the expense of adding new parks that might more readily fit into the management categories of state and local governments or private management by individuals and organizations.[7]

Former Director Russell E. Dickenson, who held that office from 1980 to 1985, has written that ". . . the 'System' must continue to evolve, sensitive to each generation's values, its heroes and heroines, and . . . it is impossible to 'blueprint' the System. With the apparent concern for environmental and conservation issues, especially by the media, I would not expect to see any dilution of public support for a truly first class NP System."[8] Dickenson has further characterized the system as "a wide spectrum of resources—natural, historical, and recreational—that taken together share a remarkable similarity to the geographic and ethnic pluralism of our culture. It is hard to imagine how even a conscious plan could have achieved so much so well."[9]

Like Dickenson, William J. Whalen, who served as director from 1977 to 1980, also did not believe a grand design was possible. Whalen maintained that the "Congress will always propose and dispose. The best the NPS can do is shape the proposals so they make sense from an operational standpoint."[10] And in the years during which Whalen served as director the size of the national park system doubled through addition of the great Alaska parks and the beginning of what were to become known as "park barrel" bills in the Congress. Under the deft legislative hand of the then chairman of the Interior Subcommittee on National Parks and Territories, Phillip Burton of California, an Omnibus Bill was passed and signed that created eighteen new parks, made additions to twenty-nine existing areas, and mandated new area studies on nine others. The Whalen years saw the most extensive growth of the national park system ever.

While Whalen was witness to much new growth, by far the most elaborate grand design for the national park system was the intellectual creation of Director George B. Hartzog, Jr., who served in that position from 1964 to 1972. Under Hartzog's tutelage the National Park Service professional staff created a thematic plan for the national park system, published in 1972.[11] The plan began with historic and cultural resources, producing an elaborate outline of the nation's history and culture. Its premise was that the role of the national park system should embrace representation of all facets of American history, either through the direct ownership and management of park units representing each facet or by designating units of national significance that would remain in other ownerships. The emphasis, however, was on National Park Service ownership. A later plan component, similarly arranged thematically, covered natural area resources, physiographic types, land forms, biotic communities, and so forth.[12]

The idea behind both plan elements was to develop an outline of a completely representative park system. Each of the then existing units of the system was categorized into the appropriate theme. Once that was done, gaps would be obvious, as well as instances of over-representation. According to NPS Bureau Historian Barry Mackintosh, the analysis sparked by the 1972 *National Park System Plan* suggested a gap of at least 196 historic site/themes and more than 300 facets of natural history. The 1972 plan was used to help support official Park Service positions on proposed park system additions, either pro or con.

Unfortunately, the plan was flawed in several aspects. First, it said nothing about the quality of theme representations, providing no clear way to decide when a theme is well enough represented. Second, there is no way to screen out proposals that although they may fill a gap, do so only poorly. Third, the plan had no way of recognizing the cumulative merit of sites that might have multiple thematic characteristics. Robert M. Utley, a former director of the Office of Archeology and Historic Preservation, who held that position in 1973, recently wrote: "Remember how silly we looked in the early seventies when our elaborate 'National Park System Plan' showed that we were over-represented in Abraham Lincoln sites and so could not support acceptance of the prime Lincoln site in Springfield."[13] Likewise, former Director Russell E. Dickenson has characterized the 1972 national park system plan as "pie-in-the-sky and overly ambitious."[14]

Although flawed in a number of small ways, the 1972 plan had two major faults that doomed it to virtual disuse, except as a general analytical support.

- It had no sanction by Congress, and
- It was never the object of formal external review by subject matter specialists, the academic community, affected and concerned interest groups, or the general public.[15]

To be sure, position papers and official testimony on proposed additions to the national park system have made reference to the thematic structure, either in support of a site or as evidence it was not needed because the theme was already well enough represented in the system. No evidence suggests, however, that Congress has taken the plan seriously, either as a device to search for new areas or as a means to evaluate the appropriateness of a proposed addition. And there is really no way of knowing how the thematic approach would be received generally if it were placed on some form of public review. Scholars and subject matter specialists would likely haggle over the details of taxonomy and terminology. Such classification schemes are subject to infinite variability, depending on the perspective or discipline involved in their creation. There is no reason to suspect, however, that the thematic outline developed by Park Service professionals is in any way technically deficient.

It is far less certain that outside interest groups and the public would share the enthusiasm of the technicians for the thematic plan. One objection was articulated by Ronald Foresta in *America's National Parks and Their Keepers:* "Perhaps some representative of exposed Silurian rock face should be preserved on a federally owned site (although I cannot see why). There is no reason for such a site to be called a park, however, or for it to be part of the national park system unless it has more to recommend it than pure representativeness."[16]

Structuring the content of the national park system around the detailed subject matter outline of an academic treatise on history or nature study, however carefully crafted, is unlikely to enthrall people whose appreciation for the system is often, and perhaps largely, emotional, aesthetic, and highly personal. It is unclear whether some version of the thematic approach might someday serve as a meaningful guide to Congress on rounding out the national park system. Congress would need to be involved in its further development for it to be so.

To the extent that the thematic approach is a useful analytical tool for National Park Service professionals it is still available today, in updated form, in two more recent publications, one on history and prehistory and a second on natural history.[17] The character and use of the new document are described as follows: "This publication is not a strategy, plan, or proposal for expanding the national park system. It provides a thematic framework for evaluating nominations for new parks and plans for managing parks already in the system. [It is] . . . intended primarily to help answer the question of suitability by outlining what examples of a specific resource type are currently represented in the National Park System."[18]

Both new theme listings retain the basic structure developed in the 1970s, with several consolidations and expansions. Changes are characterized as important for history and prehistory and minor for natural history. An extract of the theme classification system for both historical and natural areas is located in Appendix 3. The examples selected illustrate both the complexity of the thematic approach and its rather arcane structure.

The concept of a representative national park system, whether based on a thematic outline or not, leaves behind places associated with ideas, processes, and other intangibles. NPS Associate Director Denis P. Galvin has illuminated this problem in an article exploring the site-relatedness of the creative process associated with the poetry of Robert Frost. The article refers to a recently authorized study of sites associated with the early history of jazz in New Orleans and a study then underway of painters and sculptors. Galvin visited the Robert Frost farm in Derry, New Hampshire, a place where Frost lived, farmed, taught school, and wrote poetry from 1900 to 1911. The site is a National Historic Site and part of the New Hampshire state park system. Reflecting on the farm, Galvin wrote:

> visitors do not come because the farm is a rural exemplar . . . [they] come to discover something tucked away in a room perhaps or in an angle of land that inspired a thought burnished to a line and cherished for a lifetime . . . To love the poem "Mending Wall" it is not necessary to see the wall . . . but seeing it heightens my wonder at the act of creativity it inspired . . . Here creativity and place were linked. The preservation of such places can provide a measure of our culture as meaningful as battlefields or birthplaces.[19]

The site-relatedness of the National Park Service and system has posed other problems and dilemmas. For years, the Park Service had philosophical and practical problems assimilating its responsibilities for the ships and other maritime resources now part of San Francisco Maritime NHP. The vessels, some of wood and subject to extraordinary maintenance requirements and esoteric resource management, were not sites, not places in any sense familiar to the professionals in the Park Service. For nearly a decade, I can remember hearing the entreaties of the historic preservation staff in meetings of the directors' executive staff for attention to and resources for the San Francisco "fleet." The jury is still out about whether the Park Service can provide the necessary care for those valued properties. Separate legislative authorization (passed in 1988) and appropriations and its own responsible superintendent will assuredly help.

In another attempt to plan for the national park system, Congress passed legislation in 1970 that set up a process by which the Park Service would conduct new area studies on a regular basis and submit to the Congress annually a list of twelve proposed additions to the system. In this way, Congress thought, the system would be filled out on an orderly and regular basis, giving Congress a shopping list from which to make final decisions as to new areas.

However, devising a list of a dozen proposed areas, in order of priority, proved to be an impossible task. Richard C. Curry, the then associate director for legislation has observed, "In those days we would not even send up a list . . . in priority order for fear of offending the local member and/or the committee of Congress."[20] One or two lists went to Congress, but the process quickly broke down because of budget priorities and other policies of the then administration that bottled up the list time after time and month after month, sometimes in the office of the secretary of the Interior, sometimes in the office of Management and Budget (part of the Executive Office of the president.)

As a result of this failed process, no regular funding was provided for new area studies. The program was actually starved at both ends, with no studies and no lists. Soon Congress gave up expecting the list and the Park Service gave up all efforts to create one. Thus for much of the 1980s the National Park Service conducted virtually no new area studies on its own initiative. Congress did direct various studies and many of those ultimately led to new park areas—almost uniformly in spite of formal communications from the administration to Congress that it opposed the site. The Reagan-Watt-Hodel years were so consistently negative on every new area proposal that Congress began ignoring the views expressed by administration witnesses. The credibility of Park Service directors, operating under orders to oppose new areas having secure merit, was severely compromised.

The initiative for new areas has shifted almost totally from the Executive Branch to the legislative. Parks have been added without even a pretense of study by the Park Service, sometimes through the addition of substantive legislation tacked onto appropriations bills— a process that compromises legislative responsibilities in the Congress and the views of the National Park Service and the Department of the Interior.

Although, strictly speaking, the term park barrel was used to describe omnibus bills shepherded through Congress in the 1980s by subcommittee chairman Phillip Burton (D-Calif.), the term has been recently associated with other park legislation that has traveled this extraordinary path to signature. Steamtown National Historic Site (Pa.), for example, the product of skillful logrolling by Representative Joseph McDade of that state, is a classic case in point.[21] Steamtown has drawn devastating criticism from National Park Service professionals. The associate director for cultural resources characterized Steamtown National Historic Site as "absolutely not a worthy addition to the system."[22] Another Park Service official reflected a similar perspective: "Steamtown . . . deserves as much criticism as one can possibly pile on it. Steamtown has and will continue to give the Service a black eye."[23] And in a stream of continuing criticism, John White, former curator of transportation for the Smithsonian Institution in Washington, D.C., refers to Steamtown NHS as "a third-rate collection in a place to which it had no relevance."[24] Steamtown NHS therefore was relegated to the status of an affiliated area in hopes it could find another sponsor or agency.

A substantive defense of Steamtown NHS is beyond the scope of this book, but one is possible, the comments cited above notwithstanding. In 1994 the park is alive and well. With Representative McDade as its champion, the park garnered appropriations for startup and rehabilitation in excess of $60 million, all in the form of congressional budget add-ons, none of it having been requested by the administration. The operating budget for 1993, which the Park Service did solicit, was $2.3 million, and a full time staff of seventy-six members. The operating budget is projected to reach $4.3 million in fiscal year 1995! Steamtown NHS is, of course, a good example of a unit of the national park system with strong local support and a vigorous, well-placed mentor in Congress who exercises the substantial powers of seniority.

Since 1972, the Centennial of Yellowstone NP, and 1988, two of the National Park Service's most consistent support groups, the Conservation Foundation and the National Parks and Conservation Association, have attempted to fashion concepts for rounding out or completing the national park system. The Conservation Foundation, a resource-oriented think tank in Washington, D.C., enjoys a widespread reputation for its political neutrality and technical competence. The foundation focused on the Yellowstone Centennial for a major "appraisal of the National Parks as they begin their second century in a changing America."[25] Its assessment consisted of a series of five task force reports, a topical symposium at Yosemite NP that produced a series of recommendations, and a collection of several dozen papers that served as background for the Yosemite conference—six of which were published. A reading of the 1972 "Appraisal . . ." in 1994 brings into sharp focus the differing national agendas of these two periods. The 1972 assessment was undertaken amid fresh memories of the urban crises of the 1960s, and its observations and counsel reflect those concerns.

The foundation's published report called for a $100 billion "Buy Back America" program to meet present and future park and recreation needs. No specific share of that sum was identified with the national park system, which it asserted "should continue to be expanded, as in the past, by offering protection to outstanding scenic and recreational resources . . . with examples of those major landscape types and natural systems of the United States not yet represented in the National Parks."[26]

Although the foundation did not suggest a comprehensive strategy or design for the future of the system, it did propose that the national park system of the future be limited to an "environmental preservation mission," with ultimate separation and divestiture of historical and cultural sites.[27] The reason given was that "the environmental preservation focus of the national park system will surely lose clarity of purpose if the administering agency is handed an expanding . . . mission in history, contemporary culture, and the arts."[28]

Ironically, and in spite of the substantial urban emphasis in the report and accompanying papers, the Conservation Foundation recommended that Gateway NRA in the New York–New Jersey metropolitan area and Golden Gate NRA in the San Francisco area—only recently made a part of the national park system—"be transferred as soon as possible to appropriate state or regional agencies for administration."[29]

In September 1981 the National Parks and Conservation Association, one of the principal private support groups for the national park system, held a conference on the "State of the Parks." As a result of that conference, NPCA developed a program to produce a "comprehensive blueprint for the future of the national park system." Several years later, in 1988, NPCA published a nine-volume "National Park System Plan."[30] Many of the plan's elements exceed the scope of this book, but its attempts to articulate an overall context for the national park system are germane here.

According to the plan, "NPCA's vision is for a national park system that truly represents the diversity of our nation, yet is prepared for cultural evolution in this country and the sobering global changes now on the horizon."[31] The plan then notes that "NPCA is committed to the premises of the Park Service plan of 1972."[32] NPCA's reliance on the 1972 plan is based in part on the result of 1983 meetings between four conservation organizations at which the future of the national park system was discussed.[33] The group concluded that the primary justification for adding new areas to the system was the "preservation of nationally significant ecosystems, landforms, and cultural resources . . . to include representative samples of all broadly defined physiographic and biological features, or 'natural history themes,' that could be observed in different, relatively homogeneous areas, or 'natural regions,' of the United States."[34]

The NPCA plan of 1988 elaborates on the 1972 Park Service plan, adding several new levels and classes of representation based on thirty-eight natural regions and an analytical process using three types of maps. In brief, it overlaid the regional boundaries of both plans and plotted federal land management units to find out if representation existed.

The 1972 plan and its concept of representativeness lacked sound policy and political rationale for the national park system. It is particularly uncompelling as a focus for public commitment and pressure. While systematic attempts to gauge the degree to which the national park system, or any other protective umbrella, is preserving representative samples of biological and physiographic diversity in the United States may appeal to the scientific or academic community, it does not seem highly probable that it will hold great appeal for members of Congress and their constituents. It seems very likely that new area proposals based primarily on such analyses will be particularly vulnerable to attack by those who may disagree. It is far easier to say "Go somewhere else!" when the rationale is essentially based on the wish to represent an inanimate object. Successful new park proposals have a generous measure of emotional content.

Analytical processes aside, the 1988 plan by the National Parks and Conservation Association contained forty-nine natural area sites it deemed fully qualified for inclusion in the national park system "for which prompt action should be taken." It also listed an additional two hundred sites, some of which are described as being of national park system caliber, some not. Those identified as not up to national park system status are recommended for protection by another entity, often with suggested monitoring by the Park Service to ensure its long-term integrity. However, NPS has neither the legal authority nor the money and staff to accomplish such large-scale monitoring of nonpark system resources.

At the level of specific site proposals, the NPCA listing is an interesting challenge. It is also interesting because in its detailed descriptive reports on new area proposals none of the descriptive materials or evidence of significance relies on or even mentions the element of representativeness.

Other studies, conferences, and reports have offered bits and pieces of a plan for the national park system. They range from the *Report of the Outdoor Recreation Resources Review Commission* (ORRRC) in 1963 to the *Report of the President's Commission on Americans Outdoors* in 1986. The latter report, the most recent high-level examination of outdoor recreation in America, was focused primarily on local plans and action. Federal park and recreation resources were not a significant concern of the commission and no attempt was made to address the future of the national park system.[35]

In 1991 the National Park Service sponsored a Seventy-fifth Anniversary Symposium on "Our National Parks: Challenges and Strategies for the 21st Century." Working groups that included both National Park Service employees and outside experts and interested individuals met both before and during the symposium to consider reports and papers on dozens of topics relating to park system management. Subjects included four major areas: organizational renewal, resource stewardship, park use and enjoyment, and environmental leadership. A grand design or overview of the national park system was not on the symposium's agenda.[36] However, the working paper on park use and enjoyment contains an interesting background observation about the perceived foundation of the national park system. The statement asserts:

> Historically, the rationale for national parks has included scenic nationalism (our mountains are better than Europe's), efficiency (wholesome recreation is necessary for worker productivity), economic benefit (the See America First! campaign of 1910); refreshment of the populace (Muir's "tired, nerve-shaken, over-civilized people" in need of wilderness), and public training (the environmental education programs of the early 1970s). Specific arguments have been made for natural areas (open space for urban populations, savings endangered species, wilderness, preserving ecosystems, and now conserving biodiversity) and for historic areas (preserving of native cultures, paying homage to the de-

serving, teaching military strategy, and economic revitalization through tourism). It is doubtful that additional rationales would add much that is significant.[37]

Though rationales for the system (or individual parks) are not necessarily the same as a grand design for such a system, the characterizations listed above are of interest for their context and contemporary value. Is it true that further elaboration of the rationales for the national park system would not likely add anything of significance? I wonder. The final symposium recommendations call for the National Park Service to

- Revise the National Park System Plan using all previous studies as a starting place.
- Undertake "a systematic program of theme studies."
- Reinstate a new areas study program.

Other recommendations relating to the shape and character of the national park system included the suggestion that: the National Park Service consider the preservation and interpretation of cultural diversity to be significant criteria in the acquisition of new historic and cultural sites and that the National Park Service embrace the concept of "partnership parks."[38]

Since all national park system plans either pretty much failed to be systematically implemented or institutionalized, the locus of initiative for new parks today floats somewhere between the substantive committees of Congress, the Executive Branch, and outside interests with either positive or negative agendas. However, even without a plan or design there is today a national park system, now 367 units and still growing. Today's system is a most remarkable collection of sites. Even a casual glance at the inventory that makes up the national park system reveals a surprising extent and diversity of resources (see Appendix 1). It includes great natural wonders of the West and Alaska, Civil War battlefields, the homes of presidents, seashores and lakes, rivers, the Statue of Liberty, a World War II liberty ship, the home of playwright Eugene O'Neill, and the laboratory of Thomas Edison. It also includes Wolf Trap Farm Park for the Performing Arts, the White House, Alcatraz Island, the National Park of American Samoa, and parkland and beaches in Brooklyn, New York. The national park system extends from north of the Arctic Circle in Alaska to the eastern edge of the U.S. Virgin Islands and in turn to the Island of Guam, half the world away.

Absent a definition or a design idea, informed opinions on the

character of the system, its quality, and its present state of complete-
ness vary widely. One view suggests today's system simply grew like
Topsy, resulting in an uneven collection of sites unevenly representing America's natural and cultural heritage. This view comes close
to having official National Park Service sanction, as reflected in the
following characterization of the national park system by the bureau's
official historian: "All national parklands are not created equal. Besides the obvious physical distinctions among and within the basic
types of areas in the national park system—natural and cultural, urban and wilderness, battlefield and birthplace, arctic and tropical—
there are qualitative differences as well. Plainly put, some of the system's areas are better than others."[39] This view also reflects discomfort
with both the diversity of the system and the absence of uniform
selection criteria capable of encompassing every unit in the system.
As a result, this view holds some sites more significant than others
and often attributes the inclusion of some sites to park barrel legislation said to have compromised the quality of the system. And finally this view has given rise to proposals that typically surface with
almost every new administration to deauthorize various units. Some
lists are short, some surprisingly lengthy. Some are the creation of
National Park Service professionals whose philosophical discomfort
with individual sites or whole types of sites is reflected in hit lists
passed along to political appointees or influential members of Congress. Some lists are drawn up by outside interest groups intended
for the same use.

Hit lists normally appear to have been written in disappearing ink,
because within a few months each new administration discovers that
for each individual unit there is a constituency more than willing to
fight for its life in the system. Now and again, though, units are deauthorized when an effective constituency does not exist or when
local opposition or Park Service failures overwhelm the site. One recent deauthorization—Mar-A-Lago NHS in Florida—is covered in
some detail in a later chapter. Another unit, Georgia O'Keffee NHS
(N.Mex.), was authorized, then deauthorized before it was formally
established in response to local opposition that persuaded the famous
painter to renege on her earlier gift to the nation. Yet Hot Springs
NP—unique for having been the nation's first parkland reservation
from the public domain, predating Yellowstone by forty years—has
survived many such lists. Gateway and Golden Gate National Recreation Areas, two urban parks whose unconventionality has been a
difficult concept for many NPS professionals to accommodate, have
been on many lists since they were created in 1972.

Another consequence of this like-Topsy view of the national park system is that some parks are more significant than others, meriting a higher level of protection, larger staffs, and bigger budgets. This approach is sometimes based on value scales that assert resources having only local significance require less protection than those having regional significance and in turn less than those of recognized national significance. Such categorizations are, of course, the subjective judgment of NPS professionals and are not based on uniform criteria or congressional sanction. This approach was given strong support by the Reagan-Watt administration, in part because it served as what was believed to be supportable logic for budget and staffing allocations.

A further repercussion of this approach to the national park system is that it supports the concept of a hierarchy of park units, sometimes by type of park, sometimes by size, sometimes by geographic location. Stratification of park system units may leave some units in administrative and budgetary backwaters for years. Some units gain reputations as the places where people are assigned when they "goof up" in another assignment. Over the years some sixty-odd units of the national park system have been removed—deauthorized or delisted—from the system.[40] The numbers *do not* give reason to think the system is in any kind of serious danger. They *do* suggest, however, that it is possible to develop a set of conditions or a working consensus from time to time and remove a unit for reasons then good and sufficient.

Another view of the national park system holds that the system should always be viewed in its totality, that is, that the whole is more than merely the sum of its parts. This view maintains that additions to the national park system, however rationalized by the Congress and the administration then in office, reflect more than just physical assets: they are the products of the American political process at a particular time and focus of our society and culture. Accordingly, the circumstances surrounding creation of a unit are also part of the unit's substance.

The urban units came into the system in 1972, following the civil disruptions of the 1960s and the urban thrusts of the Great Society programs. The National Seashores entered the system at a time of emergent national consciousness about the disappearance of public access to beaches, especially along the rapidly developing Eastern and Gulf seaboards.

Current interest in expanding the boundaries of various Civil War battlefield sites is the product of heightened public awareness that urban and suburban encroachments are closing forever the window of opportunity to preserve these links to our history. The first glimmers of new interest in preserving sites vital to an understanding of the conflicts between the white American establishment and Native Americans at Little Bighorn Creek and Wounded Knee reflect our current position. A name change for Custer Battlefield National Monument and a new area study at Wounded Knee speak volumes about the rumbling (or sleeping?) American conscience in the 1990s.[41]

Former Chairman of the National Park System Advisory Board Robin W. Winks, a Yale University professor of history, has said that "even a unit that, at first glance, seems somewhat dubious tells us a good bit about the nation's sense of itself, of what it takes pride in, and, thus, of the political process by which we practice our democracy."[42] All units of the system, then, ought to gain an equal level of national significance by virtue of their inclusion alone. The Congress of the United States gave conclusive definition to their significance by legislative act, a standard as secure as anything in our political system short of a constitutional amendment.

In this approach there are no better or lesser components of the system, only different ones. Accordingly, all parks are created equal and all units of the system deserve the same quality and measure of protection. None may be sacrificed to appease conflicting objectives. None may be ignored or suffer disparagement. None is expendable to short-term expediency or to long-term indifference. Each has an unqualified claim on the laws that protect all units of the system and on the loyalty and skills of those who care for it.

This approach also recognizes each unit as an expression of its time, an indelible statement by one generation for those to come later, and a permanent legacy. This view of the national park system would allow no divestitures—ever. As Congress said about the early Yosemite park lands: "inalienable for all time." It represents the sort of committed integrity that could withstand any assault from any quarter, including temporal changes in social values, economic cycles, or changing perspectives on the merits of individuals, events, or resources. Within the context of manmade institutions, it is permanent. Many people feel intuitively that the parks have such permanence today. Indeed most units do. But it will take a number of changes to afford every unit the same measure of integrity.

In two ways the modern definition of the national park system is incomplete:

- It lacks a clear sense of permanence and continuity, as evidenced by proposals from its friends and custodians alike to divest existing parts.
- It lacks an overarching principle or design that gives it definition and by which criteria may be fashioned for judging future park proposals.

A new definition of the national park system should begin with a new level of discussion and debate in the Congress. Legislative history will need to make it clear as to its permanence. Debates and commentary by members of Congress will need to sharpen the understanding of national significance, leaving no doubt as to the merits of the arguments that support membership in the system. New filters will need to be devised to satisfy all interested parties that qualitative standards for admission to the system have been met.

A new tradition will need to be nurtured within the professional ranks of the National Park Service that asserts that all units have equal standing within the system, the only differences being those of geography and circumstance. Such terms as *local* and *regional* significance will exist only in other contexts, not as rationales for making otherwise difficult decisions on budgets and people. The National Park Service needs to become comfortable with a clearer understanding of its unique and important role in the processes by which new park proposals are evaluated and decided upon. Professional formats and criteria are important, including the elaborate thematic structure and its rationales. But, as Professor Winks has noted, "political issues well beyond the control of the Park Service play an important role in judgments, and even where they do not and the debate over a site is more nearly purely scholarly in nature, opinions held with good will and in good faith may legitimately differ."[43]

Park Service professionals need to have more tolerance of and appreciation for the political processes by which national values are expressed. Sometimes decisions about new park system units are just too important to leave to the professionals. Barry Mackintosh, official historian of the Park Service, does, indeed, doff his hat to the political process by which parks are created. He notes that

As a representative body, [Congress] normally and naturally will give greater weight to vocal public sentiment behind a park proposal than to abstract standards that might support a negative vote on it. A park bill backed by an influential constituency and lacking significant outside opposition is thus apt to proceed without great regard for the opinions of historians, scientists, or other professional specialists in the bureaucracy . . .

Under the circumstances, it is hardly surprising that all parks do not equal the system's "crown jewels."[44]

While there is obvious truth in such political realism, this argument misses an important point: the national park system is not intended to represent or contain only "crown jewels." It reflects a wide, and widening, spectrum of values in American society. It is no accident that the system did not stop with or is not limited to a handful of superlative scenic sites in the western states. The system would be much the lesser if it had.

Even without an official plan and even without some general level of consensus about what ought to be part of the national park system, new areas are added from time to time. The basic process is as follows: Somewhere somebody becomes convinced that something should become part of the national park system. That somebody garners the support of other individuals and groups. They may then coalesce into one or more named organizations or obtain the support of an existing association. Many groups start very local in character, but will quickly seek to enlarge the interest group to national dimensions. Letter writing and personal visits to state and federal legislators seek to gain public support and sponsorship of proposed legislation to create a new park. It is virtually essential to have the active support of the representative in whose district the site lies and at least one of the state's two senators. A bill is introduced in Congress.

NPS may already have an opinion on the subject or it may then undertake a new area study. The major result of such studies is to serve as background for a formal position on the legislation by the administration. Hearings are held, normally by the House subcommittee handling national park system legislation. Administration and public witnesses express their views. If successful, the bill is reported out of committee and sent to the floor of Congress. The Senate may do essentially the same thing, either before or after House of Representatives action—mostly after. The bill is voted on in the House and Senate. If two separate bills are involved and they differ, a conference must rationalize the two. After passage by both Houses, it goes to the president for signature. The president normally signs legislation creating new units of the national park system, even if the administration's formal position earlier opposed the bill.

In theory an administration's views begin with a study and professional appraisal of the site by appropriate experts in the National Park Service. Such studies may be well financed, in depth, take several years, and give a strong appearance of objectivity and balance.

Or they may be cursory "windshield" surveys, taken by someone who is asked to write a report whose conclusions are predetermined by an overriding policy decision. Most reports lie somewhere between these extremes.

To be eligible for favorable consideration as a unit of the national park system, sites must currently pass through four filtering criteria systems:

- A determination of national significance.
- A finding of suitability.
- A finding of feasibility.
- A judgment that no one else can do it as well or better.

Each of these is discussed below.

A central consideration in qualifying any potential site for inclusion in the National Park System is its "national significance." How is national significance defined or measured? and by whom? According to the the National Park Service, a nationally significant area or site is one that meets all of four standards:[45]

1. It is an outstanding example of a particular type of resource.
2. It possesses exceptional value or quality in illustrating or interpreting the natural or cultural themes of our nation's heritage.
3. It offers superlative opportunities for recreation, for public use and enjoyment, or for scientific study.
4. It retains a high degree of integrity as a true, accurate, and relatively unspoiled example of the resource.

The problems inherent in standards containing such subjective terminology as "outstanding," "exceptional," "superlative," and "high degree" arise often when they are applied to specific proposals. The background and perspective of the person(s) making the judgment will heavily influence the final decision. Park management professionals whose experience is widely varied will likely have a much more restricted view of what is new, different, or superlative than someone whose previous experiences are more limited. In the latter instance the exceptional are more easily found.

Often a site's outstanding qualities depend largely on the degree to which it is a rarity in the geographic region in which it is located. Or it may be outstanding to people from outside that area who are not normally used to seeing such a resource. An example would be areas of mountains and glaciers in Alaska, almost any part of which could be said to have outstanding qualities among people who do not live in Alaska. For those who live there, the choice of an outstanding site may be more difficult. Such differences were common in the debates over the Alaska parks in the years preceding their inclusion in the national park system in 1980.

The second half of the first standard, which refers to a "particular type of resource" contains an unfortunate element of singularity. Many sites—perhaps most—contain complex mixtures of resources whose value is the sum of combined elements in a unique setting. Interestingly, the added merit of complex resources is mentioned in the standards only in the context of potential National Recreation Areas.

Another problem with the "exceptional value" criterion is that the major quality of a site may only be evident or available after the site is protected and after public investments have been made in the site to protect it, to restore it, or to make it accessible to the public. Many historic buildings and sites only gain their exceptional qualities after heavy public investments. It can be similar for natural areas. Shenandoah NP was created in 1926 on lands that were then cut over, burned, and, on the whole, not very attractive as parklands. Three generations later the lands in Shenandoah NP are in many places of wilderness quality, and among the most visited parklands in the East. In 1926 they would not have met today's standard for entry into the national park system.

The third standard contains additional ambiguities. If the term "superlative opportunity" is intended to apply to "public use," it is unclear what a "superlative public use" might be. A "superlative opportunity for public use" could be interpreted to suggest a numbers game, with sites gaining significance based on the size of visitation. However, it would be very uncharacteristic of the National Park Service to suggest such a standard when a unit is proposed, though visitation numbers carry more weight in the later life of a park unit when budgets and staffing are considered.

The "high degree of integrity" standard has similar problems when applied to many cultural resources, especially those for which major restoration or rehabilitation is required. Some proponents of a specific site may argue that historical integrity is an inherent quality of a feature, unrelated to present physical condition.

Attempts are also made sometimes to define national significance in relation to the site's clientele. Such relationships are often asserted as negative evidence that a site is merely of local or regional significance because many or most of the people who would visit the area come from that part of the country. This argument has many problems, even when applied to such acknowledged nationally significant areas as Yosemite NP. Well over half of Yosemite's visitors are

Californians, and a majority of those come from the San Francisco metropolitan area. Does that fact make Yosemite merely a regionally significant site? Golden Gate NRA, located entirely within the San Francisco metropolitan area, contains attractions that appeal primarily to people from outside the region—Alcatraz Island, for example, whose visitation is estimated to be over 90 percent non-Californians.

The Statue of Liberty in New York harbor, a site whose national significance would not be a likely debate topic, is visited in large share by New York City school children, especially during the winter months when school is in session and competition from summer tourists is at its lowest.

Steamtown National Historic Site, located in Scranton, Pennsylvania, and the object of much maligning as a park barrel site lacking national significance, received 55 percent of its 1990 visitation from states other than those in the mid-Atlantic region. Over 60 percent of its visitation involved overnight stays. Foreign visitors accounted for 5 percent of visitation, a very respectable share for a newly authorized site. Total visitation was 124,508 in 1990 and 145,184 in 1993.[46]

Projected visitation patterns for areas proposed for addition to the national park system may be used as support for or evidence against a proposal, depending on the point of view of their user. High visitation numbers can suggest a positive economic impact, new jobs, increased tourism, and more money flowing into the adjacent communities. High numbers can also be cited as evidence of probable undesirable environmental impacts, increased traffic or parking problems, more crime, or larger demands on public services by non-taxpaying visitors. Low visitation numbers, such as those that might be expected at a presidential home or a historic site associated with a less widely known personage, can be used to calm the fears of nearby residents who may fear large numbers of outsiders, tour buses, and similar impacts. Low visitation projections can also be used as evidence that a site is not national in character, since it would not draw people from far away on an everyday basis.

To illuminate the standards for significance, the Park Service cited the following examples in its "Criteria for Parklands": "Nationally significant cultural resources . . . include those that . . . are associated importantly with the lives of persons nationally significant [or] . . . an entity of exceptional historical or artistic significance." A natural area may be nationally significant if it is "a landform . . . that has always been extremely uncommon in the region." These examples show the difficulty in defining national significance. It is very much in the eye of the beholder for all but a limited group of widely known, large-scale features. For proposed new areas in the future, such standards emphasize the need for well-informed judgments by open minds.

Park Service guidelines stipulate that "to be suitable . . . an area must represent a natural/cultural theme or type of recreational resource that is not adequately represented in the . . . system . . . [or] by another land managing agency . . . determined on a case-by-case basis by compari[son] . . . in the character, quality, quantity or combination of resources and opportunities for public enjoyment."[47] There are no written guidelines about what is adequate representation of a theme. That is a matter of professional judgment. The current emphasis is on saving remaining Civil War sites now endangered by other forms of development. Although much support exists for that effort, probably many people would nevertheless argue that the system already includes the best and enough adequately to memorialize and interpret those events in our history. On any subject, it must be a judgment call. Among the well-traveled professional historians in the National Park Service, it may become increasingly difficult to overcome objections when something is already represented in the system.

The feasibility of a new unit depends on it being "of sufficient size and appropriate configuration . . . to ensure long-term protection of resources, and to accommodate public use, and it must have potential for efficient administration at a reasonable cost. Important feasibility factors include land ownership, acquisition costs, access, threats to the resource, and staff or development requirements."[48]

Neither examples nor further definitions are provided. The references to costs are mandatory from a political point of view, but seldom have any major bearing on positions taken by the Park Service. Cost estimates for everything from land acquisition to long-term development and operating costs have a tradition (accidental or otherwise) of being significantly understated. Out-year costs are difficult to estimate in any event, but many such estimates in the Park Service have little credibility inside or outside the Service.

With perhaps the earliest years of the National Park Service standing as an exception, when both Directors Mather and Albright sought with vigor to expand the system into a nationwide enterprise, the Park Service has never displayed the sort of bureaucratic acquisitiveness commonly associated with federal agencies. New parks and new ventures into untapped fields of endeavor have not motivated expansion of the system. There have been several relatively long stretches when the Service rather vigorously resisted expansion.

From that perspective, the language in the formal policies governing qualifications for entry into the system is consistent with a very conservative view of the future role of the national park system. According to that policy, "New additions to the national park system and affiliated areas will not usually be recommended if other arrangements can provide protection for the resource and opportunities for public enjoyment. Cooperative management as an affiliated area is one alternative to establishment of a new national park system unit."[49]

The tone of this statement is important to understanding the combined effects of a set of strong forces within the Service that resists expansion, combined with conservative presidential administrations whose basic policy opposes expansion of the federal estate. The statement also reflects the fact that the National Park Service does not at this time see a long-term definable role for itself or for the national park system. If someone else can do it, there is no essential reason something ought to be a part of the national park system because of its inherent characteristics, or because it fits into a grand design of some sort.

The nature and extent of future growth of the national park system are uncertain. There is very little in the way of a framework within which to speculate on its nature or extent. It seems likely that new parks will come along apace, some with and some without the eager embrace of the National Park Service. Because the focus of the system is on resources and subjects and objects whose values may be invisible today and may only become apparent at some time in the future, it is unknowable what new departures will be discovered in the future. There is, however, a generous amount of old business remaining to be accomplished or disposed of, including a long list of potential additions to the national park system that is already on the books. The national park system will be what we the people wish it to be only if we the people are willing to work to make it happen.

Is the search for a plan or a rationale for the national park system another example of people (and authors) trying to find order where none exists and trying to create a pattern that is inevitably self-serving? People whose political or economic philosophy is such that they oppose all or most enlargement of federal land ownership could not agree to a plan for park expansion, no matter how it was developed. On the other hand, one of the sharpest criticisms of the 1972 plan was that it simply identified missing elements in a very detailed outline, but said nothing about priorities or costs or alternatives.

The American political system is not well engineered for plans of any type, certainly not large scale, long-term plans that require multiyear commitments. With the possible exceptions of the interstate highway system (a product of the Eisenhower administration) and the manned trip to the moon (first proposed by President Kennedy), the United States government has never embraced long-range planning or budgeting.

Our governmental system can be characterized as crisis oriented, opportunistic, and focused too narrowly on the short term.[50] Its very structure reinforces it. For example, the longest time frame in our constitutional structure is the life term of nine Supreme Court Justices. Next is the six-year term of 100 United States senators, the four-year terms for the president and vice president, and finally the two-year terms for each of 435 members of the House of Representatives. Cabinet officers, bureau chiefs, and various other political appointees serve at the pleasure of one of these constitutional officers, but tenures rarely exceed that of the appointing authority.

Nearly all federal government spending is tied to annual appropriations good only for one fiscal year. A few federal activities though are financed through Trust Funds or revenue accounts where funding generally exceeds one year. Still, all funding to the National Park Service is annual in nature, meaning that the money must be obligated in the year for which it is appropriated.

Multiyear planning and programming have been tried in the federal government, notably by President Lyndon B. Johnson in the last half of the 1960s. The effort was modeled after a system devised for the Department of Defense by then Secretary Robert M. McNamara. Dubbed "PPBS," for the Planning-Programming-Budgeting System, the effort was a radical departure for all civilian agencies. They almost uniformly resisted it because it was (1) new, (2) associated with the Defense Department, and (3) sought insistently to quantify elements judged to be unquantifiable. PPBS sought to focus on program outputs and results, not the inputs of money and personnel typical of federal budgets. It was halfheartedly carried out in many parts of government, including the Interior Department, where it was accused (with validity) of generating a profusion of paperwork in a era of budget retrenchment and program shrinkage, which the system did not handle well. As part of efforts underway to "reinvent" government, multiyear budgets may again be given a trial.

The modern politically correct view of new additions to the national park system is to search high and low for alternatives to entry into the system. Though many resources under state, local, and private jurisdiction suffer immensely from inadequate financial support, poor maintenance, and nonprofessional care, it is more desirable for the resource to remain in that ownership than to become a federal property. Many pending proposals for addition to the national park system are advanced by people knowledgeable of the shortcomings of the site's present management, and the belief that federal ownership represents a better hope of adequate long-term care.

The other side of the argument—that everything of any great value must be part of the national park system—is equally troublesome. By no means is it essential that places like Mount Vernon (owned and managed—quite well—by a private ladies' association) be owned or managed by the National Park Service. But, perhaps, in other instances there ought to be a more interventionist role for NPS in making certain that appropriate standards are maintained, that long-term maintenance and rehabilitation requirements are being accommodated, and so forth. National landmark status is, or could be, a useful vehicle, and although it does offer some color of protection, it provides virtually no actual oversight. The problem arises partly from a lack of money and adequate staffing. But NPS sees no active role for itself in any real sense of that word.

One minor irony among the effects of extended opposition to new areas has been that many Park Service professionals now share that view, not only because it is consistent with the agency's historical position but also because such opposition is well recognized to be politically correct. There is, of course, a case against expansion of the national park system. Its articulation is really beyond the scope of this book. It is also inconsistent with my biases and beliefs, though those biases do not include an overly expansionist view of the national park system.

Dissatisfactions with the National Park Service or the system as a whole do not tend to be absolute in character. Almost no one individual or group advocates abolition of the national park system or significant shrinkage of its existing extent. Major disagreements do exist, however, regarding specific sites, both proposed and sometimes existing ones. Federal acquisition of private lands within the exterior boundaries of park areas is often controversial, although such landowners are likely to do well financially in any transaction with the government. The manner in which land acquisitions are accomplished may be controversial and, for those involved, very painful. Long-established living patterns may be upset or destroyed. The government's processes and the federal employees involved have an only adequate record of compassion for the hardships and emotional consequences of new parkland acquisitions. Complaints are often valid and the remedies slow and imperfect. But matters are probably improving in the long run, in part because the agency is slowly changing, and in part because there are substantial legal and public relations pressures to do so. More generalized debates about the scope and extent of the national park system are likely to continue, particularly when the National Park Service is constrained from crafting its own agenda. The Service has played a negative role for so long, it will be difficult to change, even if its leadership wishes it. The Clinton administration has not given a clear signal on the long-term shape of the system, reflecting its concentration well into 1994 on health-care reform and deficit reduction.

NOTES

1. Barry Mackintosh, "A Historical Perspective on the National Park System," *Courier* vol. 36, no. 1 (Spring 1991): 12. Albright's words took a form familiar in government, that of a program directive written to him, by him, for the signature of his boss, Secretary of the Interior Franklin K. Lane. That memorandum is the oft-cited source of National Park Service management policies that remains in effect today. Ironically, Secretary Lane was a strong supporter of the Hetch Hetchy dam project, probably the worst intrusion on a National Park ever.

2. Abraham Lincoln NP (Ky.), now Abraham Lincoln Birthplace NHS; Lassen Volcanic NP (Calif.); and Fort McHenry NP (Md.), now Fort McHenry NM and Historic Shrine.

3. Albright, *Birth of the National Park Service*, 137.

4. Albright, Dickenson, and Mott, *National Park Service*, 11.

5. 16 USC 1a-1.

6. 16 USC 1c(a).

7. James. M. Ridenour, "Thinning the Blood," *Courier* vol. 35, no. 11 (Nov./ Dec. 1990): 1.

8. Letter to the author, Aug. 12, 1991.

9. Everhart, *National Park Service*, ix.

10. Letter to the author, July 8, 1991.

11. Rothman, *Preserving Different Pasts*, 200–201, credits Verne Chatelain, Director Horace Albright's chief historian, as the person who sought to link historic sites with broad themes constituting "patterns of history."

12. *Part Two of the National Park System Plan—Natural History*, National Park Service, Washington, D.C., 1972.

13. Letter from Robert M. Utley, June 23, 1991.

14. Letter to the author, Aug. 12, 1991.

15. The 1972 plan was the object of several meetings in 1983 that included representation from four national conservation groups. That meeting came more than a decade after publication of the original plan and was not intended to afford policy review of the underlying concepts and directions inherent in the published plan. No formal public involvement has ever taken

place on the 1972 plan or its successor documents. The plan has similarly never been the object of congressional oversight hearings or legislation.

16. Foresta, *America's National Parks and Their Keepers*, 269.

17. *History and Prehistory in the National Park System and the National Historic Landmarks Program, 1987; Natural History in the National Park System and on the National Registry of Natural Landmarks*, Natural Resource Report NPS/NR/NRTR-90/03, Sept. 1990, both published by the National Park Service, Washington, D.C.

18. *History and Prehistory in the National Park System and the National Historic Landmarks Program, 1987*, 1.

19. Denis P. Galvin, "For Those Who Long Remember," *Courier* vol. 35, no. 11 (Nov./Dec. 1990): 3.

20. Letter from Richard C. Curry, Oct. 11, 1991.

21. Representative McDade is second ranking minority member of the House Committee on Appropriations and serves in a similar capacity on the subcommittee that handles the budget for NPS.

22. Letter from Jerry L. Rogers, Feb. 25, 1991.

23. Letter from Reed Jarvis, Pacific Northwest Regional Office, NPS, Nov. 1991.

24. *Newsweek*, Nov. 26, 1990.

25. *National Parks for the Future*, 254.

26. Ibid., 20.

27. Ibid., 14.

28. Ibid.

29. Ibid., 15.

30. The nine volumes cover protecting park resources, research, parks and people, interpretation, park boundaries, planning and public involvement, land acquisition, new parks, and a final volume on the Park Service organization and its employees. See *Investing in Park Futures*.

31. Volume 8 of *Investing in Park Futures*, I–2.

32. Ibid., I–10.

33. NPCA, the Wilderness Society, the Sierra Club, and the National Audubon Society.

34. Volume 8 of *Investing in Park Futures*, II–3.

35. The Commission was created by Executive Order 12503, Jan. 28, 1985. The fifteen-member commission was chaired by Governor Lamar Alexander (Tenn.) and included two members each from the Senate and House of Representatives. The commission's 210-page report urges "a new prairie fire of concern and investment, *community by community*, that can keep our outdoors great."

36. The president of the Association of National Park Rangers, Rick Gale, said he was "disappointed that there isn't more discussion of the need to develop long range strategic objectives from which the proposed tactical actions would logically flow." From *Ranger* vol. 8, no. 1 (Winter 1991/92): 4.

37. From the Draft Report of the Working Group on Park Use and Enjoyment, in *Draft Reports of the Working Groups on Our National Parks: Challenges and Strategies for the 21st Century*, published by NPS, D-684, Oct. 1991, 77.

38. Partnership parks are parks whose ownership or management (or both) involve the National Park Service and another jurisdiction or entity. It might involve another federal agency or a state or local government or even a private institution. Arguably, NPS has been in the partnership park business for much of its history. In a September 1991 paper prepared for the National Park Service on that subject, Dr. Ervin H. Zube, a professor at the University of Arizona, asserts that some sixteen to twenty existing park units qualify as partnership parks. Zube's concept of partnerships ranges from active liaison with local interests through established advisory commissions to joint administration of an area, from formal agreements embraced in legislation to informal associations crafted by innovative or aggressive superintendents. The concept is definitely politically correct, though its application during the Reagan-Bush years served more to divert new area park proposals completely than to serve as a format for innovative affiliations with the national park system.

39. *The National Parks: Shaping the System,* (NPS, 1991), 106.

40. See Appendix 4.

41. For interesting background to the issues surrounding this name change see Linenthal, *Sacred Ground,* 129–71, 223–33.

42. Robin W. Winks, "Intelligent Interpretation," *Courier* vol. 36, no. 2 (Summer 1991): 9.

43. Ibid., 8.

44. *The National Parks: Shaping the System,* 107–8.

45. "Management Policies," National Park Service, U.S. Department of the Interior, 1988, chap. 2:2. See also "Criteria for Parklands," National Park Service folder, GPO 1990-262-100/00214.

46. "Economic Impact and Visitor Profile, Steamtown NHS," by the Greater Scranton Chamber of Commerce and the National Park Service, Apr. 1991, 8 pages. Though comparisons may be imperfect, Steamtown NHS's visitation is roughly comparable to Eisenhower NHS (Pa.), created in 1967; Saugus Iron Works NHS (Mass.), dating to 1968; Walnut Canyon NM (Ariz.), proclaimed in 1915; and Harry S Truman NHS (Mo.), established in 1983.

47. From "Report on Criteria for Affiliated Areas" National Park Service, Feb. 1990: 9–10.

48. Ibid., 10.

49. Ibid.

50. The same criticism is leveled generally at the corporate and business world, where short-term profits often prevail over long-term investments in new technology, employee training, and other changes pointed toward the future. That government reflects the same myopia should not be surprising.

TWO

Typecasting the Parks

Today's national park system is made up of twenty separate categories of sites and areas, one of which is labeled "other" and contains eleven sites that do not fit any of the other nineteen classifications. Though generalizations can be made about some categories, uniformity and consistency are not characteristics of park system nomenclature.

Reactions to the classification scheme and titles vary from bemused toleration of what is regarded as the work of bureaucrats wearing green eye shades to open hostility toward matters of no consequence at all. Though the proverbial rose may smell as sweet by any other name, the titles and designations of units of the national park system receive an uncommon measure of attention, especially in Congress and among those people in and out of government who fashion new area proposals or reconsider old ones.

Tumacacori National Monument (Ariz.), which had borne that name since 1908, was renamed Tumacacori National Historical Park in 1990, when two other early missions were added to the park. Though there is no single definition of what makes up a National Historical Park, that terminology apparently conveyed something more accurately than National Monument. The change was deemed important enough to warrant the attention of an interested clientele, Congress, and the Executive Branch.

Park names have evolved with the development of the system, reflecting not only a general desire to name like things alike but also a desire to promote more uniform public expectations concerning the way in which an area may be experienced. Classifications and titles are also useful within the National Park Service for some of the same reasons. Sometimes the selection of titles embodies major policy considerations. Although distinctions can be and often are trivialized, they can also be important parts of the negotiations leading up to a new area or a hurdle never overcome for a unit that fails. One story has it that Grandfather Mountain in Virginia never became part of the national park system because the mountain's owner, who would donate the property, wanted it to be labeled a National Park while Congress would only consider National Monument status. Classifications are assigned in the process and in the document by which the area is added to the national park system. The title given an area often represents the results of political negotiations on permitted uses or other management elements. New names have been used to expand the variety of management options once an area has become part of the system. In recent years NPS has attempted to steer Congress and others toward more consistent application of park system categories.

Broad definitions of park classifications have been published. National Parks are today defined to include areas of diverse resource values over large land areas. However, the roster of fifty-one National Parks includes several areas inconsistent with that definition, Hot Springs in Arkansas being the most extreme example. Whether Carlsbad Caverns or Mesa Verde would meet today's standard is a matter of judgment regarding just how varied the resources need be and when large is large enough.

At the first level of classification, areas of the national park system are divided into three types: natural, cultural (read historic), and recreational. These distinctions are rooted deeply in the Park Service management ethos. They are embedded in the titles assigned units in the system, in professional titles and job descriptions, and in entrenched attitudes and deeply felt opinions toward resources.

For a decade or so, the three categories of sites were the foundation of management policy and operating style. Park Service Director George B. Hartzog, Jr., concluded in 1964 that what the National Park Service needed was a separate set of management principles and policies to guide the administration of each of the three site categories.[1] In the form of a directive that he wrote for the signature of Secretary of the Interior Stewart L. Udall, Director Hartzog concluded that "each of these categories requires a separate management concept and a separate set of management principles coordinated to form one organic management plan for the entire system."[2]

Three policy manuals were written and each unit of the national park system was classified into one of the three management categories according to criteria developed by the Recreation Advisory Council, created in 1963 and composed of six Cabinet-level officials. The superintendent and staff at each park were instructed to use the appropriate management guideline as their operating policies and directions.

Though the classification system had an appealing measure of simplicity and convenience, it was soon apparent to park managers that substantially every park unit did not fit neatly into just one category, but was a complicated blend of two or all three. While Yellowstone NP was immediately classified as a natural area park, it contains cultural resources of national significance whose management required use of the guidelines and principles distinctive to historic sites. Yellowstone also has recreational resources of national significance, requiring use of policies and principles set up for the management of recreational areas.

In a similar manner, historic sites such as Gettysburg (Pa.), which shares the title of National Military Park with eight other battlefields, contains natural resource values that require treatment consistent with other natural areas. Gettysburg visitors and management alike recognize the "recreation" inherent in visiting that sublime artifact of the American Civil War. Gateway NRA, an urban park in the New York–New Jersey metropolitan region, contains a wildlife refuge, some two dozen buildings on the National Register of Historic Places, two historic districts, several noteworthy natural areas, beaches, and the nation's oldest operating lighthouse (1764). The 26,300-acre park around the edges of New York harbor defies simple categorization.

The National Seashores were all placed in the recreation area category, but all of them shared natural area characteristics that were in several instances given explicit recognition in their enabling legislation. Fire Island NS, for example, was to be administered "with the primary aim of conserving the natural resources located there."[3]

The consternation felt by many park supporters about the new management categories and policies led the Conservation Foundation to observe in 1972 that

> the taxonomic variations in national park designation—riverways, parkways, seashores, monuments, historic sites—have just about reached the limit. . . . As nominal distinctions are made between, say, a park and recreation area, some important policy judgments inevitably follow. Invariably, these judgments are such that it is difficult to retain the inherent natural values of the "recreation" area. . . . Each park unit should be examined and planned according to its own values and carrying capacities.[4]

With the passage of time and improved understandings of resource interdependencies and identification of the varied assets typical of virtually every park unit, park professionals gave less and less credence to the three management categories and their associated policy arrangement. By the mid-1970s the three management categories and the supporting manuals fell into disuse and in 1975 they were formally replaced by a new policy manual focused on resource types rather than site classifications. The new system called for zoning park areas, with each zone to be managed according to policies applicable to that zone. Some zones were identified with multiple characteristics.

The new system also represented a significant new level of planning and management sophistication as evidence of an improved understanding of resource complexities and interrelationships. The new "Management Policies" made it official: park system units "are complex mixtures of values and resources, each with its own unique qualities and purposes."[5] In 1977 Director William J. Whalen formally abolished the three-category system. In the early 1980s, in an attempt to reintroduce the less restrictive regulations associated with recreation areas (and allow more off-road vehicles at National Seashores), and in a search for a less complex approach to park management, the administration of President Reagan and Secretary of the Interior James Watt attempted to reinstate the three-category management system. However, after many months of explanations and sometimes acrimonious exchanges between NPS and the secretary's representatives, the old system's incapability of dealing with the complexities of each park's resources became apparent to Secretary Watt's staff and the effort was abandoned.

The old three categories, however, continue to be evident in the titles used for existing and new areas, in organizational arrangements, and in the budgeting and allocation of money and staff. Its roots are deep and as recently as 1988 former Director Hartzog was still bemoaning the abandonment of the three management categories, which he asserted were ended by "political bureaucrats . . . in derogation of logic and legislation." He felt that without the categorization of park units "suddenly everything had become the same and, thus, nothing was any longer special—not even Yellowstone."[6] Hartzog refers to the 1970 legislation that gave recognition to the national park *system*. That law does refer to the system as including "superlative natural, historic, and recreation areas," but it does not support separate and distinctive management policies for those areas. The 1970 law supports integration of these sites into a single system, to be administered not only under the legislation distinctive to each site but also under a unified, systemwide standard. As tidy as the three categories appear, and although they do survive in area titles and other parts of the administrative apparatus, they do not square with the realities inherent in the resources. Others doubtless share Hartzog's view, but the three management categories, when applied to entire park units, did not stand the test of professional judgment, even after a second look.

If there is little virtue in the classification system and if parks gain little in their understanding by their nomenclature, of what purpose is the naming? Why not everything simply a National Park? In practice, this book and many other references to the national park system, including Park Service publications and documents, do exactly that. They refer to all sites and areas as parks, albeit not "National Parks." The use of the generic "park," even by park professionals, normally has no technical significance. It is merely a convenience.

Natural areas within the national park system principally bear three titles: National Park, National Monument, and National Preserve. National Parks are defined to be large complex resource areas.[7] They are always created only by an Act of Congress. Their principal distinction is that essentially all consumptive uses are forbidden, including public hunting. Reflecting a curious policy inconsistency regarding wildlife resources, fishing is not usually prohibited.[8]

The National Park classification holds special meaning for many people, both in and outside of the National Park Service professional ranks. Not only does the term represent the oldest form of parkland conservation in the United States, it enjoys the most prestige elsewhere in the world and an image worthy of a major public relations campaign. The title alone implies value and permanence. In part for that reason, the National Park classification has been adopted worldwide as the designator of premier sites for protection and management, even if not always with the same level of protection.[9]

All this is true in spite of the inconsistencies evident in the classification as it has been applied in the United States. For that reason, there have been periodic moves in Congress to change the classification of one or more existing National Monuments to that of National Park or to be certain that the National Park title is used on a new area added to the system.[10] The dynamics of the political processes by which National Monuments have become National Parks have often paralleled larger trends in national environmental awareness and reflected the vigor with which an individual president or secretary of the Interior has supported the national park system as a whole.

Several existing National Monuments probably qualify for National Park status in terms of resource values and size, but existing patterns of mining, hunting, or other factors prevent reclassification in the foreseeable future. Death Valley (Calif., Nev.) with a diverse desert ecosystem is a prominent case in point.

Will there be other National Parks? Currently, there is no way of knowing, but there are several possibilities: in the southern California desert; one on Chesapeake Bay; and, perhaps, one or more areas that will begin like Shenandoah NP as, in what the Conservation Foundation has called "restoration reserves,"[11] somewhere now unrecognizable.

National Preserves have all the essential physical properties of National Parks. The National Preserve category was invented in 1974 in the Congressional give and take associated with two large natural areas in Florida and Texas (ultimately, Big Cypress and Big Thicket National Preserves). The Preserve classification recognized long-established patterns of hunting and other extractive activities in these two areas. The legislation creating the units allowed continuation of most hunting and certain other consumptive uses, when they would have been banned if they had strictly conformed to the concept of a National Park. Most of the National Preserves would qualify as National Parks based on their resource values.

Other natural areas may be labeled National Seashores, National Rivers, or Wild Rivers. Several National Recreation Areas have a strong natural area base: Bighorn Canyon (Mont., Wyo.), Ross Lake (Wash.), and others at large manmade reservoirs such as Lake Mead (Nev., Ariz.) and Glen Canyon (Utah-Ariz.).

National Monuments are often also large complex resource areas, but they may also be smaller historic sites. The Statue of Liberty on fifty-eight acres in New York harbor is a National Monument and so is Death Valley (Calif.), with over two million acres. National Monuments can be created either by Congress or by presidential proclamation. Many National Parks began as National Monuments created by a president when there was insufficient political consensus in the Congress to pass the needed legislation or because Congress simply was not interested.[12]

Eleven National Monuments once part of the national park system are no longer so. One monument in particular merits special mention. In 1922 President Warren G. Harding set aside some 320 acres for Fossil Cycad NM in South Dakota. President Harding hoped thereby to protect rich deposits of fossil cycads, a primitive seed-bearing tropical evergreen of the Mesozoic period. However, by the time the National Park Service got around to considering on-site protection thirty years later, the lands had been so stripped by fossil hunters that the site was deemed worthless as a paleobotanical reserve. In 1956 the land was returned to the public domain and in 1994 it still belongs to Uncle Sam, under the jurisdiction of the

Bureau of Land Management, with disposal of the site, according to BLM, "unlikely."

Cultural, historic, and archaeological resources within the national park system may include districts, sites, buildings, or structures, and may bear any of several classifications, each of which would be preceded by the word National.

Battlefield	Memorial
Battlefield Park	Military Park
Battlefield Site	Monument
Historical Park	Historic Site

Other cultural assets in the national park system include the White House, the Lincoln and Jefferson Memorials, and the Washington Monument, all in Washington, D.C.

The complexity of names associated with cultural sites and various historic events reflects the difficulties experienced in designing acquisition and management options capable of satisfying those who would save a site and those who would prefer less or nothing. In many instances areas of historic significance have been created using either a "foot in the door" or "a little bit is better than nothing" approach. These approaches appear to be the near-normal situation regarding Civil War battlefields. The earliest battlefield sites were set aside under jurisdiction of the army for the management of cemeteries located on the battlefield itself. As interest in and support for an understanding of Civil War history has grown, efforts to study and interpret the disposition of the opposing forces, the ebb and flow of battle, and the physical context within which the battle was fought have also grown. Commonly the land base did not include all the most relevant land, and sometimes even the most significant sites were not included.

Other reasoning behind the proliferation of historic site names relates to the need to accommodate broader land uses than those traditionally associated with the interpretation of historic events and personages. Such uses include, for example, various passive recreational uses or picnics or outdoor photography.

Some historic sites are treated as memorials, although they do not bear that title. For example, all Civil War sites, and also Little Bighorn Battlefield NM, severely restrict activities deemed inconsistent with their somber, reflective atmosphere. The "Visitor Standards of Conduct" at Little Bighorn Battlefield NM, for example, say that "visitors to these hallowed grounds will refrain from inappropriate conduct or activity that disturbs the tranquility of this place. . . . Any form of sports activity such as jogging, racing, skating or skateboarding, ball playing, frisbees, and sunbathing, is prohibited. Radios and pets are also prohibited."

The issue has two sides, however. At Manassas National Battlefield Park (Va.) in suburban Washington, D.C., the topic is heatedly debated by two sides who are both devoted to saving the Civil War site. According to A. Wilson Greene, executive director of the Association for the Preservation of Civil War Sites, "Organized games and kite flying simply do not belong on ground consecrated by blood." Mrs. Betty Rankin, president of the Save the [Manassas] Battlefield Foundation, supporting less restrictive policies, responds that battlefield "supporters were not just Civil War buffs, not just historians. They were people who have a love affair with the national parks. . . . People died so that the living would have a better life."[13]

Edward Tabor Linenthal, a professor of religion and American culture at the University of Wisconsin, thoughtfully explores the mixture of feelings and motives that people bring to battlefields and other sites associated with the war.[14] In the Foreword, Robert M. Utley observes, "Commemoration has always been a powerful motive, perhaps the most powerful, for preserving historic places. People approach these places not only as vestiges of the past, as vehicles for enlightenment, but also as shrines, as temples of veneration."[15] Policy and practice at each park are more often than not reflections of the views of its present superintendent and some changes do occur from time to time in response to local pressures. Neighbors and other local residents are likely to be more tolerant of recreational uses than Civil War buffs and scholars. Ironically, those who support the most rigorous rules against recreational uses at Civil War sites are often people who plan and participate in battle reenactments and other forms of "living history."[16]

In 1916, thirty-five areas came under the jurisdiction of the newly formed National Park Service of which six had been created primarily to protect cultural values: Mesa Verde NP (Colo.); Casa Grande Ruin Reservation (Ariz.), later a National Monument; El Morro NM (N.Mex.); Gran Quivira NM (N.Mex), now Salinas Pueblo Missions NM; Navajo NM (Ariz.); and Tumacacori NM (Ariz.), now Tumacacori NHP. All six areas contained Indian ruins. Interestingly enough, among the areas *not* transferred from the War Department to the new National Park Service until 1933 was one of the sites then designated a National Park, Abraham Lincoln Birthplace (Ky.).

National Memorials have a special place in the national park system because they are something of a contradiction to the notion that sites must have a strong associative value with the person or event they commemorate or represent. Memorials often lack such associative values. The association is often merely an intellectual artifact created wherever the memorial may be found. For example, nothing in the location of the Vietnam Veterans Memorial links that site to those memorialized. The Lincoln Memorial, the Jefferson Memorial, the Washington Monument, and others share this reality. On the other hand a measure of site relatedness can be found in other National Memorials, for example, Arlington House, the Robert E. Lee Memorial, the *USS Arizona* Memorial,[17] Hamilton Grange NMem, and others.

The National Park Service has traditionally opposed the addition of new memorials to the national park system, in part because of its general discomfort with their non-site-relatedness and in added part because of an inherent wish that such matters await a long-term period of evaluation and historical judgment. The Park Service allows for a fifty-year interval for things to gain historic significance. Memorials, in particular, are likely to surface in much less time, often within days of a person's death or the passage of an event. Standards associated with historical significance have a habit of appearing arbitrary, and exceptions often thereby gain support.

This issue can be characterized by proposals to identify a site associated with manned space exploration. Some people would like to save and interpret the last remaining launch pad at Cape Canaveral (Fla.) associated with the manned mission to the moon. Others suggest waiting to make that decision. Fifty years from now it is unlikely that any of the physical artifacts associated with space programs of the 1960s will survive. To wait or not to wait, that is the question.

The matter of site-relatedness will be important in the future—more so, perhaps, than it has been in the past. Congress and others are wrestling with the means and rationales for including in the system sites designed to commemorate or represent ideas, intellectual pursuits, and nonevents where associative values are more subtle and even unavailable. Sites relating to painting, music, and other elements of the world of art, are examples of this new frontier.

Memorials are for the living, to serve as reminders of persons no longer living, of events long past, or deeds long done. Except for the pyramids of Egypt, few memorials exist today that are the creation of the person memorialized. It seems unlikely that anyone could be a proper judge of their own memorial—common gravestones excepted. Some notable personages, though, have sought to influence later decisions about memorials. President Franklin D. Roosevelt, for example, observed in writing that he felt a suitable memorial would be a simple block of granite, about the size of a desk, located on a small downtown parcel of land in the District of Columbia. A memorial meeting that description exists, while for more than forty years committees and commissions have struggled to find and agree upon a "real" memorial to the nation's thirty-second president. An agreement now exists and the monument may actually be completed.

Although many people and editorial writers have bemoaned the time and controversy that have surrounded final decisions on FDR's memorial location and design, delay has not all been out of character for the event. While President Roosevelt's place in history is already well secured, the memorial to him may reflect a more realistic view of his presidency after the leavening effects of almost fifty years. The Washington Monument, honoring the nation's first president, was begun in 1848, 49 years after George Washington's death. The Lincoln Memorial was begun in 1911, 46 years after Lincoln's assassination. The Thomas Jefferson Memorial was undertaken 108 years after his death. Thus the timing for a Franklin D. Roosevelt Memorial seems in the ballpark with past experience.

The earliest National Recreation Area was Boulder Dam NRA, created in 1936 by an agreement between the National Park Service and the Bureau of Reclamation. It was renamed Lake Mead NRA in 1947. It is also possible to make a case that the oldest NRA is Chickasaw in Oklahoma, part of which began in 1902 as the Sulphur Springs Reservation and was later redesignated Platt National Park in 1906.

The NRAs began around the shorelines of Bureau of Reclamation and Corps of Army Engineers reservoirs. They were controversial because of their association with a manmade dam. Then in 1972 the mold was broken with the addition of two urban parks: Gateway NRA in the New York–New Jersey metropolitan area and Golden Gate NRA in and near San Francisco, California. Largely composed of surplus military and other federal lands, they were an ingenious invention and a remarkable departure from the historic pattern of rural sites serving a clientele who often traveled great distances to be there. Their ingenuity was based on recycling military bases, buildings, and waterfronts for public recreation, conservation, and historic preservation.

Gateway and Golden Gate NRAs were, perhaps paradoxically, the creation of a conservative (Nixon) administration not noted for an urban bias. But they were in part a piece of fallout from the urban unrest of the 1960s. They were not entirely welcome among professionals in the National Park Service or among the longtime constituencies of the national park system. Within NPS, assignments to one of the Gateways were shunned and disparaged by many older employees for at least a decade. Versions of those biased attitudes survive today. And many quarters expressed a great fear that the two urban NRAs were the beginning of a move for every city insisting on its own NRA. It did not happen, though three more were added: Cuyahoga Valley in the Akron-Cleveland region of northern Ohio, Santa Monica Mountains NRA near Los Angeles, California, and Chattahoochee River NRA beginning in the northern suburbs of Atlanta, Georgia.

The designation National Recreation Area was intended to differentiate these sites from parks whose reason for existence is a natural resource base. The early NRAs, at manmade reservoirs, were widely regarded as areas of less merit than sites all natural. The word *recreation* has always contained a touch of something pejorative in it for many Park Service professionals.[18] That attitude is implicit in the somewhat relaxed standards of quality associated with National Recreation Areas and the significantly longer list of possible permitted uses, including public hunting, trapping, and other consumptive activities. In practice, not much of any of those things actually goes on in NRAs, but the basic ground rules allow them to be considered on a case by case basis.

Because there is a less rigorous standard by which they are judged and because the negotiating room for permitted uses is much broader, it seems probable that the number of NRAs will increase in the future. However, there is not a very high possibility that the trend defined by the existing urban NRAs will be revived, though the closing of many military bases and facilities may reopen that possibility. The Presidio of San Francisco is now on its way to becoming an urban unit of the national park system. This large military complex in the heart of San Francisco poses incredibly complex problems and opportunities for park planners and the political forces that shape park developments. It will take a great deal of money, either public or private, to convert this site to nonmilitary public uses.

There are four parkways in the national park system: Blue Ridge; George Washington Memorial; John D. Rockefeller, Jr.; and Natchez Trace. All are narrow corridors straddling roads intended for leisurely driving for pleasure. In all cases the parkways have been designed and are maintained to provide a scenic experience along the way. Speed limits are well below those of the interstate highways on what are mostly two-lane roadways.

The Blue Ridge Parkway, a 470-mile drive along the crest of the Blue Ridge Mountains of Virginia and North Carolina was only recently completed after more than fifty years of segmented construction. It is one of the great driving experiences of the world. Natchez Trace, which will be about 445 miles when completed, may rival it.

The parkways began as federal employment programs in the years of the Great Depression. By many measures they have been expensive, not only because of their protracted acquisition and construction schedule, but also because a lot of money has been spent preserving or, sometimes, reconstructing the nearby environment. Such elements as bridges and overpasses have been constructed of native stone, using both designs and technologies intended to be respectful of the setting. In one segment of the Blue Ridge Parkway that traverses the slopes of Grandfather Mountain a unique bridge-building technology was used to reduce the visual effects of the roadway and virtually eliminate the unsightly scaring typical of hillside roads. The roadway at that location is an engineering achievement in its own right.

Driving-for-pleasure is one of America's most important forms of outdoor recreation. The parkways are therefore among the most-visited places in the national park system, the Blue Ridge Parkway holding the distinction of being the most-visited unit in the system at 17.9 million in 1993. Also among the most-visited units at the southern end of that parkway, Great Smoky Mountains NP (Tenn., N.C.), had visitation of over 9 million that same year.

Will there be other parkways in the future? Perhaps, especially in the context of efforts now emerging in various locales to preserve historic corridors, linear systems (such as canals and rail links), and similar features. Possibly, such developments might again be seen as a means of providing some form of jobs programs or economic stimulation. From time to time legislative proposals emerge for modern versions of the Civilian Conservation Corps or the Works Progress Administration, two New Deal jobs programs whose constructed works remain today in many parks—used and respected for their quality and for the employment they provided. None of those proposals has taken hold yet, but even many critics of federal pump priming regard the CCC and WPA as useful successes. The general deterioration of the American highway, bridge, and other public facility infrastructure may lead to some new form of jobs program that could have spillover benefits for the national park system.

Both the National Seashores and National Lakeshores are the product of the new environmentalism of the 1960s. Though Cape Hatteras NS had existed since 1937, all the remaining units of both types of park areas were accomplished during the administration of Presidents John F. Kennedy and Lyndon B. Johnson and then Secretary of the Interior Stewart L. Udall. Both types of areas were seen as means for preserving public access to beach and waterside resources that were rapidly being closed by private ownership and development. It now seems highly probable that if these units had not been created when they were, the two decades of development that followed would have made them impossible to achieve by the 1990s. It was a last chance well taken, adding nine National Seashores and four National Lakeshores, the latter on the Great Lakes. It is unlikely there will be new areas in these categories on any scale resembling the burst of concern three decades ago, though proposals are already in existence involving shoreline areas in New England and along the Oregon coast.

National Wild and Scenic Rivers and Riverways, National Rivers, and National Scenic Trails encompass linear parks, some hundreds of miles in length, intended to preserve river segments still wild in character or to provide long distance trails along scenic or historic corridors. Several are new and await development on the ground. Only the Appalachian Trail is in usable finished form, though that one, too, is constantly changing as land acquisition proceeds and external developments take place along its 2,100-mile length between Maine and Georgia.

Some of these units of the national park system are currently in a state of policy flux. For example, the National Park Service is considering reclassification of the Potomac Heritage National Scenic Trail as an affiliated area. If the trail is a valid program objective, it will certainly take a type and level of planning, land acquisition, development, and cooperative activities with local governments not even considered so far.

The 1989 *Index* did not list National Reserves, but since publication of that listing, one National Reserve has been authorized anew and another reclassified from the category of affiliated areas. The former is City of Rocks National Reserve in Idaho; the latter is Ebey's Landing National Historical Reserve on Whidbey Island, Washington.

The classification was first defined in 1976 in the Service's revised land acquisition policy dated April 26 of that year. The category was intended as a device to intervene in land development processes in the developing areas surrounding major metropolitan regions, particularly to help in the preservation of agricultural land uses and small rural communities. The descriptive language in the policy reads:

National Reserve (Areas of National Concern)—Federal, State, and local governments form a special partnership around an area to be protected. Planning, implementation and maintenance are a joint effort and are based on a mutual desire to protect the resource. Under this concept, the Federal Government, through the National Park Service, may acquire core zones intended to protect and allow appropriate use of the most vital physical resources within authorized boundaries of the area. The balance of property within these areas may be protected through a combination of acquisition and management by the State and local governments, and the development of zoning or similar controls acceptable to the Secretary of the Interior.

The concept has been carried out at Ebey's Landing NHRes through a 1988 agreement between the National Park Service, Island County, the Town of Coupeville, and the State of Washington Parks and Recreation Commission. The agreement set up a governing board to manage the reserve according to a plan approved by the Park Service in May 1980.

In this instance the Park Service now owns a core area of about 1,300 acres in fee and has easements or controls development rights on additional lands. The area was set up by law in 1978, but since then the site has been in a state of continuing flux regarding its legal status. For years it was treated as a part of the national park system and was later classified as an affiliated area. The official park brochure, written by the Park Service, characterizes Ebey's Landing as "officially a unit of the National Park Service [sic] . . . a completely new kind of park." More information about this on-again-off-again park is contained in the chapter on affiliated areas.

The other reserve in Idaho is in a rural area, embracing about 14,400 acres and including a state park. Created in 1988, City of Rocks NRes will be managed under a cooperative arrangement with the State of Idaho Parks Department. The management plan for the reserve will turn day-to-day administration of the site over to the state, under an agreement that requires the state to meet all NPS standards and legal requirements.

As new park proposals emerge in and near sections of the U.S. already developed or in other forms of land uses, it seems probable that this classification will grow in usage. Its terms afford great flexibility in land ownerships and uses, management styles and formats, and cooperative mechanisms among multiple levels of government and (potentially) the private sector. Though such arrangements often appear less disciplined than more conventional formats, familiarity with such devices may make them less feared by those who seek more conventional assurances of long-term protection.

Such alternative park formats are not universally welcomed within the National Park Service, however. Old management styles are shaken up. Roles change. Responsibilities vary. As a former manager of Ebey's Landing NHRes observed, "I spent more time fighting those within the Service [than] I did fighting our detractors outside the Service."[19]

The above classifications account for all but eleven units of the national park system. The remaining parks whose names and titles do not conform to other patterns are located in the Washington, D.C., metropolitan area. Catoctin Mountain Park (Md.) and Prince William Forest Park (Va.) were created from submarginal agricultural lands in the 1930s, designated National Recreation Demonstration Areas. A total of forty-five such areas were acquired at the time to retire lands no longer productive for agricultural uses. NPS typically developed the parks, often through the CCC or WPA, and subsequently transferred them to the states in which they were located. Catoctin Mountain Park and Prince William Forest Park remained with the National Park Service, perhaps because they were seen as one way of strengthening the system near the nation's capital. Part of Catoctin was set aside as President Roosevelt's Shangri-La hideaway, later renamed Camp David by President Eisenhower. They remain today as well-visited units of the national park system.

Other miscellaneous sites include such notable assets as the White House itself, for which NPS has physical responsibility. Also included are the Kennedy Center for the Performing Arts in Washington, D.C., and Wolf Trap Farm Park for the Performing Arts in the nearby Virginia suburbs, whose maintenance is NPS's responsibility (not artistic programming).[20] The substantial park system in the District of Columbia is part of the national park system as well.

In the years ahead it seems likely that there will be more, not fewer, classifications and titles within the system. Titles may represent new formats negotiated for new areas. They may signal new management styles. What, for example, might a new unit be called of the national park system created on Indian-owned lands at Wounded Knee for which management responsibility rests with the Indians? Such a format would be an innovation for which an equally innovative title would probably emerge.

As some existing parks mature, they will also sometimes gain new names, perhaps to reflect cumulative changes in management style or to illuminate some previously forgotten or unknown historical association. Some proposed changes will be controversial, and, perhaps, not all changes will be welcomed by the National Park Service and others. For example, since shortly after the Battle of the Little

Bighorn on June 25–26, 1876, the site of that Montana battle between the Seventh U.S. Cavalry and Sioux and Northern Cheyenne Indians has been named for and has served as an unabashed memorial to Lt. Col. George Armstrong Custer, who died there with about 268 others under his command. Long called Custer Battlefield NM, the site and its associated events have essentially glorified Custer, at the expense of larger issues surrounding his mission at the time and their effects on contemporary American life.

New self-awareness by Native Americans both near the battlefield and elsewhere, along with others who lend support to their concerns, pushed legislation in Congress to change the name of the park to Little Bighorn Battlefield NM in late 1991 and provide a monument to the forty or so Indians who died in the battle.

These events and the tug of war to rename an old park say much about the importance of names and about the significance that many people attach to places in the national park system. Those who urged change at Custer Battlefield NM clearly reflected newer understandings of American history and new sensitivities to Native American people and their culture. Those opposing change call it efforts to rewrite history in a fashion deemed more politically correct.

If the National Park Service and others have experienced some discomfort with nontraditional park formats, it seems likely there will be more discomfort in the future. Consider a park where one of the primary resources for which the park is created is *people*. It is already happening at several locations elsewhere in the world (Africa, Australia, and South America). Many new parks (sometimes with very different labels) are being created or considered in parts of the world that are already settled. They are the home or the hunting grounds or the sacred territory of indigenous peoples whose association with the land and its resources may be older than any industrialized society.

New parks or other conservation reserves in the area of ancient indigenous peoples pose policy and political issues of great importance, not only to the people directly affected but also to the larger society. Many of the affected peoples are "primitive" or tribal, often living a lifestyle sharply at odds with current assumptions by the dominant majority about civilization and social values. They are often regarded as curiosities and as people who should be converted or educated in the ways of modern industrial culture. The National Park Service faces such people in many Alaska parks and in its relationship with Native Americans at several parks in the lower forty-eight states.

Conventional park management wisdom asserts that the proper

format for all parks is to eliminate all the people from the site. If that is impossible, as it often is politically, the goal then is to work out some accommodation that restricts land uses by the indigenous population to its minimum possible levels. In U.S. parks such uses are limited to subsistence levels, with some additional recognition of sacred or religious uses, when they can be asserted as part of the native culture. The clash of values can be illustrated by a common example from experience at several Alaska parks. Snowshoes and dog sleds are allowed, snowmobiles are not. Indigenous peoples are almost universally regarded as the problem, and the goal of park managers or those seeking to create the park is to minimize all evidence of prior human uses and future human impacts.[21]

The world needs a new park concept that includes indigenous peoples as one of the primary park resources. The people and their culture should receive not only the same attention and care but also the same legal protection as any park resource. They should be fully engaged in its management and be a part of the decisions affecting the lands. Many such people hold nothing resembling legal title to the lands. They may be nomadic or have other reasons to move about the land from time to time. They may very likely have lived on the land for many centuries in some form of equilibrium with their environment. Unfortunately well-intentioned conservationists, who see in the land only its physical resources, have displaced populations in Africa and elsewhere, creating thereby major disruptions of indigenous peoples. This syndrome has characterized U.S. park policy from the beginning.

The notion that people can continue to live within a park or conservation reserve is not entirely new. It happens today on a minor scale as a temporary accommodation to people who may be granted life estates or other long-term residential privileges in new park areas. The difference is that the idea needs to deal with *permanent* residential uses and long-term other uses, some of which are consumptive, and with some form of self determination that gives dignity and recognition to lifestyles that may be very different from modern industrial society. However, such parks are not museums for people, and they ought not be regarded as devices to preserve curious lifestyles or novel cultures. They deserve more respect than that. They must be capable of evolving in their own time and way and change must be an accepted part of the undertaking.

This concept first came to my attention in an essay by Raymond Fredric Dasmann: "Parks, Nature Conservation, and 'Future Primitive.'" Dasmann's interest was principally directed to park proposals in the western Pacific, where he saw old park management formats as impossible on those small, settled islands.[22] Yet faced with the prospect that almost any new park of any size in the United States may overlay lands already settled, the idea is likely to be apt in this country, too. It may even have applicability to the Alaska parks and those associated with Indian-owned lands elsewhere. What would such a peoples' park be called? Maybe the affected people should themselves decide.[23]

There is, of course, another element of every name associated with units of the national park system: the locale, feature, person, event, or other distinguishing characteristic for which the park is named. Many park names come from a geographic feature or natural element in the park. For example, Yellowstone NP was named for the color of rock that distinguished the area, Sequoia NP was named for the great trees that it harbors, and so forth. Such names are not likely to change. Some people argue that names can play an important part in the sense of place that a unit evokes. Historic sites may be named after an event (Independence NHP or Theodore Roosevelt Birthplace NHS) or a place (San Juan Island NHP), a manmade feature (various forts, for example), or a person (the Jefferson Memorial). In the Director's first formal annual report to the secretary of the Interior, written by Acting Director Horace M. Albright in 1917, he asserted that "all of the [national] monuments would mean infinitely more to the American people if their funereal surname could be changed."[24]

Some names are not self-explanatory for people who come to them without prior knowledge of their association: Ninety Six NHS (S.C.), Hamilton Grange NMem (N.Y.), and Poverty Point NM (La.) are examples. The first was a Revolutionary War site; the second was the home of Alexander Hamilton; the third is a park at the site of a culture that thrived in the first and second millennia B.C.

The issue of a name was very important to the National Park Service itself at the time of the major federal reorganization in 1933 that added some fifty-six sites to the national park system. The Executive Order signed by President Franklin D. Roosevelt that accomplished this massive growth of the system also changed the name of the National Park Service to the Office of National Parks, Buildings, and Reservations. The Park Service, however, did not like the new name, and on March 2, 1934, it got its old name back.[25]

The national park system has been the object of many complaints about the complexities of its nomenclature. It has been suggested that designations be simplified to no more than two or three classifications: perhaps National Parks, National Historic Sites, and National

Memorials (which would include all the battlefields and other commemorative areas). Simplification of park classifications has an orderliness about it that is attractive at first glance. It would certainly make remembering names easier sometimes. But simplification by any great amount would lose many assets that differing classifications affords, especially when it is used as a means to signal to the public what they may expect of and at the park.

Descriptive titles are also an important part of the process of commemoration in our culture. Having something named after a person, place, or event is a widely valued expression and symbol of respect and value. The political significance of national park system names can be illustrated by a long-standing controversy surrounding a proposal to change the name of Alaska's Mt. McKinley to Denali. Denali is the Indian name for the mountain, meaning the Great One. The mountain, the highest in North America was, however, named Mt. McKinley after the twenty-fifth president (1897–1901), and the National Park was similarly named until 1980, when Congress renamed the park and its adjoining National Preserve. Members of the congressional delegation from Ohio, from which McKinley came, however, have consistently objected to legislation to change the name of the mountain. The U.S. Board on Geographic Names, the federal institution responsible for standardizing name usage on maps and in publications, always defers making name changes when they are embedded in pending legislation. Therefore, Mt. McKinley retains its older name, though the park was renamed.

So far, the National Park Service has rather successfully warded off attempts to name parks and park features after famous and not-so-famous people. The Service relies in significant part on the policies of the U.S. Board on Geographic Names to resist such actions—even if not 100 percent effectively.

But with efforts by recent administrations to encourage new levels of philanthropy in support of the parks, there is increasing pressure to recognize the beneficence of donors through plaques and other memorials and the placing of names on (particularly) buildings. Visitor centers are a major focus. Though Park Service policies generally discourage such memorialization, there are just enough exceptions and loopholes to present the appearance of inconsistency.

For all their obvious capacities to obfuscate more difficult issues or mask other problems or divert the attentions of people who simply do not want to be bothered with such details, names and titles are important for the units of the national park system.

NOTES

1. See Hartzog, *Battling for the National Parks*, 102–3. Hartzog credits staff aide Bob Coates with the idea.

2. Memorandum from Secretary of the Interior Stewart L. Udall to the director, National Park Service, July 10, 1964.

3. Act of Sept. 11, 1964.

4. *National Parks for the Future*, 15.

5. "Management Policies," U.S. Department of the Interior, National Park Service, 1988, 1:3.

6. Hartzog, *Battling for the National Parks*, 254.

7. Former Director Horace M. Albright has asserted that the first director, Stephen T. Mather, always felt that size was not an important criterion for National Park status. Though both Mather and Albright worked hard to divest two early (and smallish) National Parks—Sully's Hill and Platt—they were rather ardent visitors to and users of the Hot Springs Reservation, whose name was changed to Hot Springs National Park during Mather's directorship. Mather made it a point to take senators and congressmen to Hot Springs in the course of his many "Show Me" tours of the parks in those early days. Interestingly, Hot Springs NP was the most visited park in the system for many years. See Albright, *Birth of the National Park Service*, 30.

8. For reasons unclear to me, most people do not afford fish a place in the animal kingdom as valued as mammals or birds. Many dictionaries do not include fish in the definition of "animal." Ecologically, fish occupy a niche that is in no way less significant than any other large group of living creatures. National Park Service policies regarding fishing in the National Parks are clearly at odds with its mission to preserve other species and prevent their "harvesting" for sport by the public.

9. The International Union for the Conservation of Nature (IUCN) has for a number of years sought to standardize the nomenclature associated with National Parks and other conservation reserves. Progress has been made, but the wide variations in application of the terms worldwide have made uniformity a difficult goal.

10. In 1992 the name of Fort Jefferson NM (Fla.) was changed to Dry Tortugas NP, to recognize and protect the "pristine subtropical marine ecosystem, including an intact coral reef community . . . populations of fish and wildlife . . . [and] submerged cultural resources," along with the fort. 106 STAT. 3439. The name change involved no boundary change, however.

11. *National Parks for the Future*, 20. At a time when consideration was being given to Acadia NP and Great Smoky Mountains NP, Shenandoah was disparaged by park supporters in and out of government. "To recognize Shenandoah as a national park, its value for outdoor recreation aside, would be, in effect, to condone 'the fatal belief that different standards can be maintained in the same system without the destruction of all standards.'" Quoted in Runte, *National Parks*, 219.

12. For an interesting history of the national monuments see Rothman, *Preserving Different Pasts*. Rothman asserts that "the Antiquities Act [under which virtually all national monuments were proclaimed] is the most important piece of preservation legislation ever enacted by the United States government. . . . Without it, there would have been little flexibility in the preservation process, and many areas of significance would have been destroyed before Congress passed legislation to protect them" (p. xi).

13. Ft. Lauderdale (Fla.) *Sun-Sentinel,* Oct. 6, 1991.

14. Linenthal, *Sacred Ground,* contains studies of five such sites: Lexington and Concord, The Alamo, Gettysburg, The Little Bighorn, and Pearl Harbor. All except The Alamo are units of the national park system.

15. Ibid., x.

16. Under present NPS policies battle reenactments are not permitted in national park system sites. See the NPS "Management Policies," chap. 7, p. 3 (Dec. 1988). Civil War battle reenactments, some of them very elaborate undertakings, in which participant garb and arms have acknowledged replicate or historical authenticity, have become increasingly popular in the last two or three decades, though they have gone on at some Civil War sites since shortly after the actual battles. Reenactments are inherently dangerous, not only for the participants, but often also for spectators. Reenactments also trample the landscape and require much staff support. On more philosophical grounds, battle reenactments are by their nature an inaccurate portrayal of a dirty, deadly, bloody event. The acknowledged fun and attempts at historical accuracy notwithstanding, reenactments trivialize the horror and reality of war and, for young people and children in particular, they convey a false impression of war's terrible effects.

The National Park Service does sponsor or permit others to conduct living history demonstrations of nonbattle activities and events. Examples include the exhibit of black powder firearms and, perhaps with evidence of some inconsistency in the policy, field medical services (absent blood, of course).

17. See Linenthal, *Sacred Ground,* 175–212.

18. Among many people, feelings about recreation as a valid, wholesome, human activity have long been mixed with residuals from an older ethic that treated leisure as sinful and a waste of time. Though sports and recreation are a very large part of the nation's economy and recreational pursuits are an almost everyday occurrence in everyone's life, they still raise images of time wasted in fun and games. Attitudes toward recreation hold an interesting set of paradoxes in American life.

19. Letter to the author from Reed Jarvis, Nov. 1991.

20. The fiscal year 1995 budget proposes to transfer the Kennedy Center to the Smithsonian Institution.

21. For a discussion of one such population, the Bajau in the Sulu Archipelago, see Hamilton-Paterson, who observes: "It is beyond understanding why governments and their agents should imagine that cultures which have taken millennia to attune themselves to such ways of life might cheerfully renounce them in as little as a generation. The world is dotted with groups

of demoralized tribespeople, drunk in shacks and shanties at the margins of the societies that have disinherited them. Exasperated and not always unsympathetic officials complain about the inertia and fecklessness of Aborigines or American Indians, how pathetically they connive at their own degradation" (*The Great Deep*, 275).

22. See Brower, *Micronesia: Island Wilderness*. I expanded on Dasmann's concept in a proposed policy paper in the *Courier* vol. 32, no. 2 (Febr. 1987).

23. I would like to suggest that Vice President Al Gore was thinking about something compatible with this idea when he wrote in *Earth in the Balance* that we "cannot treat the earth as something separate from human civilization; we are part of the whole too" (p. 2).

24. Annual Report of the Director for F.Y. 1917, in *Annual Report of the Secretary of the Interior* (Washington: Government Printing Office, 1917), 787.

25. 48 STAT. 389.

THREE

Affiliated Areas

The 1970 definition by Congress of the national park system—any area administered by the National Park Service—however simple in its terms, has not turned out so simple in practice. At that time, the National Park Service cared for, more or less, 250 areas and sites. The number is only approximate because, in fact, there was no formal list or understanding in Congress or in the National Park Service regarding what was in or out of the national park system. A formal list was not drawn up until 1973. At that time the National Park Service did not wish to include several sites under its jurisdiction in the system. The reasons are unclear, but in that year a classification dubbed "Affiliated Area" was invented by NPS and nine areas were initially so designated.[1]

According to a 1990 Park Service report on affiliated areas, the "category developed by default to encompass areas that did not fit the definition of park system units rather than areas that did meet some specific criteria."[2] The report went on to explain that "the term 'affiliated area' has no clear basis in legislation and does not confer any legal status or importance to a site.... The concept ... is based on the character of a relationship with the National Park Service rather than a description of resources, significance, or appearance on an official list."

From that beginning in 1973 through the present time, the only official list of national park system areas is an occasional publication of the Park Service's Office of Public Affairs and Division of Publications *The National Parks: Index 1989* (and other years).[3] Until very recently the actual decisions about which units would be classified as affiliated areas were made by the Office of Public Affairs based on informal consultations with other offices, especially the Division of History.

The affiliated area category was rationalized on the grounds that the

1970 law that defined the national park system "specifically excludes 'miscellaneous areas administered in connection therewith,' that is, those properties that are neither federally owned nor directly administered by the National Park Service but which utilize NPS assistance."[4]

The Act of August 18, 1970, not only deleted all references to "miscellaneous areas," but also redefined the national park system by eliminating all references to park system "categories" such as National Parks, National Monuments, and so on. This action is consistent with the new definition of a single system "united through their interrelated purposes and resources."[5] It is a major stretch of purpose to argue that such language supports a separate category of affiliated parks. Notwithstanding an early misreading of the statute, the National Park Service has continued to rely on the supposed exclusion of "miscellaneous" areas, up to and including its 1989 instructions regarding the classification of national park system units,[6] its 1990 report to Congress on affiliated areas, and the latest official list of park system units contained in the *Index 1989*.

The Park Service acknowledges that the classification has been applied inconsistently in the past. There is a rather long list of areas and facilities not in the system that have received federal financial support through appropriations made to the Park Service: the Folger Library, Arena Stage, and the Corcoran Gallery of Art, all in Washington, D.C.; the Martin Luther King, Jr., Center for Non-violent Social Change in Atlanta, Georgia; Jubilee Hall at Fisk University in Nashville, Tennessee; and Balboa Park in San Diego, California, among others.

While some areas now on the affiliated area list receive no financial or other support from NPS, some do. American Memorial Park in Saipan, Marianas, is staffed and managed by the Park Service, but until 1994 it has been variously carried first as a unit of the system, then as an affiliated area "because the authorizing legislation envisions that this park will eventually be transferred to the Territorial Government."[7] Boston African American NHS (Mass.) is also administered by the Park Service but was carried as an affiliated area for many years. In 1994 it is classed as a national park system unit.

Steamtown National Historic Site in Pennsylvania was created by Congress in 1986, but was carried by the National Park Service as an affiliated area until 1988. According to a Park Service official who asked not to be identified, "The law authorized, but did not require, NPS to own the land, and some of us hoped a way would be found to avoid having the site in the system. When, in 1988, we actually acquired the site we had no choice."

Ebey's Landing National Historical Reserve, located on Whidbey Island, Washington, is an interesting case in point and one that was only recently resolved. The law that created Ebey's Landing NHRes specifies that NPS will administer the site under terms of the National Park Service organic act "as long as responsibility for management and administration remains with the United States."[8] NPS shares membership on the governing trust board, provides on-site staff, and supplies up to half the reserve's operating budget through the regular appropriations process. Also, it is charged with conducting an annual "appraisal of the management and operation of the Reserve."

Established in 1978 as an acknowledged part of the national park system, Ebey's Landing was reclassified as an affiliated area in 1989. The Pacific Northwest regional director "strongly" recommended reclassification back to park system status. In a memorandum to the director, the regional director noted: "We have been telling area residents and support groups for many years that this is a full unit of the system."[9] Because Ebey's Landing was conceived to preserve and protect a cultural landscape through the cooperative efforts of federal, state, and local laws, regulations, and management, it is distinctive and does not fit the conventional format of national park system units. The principal means by which this historic pastoral landscape is to be preserved is through zoning and other land use controls, not the fee ownership of land by the National Park Service. In current political parlance, Ebey's Landing is a "partnership park." Many people believe this type of unconventional park acquisition and management format will become increasingly common in the future, in part because fee acquisition is so expensive and in part because other means may be found to protect valued resources without full-scale public ownership.

The regional director's appeal for reversal of the action to exclude Ebey's Landing NHRes from the national park system was turned down. He appealed again on January 20, 1990, and on February 13 was again turned down, in the course of which the director's memoraadum noted that "Ebey's Landing certainly does not fit the neat definitions that we would like to have for distinguishing units from affiliated areas or other designations."[10] The memorandum went on to note that formal classification procedures had been adopted in 1989, containing criteria that Ebey's Landing did not meet. The new classification procedures spelled out roles for the Park Service Division of Legislation and others before printing the *Index*. The memorandum also listed seven criteria in the form of questions:

Exactly what does the authorizing legislation provide?
Does NPS own any land or interests in land in the area?[11]
Are [NPS] funds being used to support management of the area?[12]
Are uniformed or other NPS personnel assigned to the site?
Has NPS delegated administrative responsibilities through a cooperative agreement?
Does NPS retain ultimate responsibility for administration although some operations have been delegated?
What implications does the classification as a unit have for fee collection, legal liability, law enforcement, or public understanding?

Unfortunately, the memorandum does not spell out how the questions are to be used. Must a site meet any or all of the criteria? If NPS owns land at a site, does it matter how much land is involved or whether it is in fee or less than fee? What if it meets some criteria but not others? Do they all have equal weight?

NPS does own land at Ebey's Landing. Park Service funds pay for about half the operating costs at the site. The principal staff person, called the project manager and equivalent in grade and responsibilities to a superintendent, was until 1993 a uniformed NPS employee. Yes, certain administrative responsibilities have been delegated through a three-way agreement. Yes, NPS does retain ultimate responsibility for the site, makes inspections and monitors actions. The body that serves as the site's governing board (called the trust board) reports to the NPS regional director. So why was Ebey's Landing an affiliated area? Perhaps the answer is best captured by a handwritten note on the bottom of a memorandum sent to the regional director further reinforcing the denial of his request (but leaving the door open a crack "if the Regional Solicitor can find that Ebey's Landing fits the technical definition of a unit"). On the bottom of the memo, then Director James M. Ridenour wrote a note to the regional director, Charles Odegaard: "Chuck—I have to admit that I haven't an opinion on this matter. Other subjects seem higher on the list of importance. If you are fired up about it, feel free to make a crusade."[13]

Regional Director Odegaard persisted, however, and in spite of opposition from some of the director's staff in Washington, a legal brief by the regional solicitor prevailed and on October 7, 1992, the unit was again declared a full unit of the national park system—perhaps permanently this time.

There are no written policies or ground rules covering affiliated areas. Accordingly, the sites do not enjoy the full legal and administrative protection afforded all other units of the national park system. In fact, they generally receive no NPS oversight and are not given periodic inspections or audits. Most have no formal master plan, and any plans that do exist are not usually given formal approval by the National Park Service.

Some sites classed as affiliated areas have long been disparaged within the Service as unworthy of NPS involvement. The David Berger National Memorial in Cleveland (Ohio) is an example. This site was recognized by Congress in 1980 and honors the eleven Israeli athletes assassinated at the 1972 Olympic Games.[14] The memorial is a sculpture by David E. Davis on the entrance lawn of the Jewish Community Center in Cleveland Heights. The law relating to the national memorial reads as follows: "The Secretary of the Interior shall designate the David Berger Memorial located at the Jewish Community Center in Cleveland Heights, Ohio, as a national memorial. The significance of the memorial in preserving the memory of the eleven Israeli athletes who were assassinated at the Olympic games in Munich, Germany, in 1972 is, by this designation, recognized by the Congress."

Does such a law make the David Berger NMem a unit of the national park system? Are there even grounds for classifying it as an area affiliated with the system? In researching the site I was unable to locate anyone associated with the Cleveland Jewish Community Center who knew of a relationship with the National Park Service or system. The community center cares for the memorial as part of the grounds of its building, occasionally planting flowers nearby. A plaque, approved and paid for by the National Park Service, identifies the sculpture as a national memorial.

It would appear that the disparagement directed toward this national memorial is unwarranted. There seems to be little evidence Congress ever intended it to be associated with the national park system in any way. Such ambiguities of purpose and effect argue powerfully for more disciplined action by the Congress, including greater clarity of intent, and clearer policies of the National Park Service regarding temporary or one-time roles it may play in the nation's commemorative processes. Port Chicago National Memorial (Calif.) is a recent example almost identical to David Berger NMem.

The National Trails System contains additional inconsistencies in classification. The *Index* typically lists national trails—historic, scenic, and recreational—under a separate heading, and their resources are not included in statistics for the national park system. Since there is separate generic legislation covering the trails system, such separation is logical. Many trails contain no federally owned lands other than lands previously acquired for another purpose, such as a military installation. Much trails legislation specifically prohibits federal land acquisition. One wonders how its congressional sponsors envisaged the trail ever to come about.

The National Trails System Act of 1968[15] set up a class of National Recreation Trails, managed by public or private organizations, and designated officially by the secretary of the Interior only after they have been fully developed and are open to the public. As of January 1, 1993, the most recent year for which statistics are available, 804 National Recreation Trails have been designated throughout the United States. Most of the trails (525) are on federal lands, 151 on state lands, 85 are local, 31 are private, and 12 involve some form of joint sponsorship.

There are eight national scenic trails and eight national historic trails.[16] Curiously, three of the eight scenic trails are included both as part of the national trails system and as units of the national park system: Appalachian, Natches Trace, and Potomac Heritage. A reading of the authorizing legislation for those trails does not immediately reveal how they are different in a way that would qualify them for membership in the national park system. The 1990 report of the Park Service on affiliated areas also suggests the Santa Fe NHT and the Trail of Tears NHT "appear to fit the definition of a unit" of the national park system. No specific reasons were mentioned.

The North Country NST, authorized in 1980[17] states that "the trail shall be administered by the Secretary of the Interior." The language for the Potomac Heritage NST, Overmountain Victory NHT, and the Natchez Trace NST say the same thing. The qualities that make these trails in or out of the national park system are not obvious.

The same issues apply in some part to ten wild and scenic rivers administered by the National Park Service and classified as units of the national park system. A total of twenty-six wild and scenic rivers is listed as "administered by the National Park Service," but sixteen of them are not included in the national park system. The reasons are unclear because most of them lie within the exterior boundaries of national park system units.

The 1990 affiliated areas report notes that if such areas are taken seriously, "Maintaining oversight on these [sites] will require allocations of staff, funds, and time in the regional offices or nearby park system units. This could include a formal annual operations evaluation. Funding for affiliated areas must compete with other priorities for existing units of the national park system."

In the 1990 study and report on affiliated areas the National Park

Service has made a valid and important effort to clarify the subject, including a candid admission transmitted to Congress that justification for the category was an administrative artifact inconsistently applied. The report was transmitted to both Houses of Congress by then Secretary of the Interior Manuel Lujan, Jr., containing criteria "for the elements of national significance and other factors necessary for a proposed area to be considered appropriate for inclusion as an affiliated area of the national park system."[18]

Unfortunately, the secretary of the Interior did not specifically ask the committees for their comments on or agreement with the affiliated areas classification or with the criteria used to include areas within it. Further, the document sent to Congress did not by itself change anything. The recommendations contained in the report remain unapproved. Nothing has changed internally, including several proposed reclassifications from affiliated areas to units of the system. The next edition of the *Index* will not reflect the recommended changes.

The study does not, however, resolve the issue in any legally sufficient way. Does the National Park Service have authority unilaterally to classify areas authorized by Congress as either units of the national park system or affiliated areas? It has exercised that authority in the past, without consulting Congress. Does NPS have authority to change the status of a unit from affiliated area to unit of the system without explicit action by Congress? It has done so in the past. And, what is much more important, does the body of law that governs and protects units of the national park system apply with equal force to affiliated areas? Included are: the National Park Service Organic Act, the National Environmental Policy Act, the Clean Air Act, the Clean Water Act, the Endangered Species Act, the National Historic Preservation Act, Executive Order 11990 (relating to wetlands preservation), and others.[19] Applicability of these statutes to affiliated areas is an important policy decision for both Congress and the Executive Branch. It is uncertain how the Clinton administration and Congress would decide.

It is also uncertain whether the general body of national park system law applies to national scenic or historic trails (established under authority of the National Trails System Act of 1968) and to Wild and Scenic Rivers (created under authority of Public Law 90-542 but classified by the National Park Service as units of the national park system). When an Interior Department lawyer versed on National Park Service matters was asked that question, he said only that he did not know and that as far as he knew, the issue had not been raised in any formal way. Such a response probably means the answer is "no, national park system law does not apply to national scenic trails even if they are classified for *Index* purposes as units of the national park system." Publication in the *Index*, after all, has no legal significance; its purpose is strictly for public information.

It seems highly probable that Congress will opt for expanded and enlarged use of the affiliated area concept in the future. It has the advantage of affording a site the status of being a "national" something or other. Simultaneously, it does not carry with it assurance of federal financing and operation. It could stimulate private or corporate philanthropy in support of a locally sponsored project. The kicker is that the site will still need to meet the definition, however described and by whomever decided, of being nationally significant. Such a conclusion is far easier when there is no money attached to the judgment, though it could easily be used in that form as a means of getting the proverbial camel's nose into the tent.

In that spirit, it is very important that Congress consider the terms proposed by the National Park Service for affiliated areas. Those terms ought to be defined in law. Then Congress needs to abide by those criteria and be very clear in its legislative enactments as to its intentions. It has failed on many occasions to do that in the past. Steamtown NHS is a good example. That site's authorizing legislation did not make it clear that the site was to be a part of the national park system, and the National Park Service promptly relegated it to status as an affiliated area. The Park Service should not have that option, but Congress needs to be much more precise about its intentions.

To whatever extent authorizing legislation is unclear or inexact, Congress needs to be more precise. It would be a constructive act for Congress and the National Park Service to come to an official agreement concerning the exact extent of the national park system—all 367 units, by name and number. The next unit enacted would be No. 368, then 369, and so forth. Such agreement would serve several useful purposes, including a clarification of the real status of the present list of affiliated areas. It would also serve as a public reminder regarding the extent of the system and recognition of the additional responsibilities that each new area gives to those who finance and care for the system.

The existence of the affiliated area category in its present form is a disturbing phenomenon. Created by administrative fiat, and not an explicit one at that, the category has been used as a "parking lot" in which to put areas and sites for which the National Park Service's commitment is hesitant, limited, or nonexistent.

As shown in the study by Alan Hogenauer cited in the bibliography, NPS has accumulated some ten sites that have been authorized but never established. Nevertheless, although there were acceptable excuses for things not happening at various times in the past, there is similarly no follow up later when conditions may have changed, no tickler to remind the Park Service periodically of unfinished business. Memories are short and in an organization where even the most senior positions turn over fairly rapidly, previous agendas and old business can be easily lost and forgotten.

Ancillary systems managed by the National Park Service, including the wild and scenic rivers system and the national trails system ought similarly to be clarified as to their status vis-à-vis the national park system. Is the distinction intended to be more than one associated with nomenclature? What body of law applies? Do wild rivers within units of the national park system enjoy the full protection of law associated with the surrounding lands?

Congress and the bureau need total and unequivocal agreement on what is in the system and what is not. If there are hangers-on areas defined so that they are affiliated, but not members of the system, Congress and the Park Service need to understand jointly *and* clearly the legal and policy implications of that affiliation. What laws do or do not apply? What obligations does NPS have to police the terms and conditions of their affiliation? Who hollers "Hold!" when a site is endangered?

There will be more affiliated areas, by whatever terminology they are labeled. What is important is that they end up better off as a consequence—not shoved off into an undefined limbo of future expectations. Sites recognized by Congress for their national significance merit a full professional and legal commitment by the National Park Service. The present policies governing affiliated areas fail completely to serve the integrity of the national park system. The remedy lies with Congress.

NOTES

1. For a description of each, see Appendix 2: (1) Chicago Portage NHS (Ill.); (2) Chimney Rock NHS (Nebr.); (3) Gloria Dei (Old Swedes') Church NHS (Pa.); (4) Ice Age National Scientific Reserve (Wis.); (5) International Peace Garden (N.D.); (6) Jamestown NHS (Va.); (7) McLoughlin House NHS (Oreg.); (8) Roosevelt Campobello International Park (New Brunswick, Canada); and (9) Touro Synagogue NHS (R.I.).

2. *Report on Criteria for Affiliated Areas,* to Committee on Interior and Insular Affairs, House of Representatives, and the Committee on Energy and Natural Resources, U.S. Senate, pursuant to P.L. 100–336, National Park Service, Feb. 1990: 1.

3. The booklet is published every two to four years and includes a general description of the national park system and its nomenclature; a listing and description of current units; and a listing of affiliated areas, units of the Wild and Scenic River System, and units of the National Trails System. As this book goes to press the *Index 1993* is in print.

4. *The National Parks: Index 1989*, 87.

5. Sec. 2(a), P.L. 91-383 (84 STAT. 826) amending Sec. 2(a) and 2(b), P.L. 230 (67 STAT. 496).

6. Memorandum to the directorate and field directorate from the director, Subject: Classification of NPS Units and Related Areas, File: L58(763), June 9, 1989: 1.

7. The quotation is from the study cited in note 2, p. 3. The authorizing legislation is contained in P.L. 95-348, approved Aug. 18, 1978 (92 STAT. 491).

8. Section 508(d), P.L. 95-625 (92 STAT. 3508).

9. Memorandum to the director, National Park Service, from the regional director, Pacific Northwest Region, Subject: Ebey's Landing NHRes, File L3215 (PNR-PL), May 26, 1989.

10. Memorandum from the director to regional director, Pacific Northwest Region, Subject: Status of Ebey's Landing NHRes, File D18(773), Feb. 13, 1990.

11. The National Park Service owns land or has an interest in land at three sites currently listed as affiliated areas: (1) Gloria Dei Church NHS (Pa.), 2.08 acres in fee; (2) Green Springs Historic District (Va.), NPS holds easements on 5,490.59 acres; and (3) Lewis and Clark National Historic Trail (Ill. to Oreg.), 39.11 acres in fee. All acreage as of Sept. 30, 1991. Source: Land Resources Division, NPS, WASO.

12. Four affiliated areas were included in the 1995 NPS budget: (1) American Memorial Park (Saipan), $149,000; (2) Gloria Dei Church NHS (Pa.), $28,000; (3) Pinelands NRes (N.J.), $297,000; and (4) Illinois & Michigan Canal National Heritage Corridor (Ill.), $152,000.

13. Memorandum from Denis Galvin to the director, Subject: Status of Ebey's Landing NHRes, Apr. 4, 1990, and the note thereon initialed "JMR," Apr. 9, 1990.

14. Sec. 116, P.L. 96-199, approved Mar. 5, 1980. (94 STAT. 71).

15. P.L. 90-543, as amended.

16. The eight national scenic trails: (1) Appalachian (Maine to Ga.); (2) Continental Divide (Canadian border to Mexico); (3) Florida (from Everglades NP north); (4) Ice Age (Wis.); (5) Natchez Trace (Nashville, Tenn. to Natchez, Miss.); (6) North Country (N.Y. to N.Dak.); (7) Pacific Crest Trail (Canadian border to Mexico); (8) Potomac Heritage (Potomac River, Md., and Va. to Pa., but not W.Va.).

The eight national historic trails: (1) Iditarod (Seward to Nome, Alaska); (2) Lewis and Clark (Mississippi River to Pacific Ocean); (3) Mormon Pioneer (Nauvoo, Ill. to Salt Lake City, Utah); (4) Nez Perce (Oreg. to eastern Mont.); (5) Oregon (Independence, Mo. to Portland, Oreg.); (6) Overmountain Victory (Va., Tenn, N.C., to Kings Mountain, S.C.); (7) Santa Fe (from Arrow Rock, Mo., through Kans., Okla., and Colo., to Santa Fe, N.Mex.); (8) Trail of Tears (N.C., Tenn., Ga., Ala. to Okla. and Ark.).

17. P.L. 96-199, approved Mar. 5, 1980 (94 STAT. 67).

18. Letter from Secretary of the Interior Lujan to Hon. George Miller, chairman, Committee on Interior and Insular Affairs, House of Representatives, June 17, 1991. An identical letter was sent to Senator J. Bennett Johnston, chairman of the Senate Committee on Energy and Natural Resources, in response to P.L. 100-336, approved June 17, 1988 (102 STAT. 617.)

19. See also the list of statutes recited in Sec. 2(b) of the Act of Aug. 18, 1970 (84 STAT. 826).

FOUR

The Crown Jewels

Both within the National Park Service and among various publics, the units bearing the title "National Park" have a special mystique. In turn, some National Parks are often called the "crown jewels," usually understood to include Yellowstone, Yosemite, and Grand Canyon National Parks, and perhaps others, depending on one's background or perspective. The term is normally confined to the large natural area parks in the western United States, and would not include even the most renowned historic sites, the Statue of Liberty and Independence Hall included. Nor does it usually extend to the National Parks in Alaska.

The term "crown jewels" is intended to bestow on those parks a supremacy of regard and reflect a special loyalty toward them. They are the crème de la crème. Outside the National Park Service they are often regarded as the central theme of the national park system. In times past various national park supporters, including the National Parks Association,[1] have advocated that the system be limited exclusively to the crown jewels and that everything else in the system be transferred to another agency or jurisdiction.

Within the Park Service the crown jewels cast a similar aura. As a result, many professionals in the Park Service feel that the crown jewels may legitimately assert a more forceful claim on the National Park Service budget than other parks in the system. The crown jewels are the parks whose Superintendents are at the apex of the career ladder. They typically have the largest staffs, the largest operating budgets, and the largest annual construction programs. The crown jewels are often referred to in public statements, testimony, and publications of the Park Service and Park Service officials, including its directors.

Many of the maxi-attributes assigned to the crown jewels are, indeed, valid translations of physical and historical realities. Yellowstone *was* the premier park in the system, first in time and first in size (in the lower forty-eight states). Until the parkways and urban park units came along, Yellowstone, Yosemite, and Grand Canyon National Parks were also first in visitation. One reason for the wide name recognition they enjoy is the media attention they receive, both good news and bad.

There is, however, a dark side to the crown jewels phenomenon. By bestowing a special status on a handful of large, western natural area parks, every other park unit in the system becomes second fiddle. But it can even be worse than that. Other parks become involved in a stratification process that devolves an order of merit among park units that makes stagnant backwaters out of some parks, personnel dumping grounds out of some, and neglected stepchildren out of many others.

One case in point is mentioned by former Director Horace M. Albright in his autobiographical account of the founding years of the Park Service. In a story used as an example of policy differences between him and Newton Drury, the fourth director, Albright noted that for years it was practice in Carlsbad Caverns NP for the staff to sing "Rock of Ages" in the darkened cave near a giant stalagmite given that name, some seven hundred feet underground. According to Albright, "[Director] Drury ordered Superintendent Tom Boles to stop the practice of the hymn singing and lights going on and off. But Boles, who believed the ceremony added greatly to the visitor's park experience, did not comply with the director's order. Drury finally got exasperated and transferred Boles to Hot Springs National Park, despite outcries from New Mexico congressmen. Boles retired from the Park Service soon afterward."[2]

Some Park Service people dismiss the derogatory aspersions cast at lesser parks as mere joking or making harmless fun of sites whose geography or costs of living or climate make them less desirable places to live and work. The reality is more harsh. The reasons some parks are "lesser" or "unworthy" of membership in the national park system is because the professional and supervisory leadership of the Service cast doubts about the validity of a park's existence, or about its historic or resource bona fides, or about its future as a unit in the system. The following examples are a matter of record.

In 1973 the then director of the Park Service Office of Archeology and Historic Preservation—the organization of professional historians, archaeologists, and historical architects in the Service—wrote a memorandum to the associate director for professional services, the number three official in the Park Service. He recommended that eleven National Historic Sites be dropped from the system.[3] (All but two were eliminated in due course, though several remain as affiliated areas.) In addition, he advised that nine national cemeteries, then units of the national park system, lose their separate identity and be absorbed into the larger unit nearby.[4] (All nine were later absorbed in that manner.) Further, he wrote that ten National Memorials were of "dubious merit as components of the National Park System."[5] (The list included Johnstown Flood NMem [Pa.], which had 131,832 visitors in 1993; and Lincoln Boyhood NMem [Ind.], with 177,320 visitors in 1993. None has yet been divested.)

In his memo, he went on to assert that twelve additional historic sites and monuments that "did not meet standards of national significance . . . should not have been added to the System in the first place and should now be dropped." (One site, Mar-A-Lago NHS, was divested seven years later.)[6]

The memorandum did not spark great action in 1973, though it can perhaps be credited with sowing seeds that took root and bloomed years later.[7] In November 1990 the official bureau historian revived the memorandum and brought it to the attention of National Park Service Director James M. Ridenour. The historian observed that "it's safe to say that many more would not pass professional muster now."[8]

In 1990 Director Ridenour accused the Congress of "thinning the blood" of the national park system. He went on to charge the Park Service with "being willing to accept something that is less than nationally significant into our park system." Recognizing the possible negative effects on congressional leaders and NPS personnel, he added, "Obviously I am not going to name any specific parks or park proposals here."[9]

In his editorial Director Ridenour asked his readers to reflect on recently added parks and to "compare them to the 'crown jewels' with which we long have been entrusted." In 1991 he further elaborated on his views about the place of the crown jewels, writing, "I don't want to see our 'crown jewels' suffer further deterioration as we drain staffing and budgets to support new parks that might appropriately be managed by state and local government or even developed privately by individuals or organizations."[10]

Director Ridenour's view was reflected in official testimony before Congress by the vice president of the association representing the Park Service's professional rangers. Testifying on November 21, 1991, Bill Wade expressed the view that "areas of less than national significance—sometimes far less . . . have been brought into the system, thereby diluting our original mandate, mixing the truly wondrous with the truly mediocre, and stretching our funds and staff beyond the breaking point."[11] He did not name names.

In *America's National Parks and Their Keepers,* Ronald A. Foresta declared that[12] "the entire urban wing of the National Park System was, in essence, an experiment . . . and [NPS ought] to . . . write off failures when the time comes to do so. . . . Indiana Dunes [National Lakeshore] is probably such a failure. Fire Island [National Seashore] is also without doubt a failure."

A contrasting view was expressed recently by longtime national park system supporter Robin W. Winks, former chairman of the National Park System Advisory Board. Dr. Winks noted that he has, remarkably, visited 333 units of the national park system, including about 20 that he had thought were "bad ideas." He went on to observe that "at least 75 percent of them have turned out to be very good ideas indeed, through intelligent interpretation. Some need more funding. . . . one or two . . . need to be interpreted more broadly. . . . conceivably three or four will not make the grade. That is hardly a [recent] decline in quality, since three of my 'three or four' came into the park system more than thirty years ago"[13] Fortunately, Professor Winks, also, did not name names.

Consequences flow from the crown jewels concept. The most obvious effect is a broad stratification of parks into two groups: the crown jewels and everything else. But the concept is carried even further. It pervades other differentiations and affects the allocation of funds, the assignment of personnel, and the futures of both sites and career staff. Foresta cites an example: Thaddeus Kosciuszko NMem in Philadelphia. The memorial was authorized by Congress in 1972 and, according to Foresta, "[NPS] was not particularly interested in the site. . . . there was already a glut of Revolutionary War memorials and sites in the system. . . . All [the Service] could do was tastefully ignore the site once it was in the System."[14]

There are, unfortunately, other examples of park sites created by Congress that the National Park Service has managed to "tastefully ignore." In his scholarly history of the national monuments, Rothman documents how *all* of the early national monuments "were largely left out of the development of the park system" until the Park Service received new money and people through the Civilian Conservation Corps (CCC) and other employment programs in the 1930s.[15]

One such site, Fossil Cycad NM, was so ignored it never received any form of on-site protection and was ultimately looted of its reason for existence and later abolished. Another site, Mar-A-Lago NHS, was divested eight years after its creation, without a uniformed NPS employee ever having served there. The story of this modern failure of the park system is told in the chapter that follows.

Reflecting the belief that Congress was causing the addition of sites lacking appropriate merit, Foresta went as far as to suggest to a Park Service official "that perhaps the Service could discourage the addition of sites of little merit by giving less than its complete attention to some of the unworthies already in the system."[16] Fortunately, the official involved in the discussion declined the suggestion as a "dangerous strategy."

An internal example is taken from the working papers of the Seventy-fifth Anniversary symposium in Vail, Colorado, in October 1991. Addressing what it calls the National Park "culture" the paper asserted that "superintendents in smaller parks talk about the difficulty of getting timely assistance from headquarters and the regions. . . . and these same superintendents said bureaucratic retribution would follow if they complained too loudly about lack of support and assistance. . . . In this world the big parks—the crown jewels—will do fine. They have extensive networks of supporters and substantial professional resources, are politically sensitive, and (often) are led by the most experienced and savvy superintendents. But smaller and newer national park system sites will suffer."[17]

These writings and statements reflect a dangerous, unfortunate, and legally questionable disregard for the integrity of the national park system. The "maintenance of the integrity of the system" is a central concept associated with the 1970 amendment to the Organic Act of 1916.[18] The 1978 amendments to the Organic Act further called for National Park Service "management and administration of these areas . . . in light of the . . . integrity of the National Park System."

What does "integrity" mean when applied to the national park system? Integrity begins with the selection and creation of sites that enter the system in the first place. Because that process has brought units into the system that did not enjoy a broad consensus of National Park Service professional support, many NPS employees and other park supporters argue the integrity of the system has been compromised from the beginning. A major problem in dealing with this argument is that often in the past the National Park Service was largely or completely uninvolved in the processes by which a new unit was identified and added to the system. Without financing for new area studies, the Park Service has not crafted its own agenda for over a decade. Under pressures from the Reagan and Bush administrations, during which *all* additions to the national park system were not welcome, virtually no new area studies were done, resulting in the initiative for new parks resting entirely with Congress.

Within the National Park Service the absence of an agenda of its own was not entirely unwelcome, reflecting a concern that the wrong areas were getting into the system and that the additions already made were putting too much stress on NPS funding and staffing. Bureau Historian Barry Mackintosh wrote that "the virtual moratorium on new areas from 1981 to 1986 came as a relief to many."[19]

Another reason for noninvolvement is because a site may have represented a new departure from old norms. It would not be unusual for the Service to be a reluctant recipient of the new responsibilities represented by the site. Such reluctance served as a force opposing entry of the reservoir recreation sites in the 1950s, of the urban recreation areas in the 1970s, of sites associated with the world of arts and letters in the 1980s, of maritime resources in the late 1980s, and of sites associated with industry and commerce in the 1990s.

With few exceptions, the National Park Service has institutionally resisted the expansion of its mission to include new themes and new environments, in spite of theme studies and lists designed to identify important natural resource areas and historical events and trends important to the flow of American and world history.

However, once a part of the system, in almost all instances, as the Service has gained experience and developed a cadre of informed professionals whose values include the new departures, the resistance has moderated. But the process is slow and old discomforts do not disappear easily or completely. The crown jewels syndrome makes that integration more difficult.

During the last two years of the Bush administration the National Park Service attempted to regain a share of the initiative with Congress. It crafted a list of proposed new area studies and sought approval from the Office of Management and Budget to submit them to Congress. The Service has also worked to redefine the types of new area studies it makes to distinguish those sufficiently detailed to support a new park proposal from those made essentially as a service to a local entity that is looking for a way to protect a valued property.

A second element in defining the integrity of the system relates to its permanence. Virtually no one regards the national park system as a temporary phenomenon. But would everyone agree that it is *permanent?* People who support divestitures must countenance something less than forever, at least for selected (by them) sites. Is the national park system to be something whose content can be changed in the future for good and sufficient reason? Just as new areas are added in response to new understandings of a resource or event or new values ascribed to a resource or event, ought the system be purged of sites less valued or less appreciated at some future time?

We are, in the 1990s, rounding out the boundaries of sites significant to the Civil War, in part because of widening public knowledge of and appreciation for that war as a force that has shaped our lives and culture. Also, we move now because the sites associated with that war are being infringed upon and obliterated by population growth and economic development. Often, it will be now or never. But will the national interest in the Civil War be as high on the preservation agenda (say) fifty or a hundred years from now? Should the acquisitions and preservation actions undertaken now be carefully framed as decisions we make that we intend to be permanent—forever? Neither Congress nor the Executive Branch is clear and certain on the point. There would be no hit lists if the matter were clear.

A third and final element of integrity is, of course, the quality of care afforded each site in the system and the degree to which it is faithfully protected from the natural and manmade forces that would compromise or destroy it. This final element in support of the basic integrity of the national park system cannot exist without the other two elements preceding it. It must be a valid entrant to the system, and it must be there permanently. If the system can be attacked and potentially dismantled by its own custodians and supporters, what hope is there for defending it from people and forces who are not sympathetic to its values?

The process by which units are added to the national park system currently fails to satisfy many people. Some units are said to have been given inadequate study. Others have been compromised by incompatible developments or the weather. Still other units, while associated with a valid theme, should have been located in another place. Many units are of only regional significance, with events or persons lacking the "transcendent" importance to merit memorialization at a unit of the national park system. Some units of the system were added without hearings before the appropriate committees of Congress and consequently were passed without adequate debate. Or some passed Congress when only a handful of representatives was on the floor of the House or only a few senators present in the chamber. So the arguments run.

However, every site in the national park system—every law on every subject passed by every Congress—is an expression of our political culture at a particular time in our history. Each site is associated with a distinct moment in our history and the cumulative product of singular events whose timing and circumstances are unique and not reproducible. Yellowstone did not become a National Park in 1871 or 1873. It happened on a particular day in 1872.

The value of no legislation is measured by the number of senators present and voting or the length of committee hearings. Our governmental system is structured in ways that give and require equal enforceability and effect for all legislation passed by both Houses of Congress and approved by the president or by overriding his veto.

By passage of legislation creating a new unit of the national park system, the Congress has declared its "national significance." Most authorizing legislation contains explicit language to that effect. The political judgment has either ratified or taken precedence over the opinions of "experts." Recognition of that reality and commitment to live within it can be an important foundation for the long-term integrity of the national park system. However, the certitude and often arrogance of expertise make acceptance of that principle a difficult object of institutional change within the ranks of the Park Service.

Two recent directors of the National Park Service have attempted in their own discourse to temper the crown jewels syndrome. Both Russell Dickenson and the late William Penn Mott, Jr., have maintained that on the level of merit all units of the national park system begin and end on a level plain. Every park is "a jewel in the crown." What the system represents are differences among equals— different resources, different events, different characteristics. But the parks are equally demanding of National Park Service loyalties and equally subject to the protection of national park system law and its professionals.

Both Dickenson and Mott used the analogy of the family. As new members are added, parental love and attention expand to embrace the new member. Children, like parks, are not alike in structure or form. They are always different, to be loved and cared for with equal passion according to their individual needs and potentials.

The concept of equal "jewels in a crown," which former Director George B. Hartzog, Jr., interprets to mean "an amorphous policy . . . reduced to the lowest common denominator,"[20] asserts only that all units of the national park system have an equality of membership in the system. Beyond that lay differences in resources, in needs, and in potentials. Difficult decisions on management strategies, budget allocations, personnel, and so forth, remain. But no park is a lesser member of the "family." Just as in a family, such a policy and attitude can make a difference, not only in levels of self-esteem but in performance.

On another level, similar attitudes and differentiation occur in the titles assigned to units of the national park system. Some park advocates and members of Congress share this perspective regarding the advantages of National Park status, and proposals are advanced from time to time to change the name of an existing unit to that of a National Park to capture the aura and prestige associated with that class of parks. It is widely believed that the National Park designator will also more readily assure that a site is regarded as a "destination park," at which people will plan overnight stays or longer visits. Recent examples of sites redesignated as National Parks include Biscayne and Fort Jefferson NMs (Fla.), the latter now Dry Tortugas NP.

Some purists have long asserted that there is something fundamentally wrong with Hot Springs NP (Ark.) having that designation. Director Drury thought it was far enough down the totem pole that being named its superintendent was an appropriate penalty for insubordination, as related earlier. However, that site is contemporary testimony to the foresight of people in the mid-nineteenth century in preserving lands from the once vast public domain for a public purpose. In the context of the nation's westward expansion and land giveaways of the nineteenth century, the Hot Springs Reservation was a monumental achievement and a fitting precursor to creation of the first National Park in 1872. Hot Springs was first set aside in 1832—two generations before Yellowstone! Both of the first two directors, Stephen T. Mather and Horace M. Albright, went there to "take baths, rest and talk out the situation" in the hectic formative days of the National Park Service.[21] Perhaps absent the Hot Springs precedent, Yellowstone would have been less likely.

The crown jewels syndrome—doing the best for what we regard as the best among equals—is a widespread phenomenon in almost every facet of public and private life. Concepts of "jewels in a crown" notwithstanding, even parents do not uniformly treat their children in a manner based on equality, even when they may wish sincerely to do so. The allocation of attention and caring involves subtle and often hidden values, almost never made explicit. One reason such judgment factors are not treated openly is because we know that to do so would hurt someone's feelings or instill a sense of inferiority in ways that are neither needed nor intended. In many instances of interpersonal relationships the disclosure of such factors is consciously suppressed—sometimes the subject of "white lies"—to avoid the negative effects we believe might otherwise result. But application of those restraints to public policy decisions and to the allocation of public resources denies information needed for accountability to the public served. If the crown jewels syndrome results in allocating a disproportionate share of resources to a few parks, and a consequent shortfall in others, it is very important for the factors that caused such decisions to be opened for debate and public examination. That is the nature of accountability.

There is a strong sense of hierarchy in the National Park Service that ranks types of units in the system and, within types, by groups of units. Listings are largely intuitive and would on only the rarest of occasions be put in writing or articulated in any coherent way. Ranked comparisons are, however, very common in everyday conversations.

Many lists are constructed ad hoc in response to a specific issue or decision. Hierarchies are not cast in stone and over time the merits of specific sites may change. Normally a site rises in its merits with the passage of time, partly because staff who once worked there may now say good things about it and partly because extended familiarity reduces discomfort levels. Albeit, some parks that have been around a very long time never get out of the institutional cellar.

Measuring the effects of hierarchy in the National Park Service is more difficult because it is so implicit in everyday life. One piece of strong evidence is suggested in a study conducted in 1990 by Denis P. Galvin, NPS associate director for Planning and Development. Galvin concluded that during the 1980s, a time when the Park Service budget increased overall at a rate substantially above the rate of inflation, almost one-third the parks failed to keep pace with inflation.[22] Though Galvin is reluctant to define "winners and losers" based on his analysis, the director's 1991 budget request for the National Park Service specifically asked for "a modest overtarget amount ... [of $10 million] to make inroads against the gradual erosion of the park operating base, focusing on ... nearly every small and medium-sized park."[23]

The 1991 budget request attributed the shortfalls experienced by small- and medium-sized parks to the increased costs of pay and retirement, infrastructure backlogs, and the failure of such parks to benefit from an expanded fee collection program. Many of those factors apply to every park, however, and one suspects other less obvious forces underlie the reality.

A late 1991 Associated Press report, headlined "Grant's Tomb Falls on Hard Times," recounts the following:

NEW YORK—If Ulysses S. Grant could see what his tomb looked like these days, the nation's 18th president would be rolling over in his sarcophagus.

Spray-painting vandals and the federal government's tightening purse strings are blighting the final resting place of the Civil War hero and his wife. . . .

Graffiti . . . stains . . . a stark obscene message . . .

"It's such an embarrassment. People get off their tour buses, and this becomes their image of New York. . . . *At the Washington Monument [in Washington, D.C.] this would never be allowed to happen,*" said Georgette Nelms, a supervisor for the National Park Service.[24]

General Grant NMem is located on Riverside Drive at 122nd Street in New York's Manhattan. Overlooking the Hudson River, the three-quarter-acre site affords a spectacular view, and records official visitation of some one hundred thousand a year. Its 1991 budget was some $109,000 with a full-time staff of four to care for it. Grant's tomb has long been regarded as a lesser site in the national park system. As a "mere" memorial it lacks the site relatedness so many people feel is necessary to validate a park system site. It is also very small and very urban, a neighbor to Harlem.[25]

Is it possible to live with the crown jewels concept without its potentially damaging consequences? The answer must be an emphatic "Yes." It is probably unrealistic to even think about eliminating the phenomenon. The concept is too firmly established and too much a reflection of values no one would really wish to destroy or deny. The answer lies perhaps in examining the issues it raises, understanding the subtleties of its effects, and devising systems and processes that level out the playing fields of budgets, personnel assignments, and so forth. Simply talking about it will help. Institutional systems must follow.

Appendix 6 offers several samples of unconventional ways of looking at the national park system. Hierarchies have been established by budget size and by total visitation. Sample correlations with budget costs have been computed and are displayed in Appendix 7. Even this small sample of comparative data suggest the need for much further analysis.

If, on the other hand, explicit ranking is justifiable as public policy, it is essential that it be accomplished in an open public process, exposed to argument and the competition of opposing points of view and perspectives. Minority interests compel illumination if they are to be protected from domination by those in the majority or those representing the crown jewels. The expression "many jewels in the crown" protects even the smallest and most obscure element of the system. Too much evidence already exists that it is too easy to allow harm to wheels whose squeak is too dim or whose clientele too small. The national park system gains larger meaning and importance in its diversity, as a reflection of the nation's pluralistic citizenry and values. Park professionals must respect those values as their own.

NOTES

1. Now the National Parks and Conservation Association, a nonprofit support group, headquartered in Washington, D.C. NPCA has a membership approaching half a million. It performs a range of interest group functions: testifies on pending legislation, educates legislators on matters of concern, conducts or sponsors research and publications, holds conferences, and serves as external champion of the national park system while often simultaneously prodding NPS officials and staff to make changes or not to make changes, as the case may be.

2. Albright, *Birth of the National Park Service,* 326.

3. The following units were recommended to be dropped from the national park system: Chicago Portage NHS (Ill.), now an affiliated area; Chimney Rock NHS (Nebr.), now an affiliated area; Dorchester Heights NHS (Mass.), now part of Boston NHP; Gloria Dei (Old Swedes') Church NHS (Pa.), now an affiliated area; Jamestown NHS (Va.), now an affiliated area; McLoughlin House NHS (Oreg.), now an affiliated area; Pennsylvania Avenue NHS (D.C.), still a unit of the system; St. Paul's Church NHS (N.Y.) still a unit of the system; St. Thomas NHS (V.I.), divested in 1975; San Jose Mission NHS (Tex.), incorporated in San Antonio Missions NHP in 1978; and Touro Synagogue NHS (R.I.), now an affiliated area. Memorandum from the director, Office of Archeology and Historic Preservation to the associate director, Professional Services, Subject: Scope of the National Park System, Mar. 8, 1973.

4. The nine national cemeteries were Antietam NCem (Md.); Fort Donelson NCem (Tenn.); Fredericksburg NCem (Va.); Gettysburg NCem (Pa.); Poplar Grove (Petersburg) NCem (Va.); Shiloh NCem (Tenn.); Stones River NCem (Tenn.); Vicksburg NCem (Miss.); and Yorktown NCem (Va.).

5. The other eight were Arkansas Post NMem (Ark.); Chamizal NMem (Tex.); Coronado NMem (Ariz.); Desoto NMem (Fla.); Fort Caroline NMem (Fla.); Fort Clatsop NMem (Oreg.): Roger Williams NMem (R.I.); and Thaddeus Kosciuszko NMem (Pa.).

6. The eleven other units were Abraham Lincoln Birthplace NHS (Ky.); Booker T. Washington NM (Va.); Cabrillo NM (Calif.); George Washington Carver NM (Mo.); Pipe Springs NM (Ariz.); San Juan Island NHP (Wash.); Saugus Iron Works NHS (Mass.); Theodore Roosevelt Birthplace NHS (N.Y.); Theodore Roosevelt Inaugural NHS (N.Y.); Tupelo National Battlefield (Miss.); and Tuzigoot NM (Ariz.).

7. By 1991 the author of the 1973 memorandum, now retired, had con-

cluded that making up lists of unworthy parks "always shattered on the twin shoals of political reality and internal disagreement. As a waste of staff time, such an exercise is surpassed only by attempts to tinker with nomenclature." Letter to the author from Robert M. Utley, June 23, 1991.

8. Memorandum from the bureau historian to the director, Subject: Plaudits and a Plea, K3815(418), Nov. 14, 1990.

9. From "Thinning the Blood," *Courier* vol. 35, no. 11 (Nov./Dec. 1990): 1.

10. From "Building on a Legacy," by James M. Ridenour, *National Parks Magazine* vol. 65, nos. 5–6 (May/June 1991): 23.

11. *Ranger* vol. 8, no. 1 (Winter 1991/92): 10.

12. Foresta, *America's National Parks,* 280–82.

13. From "Intelligent Interpretation," *Courier* vol. 36, no. 2 (Summer 1991): 9. Professor Winks goes on to say, "I have never met a park I didn't like, and, though vigilance is the price of quality, we need not despair."

14. Foresta, *America's National Parks,* 135.

15. Rothman, *Preserving Different Pasts,* xv.

16. Foresta, *America's National Parks,* 79.

17. "Draft Report of the Working Groups on Our National Parks: Challenges and Strategies for the 21st Century," prepared for consideration by a working Congress on National Park Management, Vail, Colo., Oct. 7–10, 1991: 16, 18.

18. See especially House Rept. No. 95–581: 21.

19. Barry Mackintosh, "A Historical Perspective on the National Park System," *Courier* vol. 36, no. 1 (Spring 1991): 13.

20. Hartzog, *Battling for the National Parks,* 254.

21. Albright, Dickenson, and Mott, *National Park Service,* 14. If someone thought Hot Springs NP was low on the ladder, the superintendent in 1992 saw other units below him. In a letter to the author dated Feb. 21, 1992, Superintendent Roger Giddings noted that "Mather and Albright both enjoyed and touted Hot Springs. As I understand, Franklin Lane (secretary in their times) did, too. Of course, there was only a handful of parks at that time; not that some added to the system since then would be any competition."

22. *Trends in the Operating Budget of the National Park Service, 1980–1988,* (typescript) by Denis P. Galvin, July 1989.

23. Memorandum from the director, National Park Service to the assistant secretary for Fish and Wildlife and Parks, Subject: FY 1991 Budget Request, File F30(330), May 22, 1989, 2; and attachment Number 7: "Detail of Potential FY 1991 Overtarget Items in Priority Order." The amount requested was said to be enough to cover 225–75 requests.

24. Emphasis added. Associated Press dispatch, Dec. 26, 1991.

25. By fiscal year 1994 General Grant NMem had a budget of $126,000, and it was projected to increase to $578,000 in 1995, with seven FTEs.

FIVE

Mar-A-Lago
National Historic Site

On January 16, 1969, Secretary of the Interior Stewart L. Udall signed an order declaring Mar-A-Lago, the seventeen-acre estate of cereal heiress Marjorie Meriweather Post, a National Historic Site. Located in Palm Beach, Florida, Mar-A-Lago is grandiose. The main house has 118 rooms, including 17 bedrooms, and is dominated by a 75-foot tower from which panoramic views of the Atlantic Ocean and Lake Worth are afforded. The name means "between the ocean and lake." The site stretches between both, and includes a private tunnel for access to the beach under a busy thoroughfare along the ocean front.

The 37,000-square-foot building is made of Doria stone, three boat loads of which were brought to the site from Genoa, Italy. The house is profusely decorated and enhanced by more than 36,000 old Spanish tiles, some of which date back to thé fifteenth century. The house also contains many stone carvings as details at windows, doors, and other architectural elements. The grounds include landscaped lawns, a swimming pool, several outbuildings, a nine-hole golf course, greenhouses, and maintenance facilities.

The building's interior was lavish in its construction detail and furnishings, including many original works of art and individual pieces of furniture manufactured by craftsmen whose skills could no longer be assembled at any price.[1] Opening in 1927, the building took four years to build and cost a reported $8 million.[2] Except for the addition of minor outbuildings and a swimming pool the estate has been kept very close to its original configuration.

Architectural plans, measured drawings, photographs, and other permanent documentation of the Historic American Buildings Survey were completed for the estate in 1967. The estate's significance is as a "remnant of the wealthy resort culture of the 1920s, noted for its variety of opulent architectural styles and design details."[3] By the late 1960s the number of such places remaining in the United States was rapidly diminishing under the combined forces of social and economic change. When Congress considered legislation that would make the site part of the national park system, it concluded that Mar-A-Lago was "truly one of America's greatest manmade treasures . . . [that] could never be duplicated."[4] The House Report noted that "while this property may not rank among the properties which have been recognized because of their antiquity, it is one whose values will grow in future generations."[5]

Mrs. Post had for many years expressed hope that the property be preserved for the benefit of the state and the nation. She first offered the property to her three daughters, each of whom declined interest on grounds that it was too large and too expensive to maintain. In 1964, long before any national attention was turned on Mar-A-Lago, Mrs. Post approached Florida Governor Farris Bryant with a proposal to donate the property to the state. When Mrs. Post explained with studied precision that the property cost $259,512 a year to maintain, Governor Bryant politely declined interest on behalf of the state.[6] In the late 1960s Mrs. Post approached the National Trust for Historic Preservation to try to interest that nonprofit organization in the property. However, the National Trust also declined interest in the estate. She then approached her well-placed contacts in Washington, D.C., about ownership and operation by the National Park Service.

Legislation to create Mar-A-Lago NHS was introduced in the House of Representatives by the powerful chairman of the Committee on Interior and Insular Affairs, Wayne N. Aspinall (D-Colo.). The legislation was cosponsored by Congressman Paul Rogers of Palm Beach, Florida; Rep. Roy Taylor (D-N.C.), then subcommittee chairman; and ranking minority member Joe Skubitz (Kans.). The Bill was also supported by Florida senators Lawton Chiles (D) and Edward Gurney (R).

The legislation was signed by President Nixon on October 21, 1972,[7] thereby establishing Mar-A-Lago National Historic Site and authorizing acceptance of the property if it were donated to the National Park Service. The law also called for the acceptance of furnishings and other personal property and provided that administration of the site would be accomplished through funds donated to the Park Service by the Marjorie Meriweather Post Foundation, an institution established to oversee Mrs. Post's estate. At that time, Mrs. Post was still living at Mar-A-Lago, and it was understood she would continue there until her death. She died on September 12, 1973, at the age of eighty-six.

The legislation making Mar-A-Lago part of the national park system and its companion legislative history referred to use of the property "as a temporary residence for visiting foreign dignitaries or heads of state or members of the executive branch of the United States Government." The legislation made no provision for the use of appropriated funds to support the property. National Park Service and Foundation testimony clearly and strongly asserted that private funding would be sufficient to operate the estate. The committee report optimistically asserted that creation of Mar-A-Lago NHS "should result in no significant cost to the Federal Government."[8] Such arrangements for the operation and maintenance of a unit of the national park system were unique. No prior unit of the system had been created under such terms, though several units do gain partial support from private donations or endowments. Private gifts and endowments have been important to many land acquisitions and for a variety of capital developments. However, almost no endowments or gifts support general operating costs.

No units of the national park system were then or are today totally dependent on operational funding from nonappropriated sources. The language in the law and the history written during hearings on the legislation were a major factor in the site's later divestiture. A second feature of the Mar-A-Lago legislation was also unique: use of the site would be limited to VIPs. No other national park system legislation contains such restrictive language, although many sites came into the system with knowledge that visitation would be low or otherwise limited to small numbers of people having a specialized interest or need. The Palm Beach Town Council objected to the site as a public facility from the beginning, insisting it "remain closed to the general public."[9]

The house report refers to possible use of the site by the president or other dignitaries. Later it was alleged that the site was incapable of providing adequate security for such uses because of the site's location beneath approaches to the Palm Beach airport. Apparently that objection was mere speculation by local opponents of the project, not a conclusion by the U.S. Secret Service. The Secret Service says it has no record of ever having examined the issue of security at Mar-A-Lago and no record that it was ever asked to do so by the Park Service or the Departments of the Interior or State.[10]

The opulent, art-filled character of the house, replete with literally priceless furnishings, made unsupervised visitation impossible. Theft, breakage, and normal wear and tear would have most assuredly exacted an unacceptable toll on the resource. The residential quality of the neighborhood setting similarly militated against unrestricted visitation.

The Mar-A-Lago legislative history, however, recognized the possibility of use by "supervised groups on a reservation basis."[11] The law gave the secretary of the Interior authority to allow "further use" (besides that of VIPs), after consultation with an advisory commission that was to support the site.[12] The advisory commission was to be appointed by the secretary of the Interior to include one person recommended by the governor of Florida, one on recommendation of the Marjorie Meriweather Post Foundation, two to be submitted by the Palm Beach Town Council, and a chairman to be named by the secretary to represent the general public interest. Nominations were promptly received from the governor and foundation, but no nominations ever came from the town council. The commission was never appointed.

Following Mrs. Post's death, the Park Service took possession and title to the real property. To administer the site the Service retained Mr. James Griffin, the longtime site manager employed by Mrs. Post, and about a dozen others who had been employed there at the time of her death.[13] The Park Service believed this action to be the only way to keep maintenance costs at a level the annual foundation grants could cover. Though converted to government positions and paid by NPS, the local staff did not wear National Park Service uniforms or receive additional on-site supervision or Park Service training. During the entire eight years it was part of the national park system, no uniformed National Park Service employee ever served at Mar-A-Lago NHS.

From the beginning, many professionals in the Park Service expressed ambivalence about the site. Some objected to it on general grounds that it was improper to have within the system a site whose character and circumstances would prohibit public use and visitation in significant numbers. One former National Park Service official who was personally involved in the project said that after reading a document that explained how visitors to the site would be guided by docents: "I remember reacting to the term 'docent' as epitomizing the exclusivity of the showing of the place. I think the group could have one of those watercress sandwich lunches mid tour or high tea if they were on the afternoon schedule (pronounced 'shedyoual')."[14]

Exclusivity, prices that reflect upper-middle income levels, and special programs and other services for special groups or individuals have for many years been a nagging concern of many National Park Service directors and staff and the object of sometimes scathing journalistic attacks. The paradoxes and problems evidenced by such feelings can be illustrated by an example, of which there are several in the national park system.

The Ahwahnee Hotel in Yosemite NP is a magnificent one-hundred-room establishment whose grandeur and architectural splendor have made it a valued destination-within-a-destination. It is on the National Register of Historic Places, and its massive granite and pine beams give it a distinction all its own. That splendor, its elite clientele, its admittedly high costs—all give great offense to some who believe passionately that Yosemite NP (and others) must only be enjoyed on its own natural terms. Historical significance aside, some people would tear the Ahwahnee Hotel down, along with much of everything else in Yosemite Valley, in order to restore the area to something like it was earlier. In fact, the Ahwahnee is loved as emphatically and with loyalty comparable to the park itself. The joint identity is powerful in many peoples' minds.

Every Christmas season the Ahwahnee Hotel sponsors a grand Christmas pageant and celebration, modeled in rich (if not totally accurate) detail after what might have been a seventeenth-century celebration in the home of an English country squire. The event is complete with elaborate decorations and costumes. The pageant, called the Bracebridge dinner, has become an annual tradition in Yosemite, rivaling famous sports events for its popularity. Since 1977 reservations for the event have been handled on a lottery basis. In 1993 more than twenty-two thousand reservations were sought for a capacity of only 992 seats at a cost of $191 for an adult and $160 for children, plus wine and gratuity. The menu is sumptuous, accompanied by three hours of choral music, soloists, minstrels, and pomp and pageantry—all of it intended to be mostly great fun.

The event does project elitist values, and the connection between the pageant in Bracebridge Hall and the natural resource values beyond the walls of the hotel is obscure at best. However, the linkage exists for some, others simply don't require it. It did exist for one of Yosemite's most ardent supporters and someone whose dedication to the park's natural values is unimpeachable: the photographer Ansel Adams. Adams helped write the pageant's first script and directed its annual production for some forty-four years! If Adams ever saw conflict between the Christmas pageant at the Ahwahnee Hotel and the object of his love of nature he never articulated it.

Unlike Adams, some in the Park Service did not support the use of Mar-A-Lago by government VIPs and others on an exclusive basis. The Park Service is regularly importuned by White House and secretarial officials and by powerful congressional committee chairmen and others to make available facilities in the parks for personal and family vacations and similar purposes.

President Franklin D. Roosevelt's "Shangri La," now the official presidential retreat known as Camp David, began on just such an informal use basis. The land is within Catoctin Mountain Park, a unit of the national park system in Maryland that began as one of the National Recreation Demonstration Areas. Camp Hoover in Shenandoah NP was a similar retreat for President Herbert Hoover.[15] It remains today as a rustic retreat used by Executive Branch officials and congressional members and staff on a reservation basis.[16]

Special favors of this character for members of Congress and others have a long history in the national park system. The Service's first director, Stephen T. Mather, spent the modern equivalent of tens of thousands of dollars, perhaps more, on organized tours to the western National Parks and personally escorted groups to the parks. He provided transportation (often through friendly railroads that served gateways to the parks), sleeping bags, horses, food, and other necessities.[17] Park superintendents served as guides and companions, all in the name of introducing people of power to the wonders of the National Parks. Though subsequent directors did not continue comparable levels of financial support, there remains to the present a strong tradition supporting red carpet treatment for members of Congress and other important supporters by NPS directors, superintendents, and others.

Others in the Park Service were reticent to include in the system a site so opulent, representing such enormous wealth and conspicuous consumption—all in what would be a hostile environment and an uncomfortable (and expensive!) community for any resident staff of government employees.[18] According to an analysis by the National Park Service, the operating costs of Mar-A-Lago during 1972, Mrs. Post's last full year there, amounted to some $360,585, excluding personal services such as maids, cooks, chauffeurs, food, and security.[19] It is probable that this estimate was low, although it was based on data furnished by Mrs. Post's financial secretary.

Donations from the foundation amounted to $98,350 during the first year of operations and rose to $170,000 two years later. From the beginning, the National Park Service "bootlegged" appropriated funds amounting to at least $50,000 a year in support of the operation, although the site was placed in a mothballed status. The property was barely maintained, sufficient only to prevent loss or deterioration of site features. The property was not open to the public, and no tours were offered or conducted, except for show-me tours done for the benefit of the chairman of the Park Service's appropriations subcommittee, several congressmen and senators, and other involved persons. President Nixon visited the site by helicopter on July 7, 1974, from his vacation retreat at Key Biscayne, Florida, shortly before he resigned.

Local opposition to federal ownership and management of Mar-A-Lago was vocal and organized from the beginning. The Palm Beach Civic Association, characterized in one report as "the largest and most influential body of citizens" in the community was said to be "near-unanimously opposed."[20] Palm Beach Town Councilman Benjamin Oehlert was an early and persistent opponent of Mar-A-Lago as a national park system unit. Several arguments against continued Park Service involvement with the site were voiced: federal ownership denied needed tax revenues to the local government; public visitation would change the character of the community; and traffic would be increased.

As early as 1974 the local congressman, Paul Rogers, was enlisted in the effort to divest, even though he was in 1972 a sponsor of the legislation to create the site. Legislation was introduced to return the site to the foundation and private ownership. Congressman Rogers's bill, and that of his successor, Congressman Dan Mica, languished in Congress for six years without action, largely because the then chairman of the House Subcommittee on National Parks, Congressman Roy A. Taylor (D-N.C.), opposed divestiture on grounds the site merited inclusion in the national park system. A similar view was held by Chairman Taylor's successor, Congressman Phillip Burton of California.

In 1975 then Senator Lawton Chiles (D-Fla.) agreed to attach a divestiture bill to legislation in the Senate. The bill was a major piece of legislation dealing with the redevelopment of Pennsylvania Avenue in Washington, D.C., but it died in adjournment. Senator Chiles did not push for divestiture later. With pressures building to divest, in January 1976 Chairman Taylor formally asked the National Park Service to develop a planning document covering alternative management options for the site. He asked that the plan specifically address the issues of limited public visitation, transportation and access, and costs. Chairman Taylor also advised the Park Service that it "should assume the continued federal guardianship of the Mar-A-Lago estate as now provided by law."[21]

By 1976 a formal planning process for Mar-A-Lago NHS was already overdue. National Park Service planning guidelines then provided that new units of the system have a "Statement for Management" as the first step of a multiphase formal planning process.[22] The statement for management is a preliminary document setting forth the nature and significance of the resource, its purpose, and the most important management objectives. Major issues and problems are to be identified and existing conditions described—all designed to serve as an interim management guide and as the basis for more detailed site planning and its accompanying public involvement.

Public involvement during the planning process is the principal mechanism by which the Park Service communicates its proposals, policies, and intentions to the public. It is also the primary device by which the public can communicate to the Park Service its concerns and points of view. The planning process is the primary mechanism for resolving controversies that may exist for the unit: permitted uses, transportation and access, user fees, and so forth. Park planning often involves extended give-and-take, often running to second or even third drafts as issues are hammered out and consensus approached. Of course, unanimity is improbable and some plans remain unapproved for years. However, most are eventually given formal approval. The timing of park unit planning varies widely. The General Management Plan for Gateway NRA in New York and New Jersey took nearly ten years and a plan for Yosemite NP over six years. However, most plans are accomplished within three or four years. Many major investments and program decisions must await completion of the GMP and superintendents are anxious to have them completed.

The absence of an ongoing planning process with its attendant public meetings, proposals and counterproposals, and the involvement of a concerned advisory board left the growing controversy unanswered and unattended. During these times there was not even one uniformed Park Service employee on site as evidence of the agency's intentions and commitment. No official NPS sign ever identified the site.

When the Park Service Regional Office planning staff in Atlanta began to develop a document responsive to Chairman Taylor's letter, they were faced with growing local opposition and no record of efforts to be responsive to local concerns. The options paper observed: "There may be a lack of understanding in Palm Beach as to the type of operation that the National Park Service could have at Mar-A-Lago. There are fears that the grounds of the estate might be open to all comers, with picnicking on the lawn."[23]

The management options document proposed supervised visitation by no more than two hundred people a day in groups of ten, collected at an off-site location in West Palm Beach and transported to the site in a van. The site would be open only eight months a year, Tuesday through Saturday. Not only was the Service concerned about parking, traffic, security, and wear and tear, but also the house had more than nine hundred openings that took the maintenance staff two weeks to close and cover each year in anticipation of hurricane season.

The options paper proposed an admission fee of $9.50 for a major tour and $4.25 for a short tour, all by reservation only. The study noted that based on visitation experienced at comparable places elsewhere—such as Vizcaya in Miami, the Hearst Castle (San Simeon) in California, and the Biltmore Estate in North Carolina—even high admissions fees were not likely to serve as a significant damper on visitation.[24] Many people would want to visit Mar-A-Lago. The plan called for visitor services to be handled by the Historical Society of Palm Beach County, the local private volunteer organization of several hundred members, possibly with the further assistance of the Eastern National Park and Monument Association. The latter organization is a "cooperating association," chartered by the National Park Service that operates publications sales outlets at many park system units in the eastern U.S. The admission fees would go to the Society to cover its expenses. Normally, fees collected at Park Service facilities in the 1970s were deposited directly into the U.S. Treasury and were not available for use by the National Park Service. That assumption was made in this instance, though there is language in the House Report accompanying the Mar-A-Lago authorization that says, "Any revenues collected for supervised tours or use of the facilities are to be used in conjunction with the income from the endowment for the benefit of the property."[25]

The management options paper was not, however, a formal planning document. While it was transmitted to Chairman Taylor as requested, and the contents of the paper were given superficial coverage in the Palm Beach papers, there is nothing in the record to show that it was ever officially made public or that its contents were ever treated as public information. The Palm Beach Town Council knew its contents, however, and publicly opposed any and all forms of public use.[26]

Nothing in the record explains why no formal planning was done for Mar-A-Lago.[27] No specific funding was available for Mar-A-Lago planning, though none was ever requested, either within the Service or of the Congress. However, negative Park Service attitudes toward Mar-A-Lago were already formed. By early March 1973, barely four months after passage of the authorizing legislation and six months before Mrs. Post's death, the chief of the Park Service's Office of Archeology and Historic Preservation asserted that Mar-A-Lago "[does] not meet standards of national significance . . . should not have been added to the System in the first place and should now be dropped."[28] This is the same office responsible for oversight of Historic American Buildings Surveys and the professional evaluations contained in the original finding of national significance in the declaration as historic site in 1969 and findings as late as 1978 to the same effect.

In addition, the first bill to divest the property was introduced in the House of Representatives in 1974, barely a year after the Park Service had taken jurisdiction over the site. Whether the mere existence of the pending legislation served to prevent or delay formal planning seems unlikely, though it was very unusual, if not unique, for a local congressman to introduce legislation to abolish a national park system unit after Congress had already acted to authorize it. Along with the bill, statements had been forthcoming from the Park Service and departmental officials suggesting divestiture or asserting that the federal government cannot afford to maintain the property. As early as December 1974, the following appeared in the local press: "The NPS has decided that the Federal Government can't afford to keep the palatial estate in Palm Beach . . . sources say the Park Service's decision to relinquish the property has received tentative White House approval."[29] At least two members of the Florida congressional delegation supported the divestiture legislation in the House of Representatives. Senate involvement did not come until later.

Annual contributions to the Park Service from the foundation were well below the total financial requirements for the site. Could the foundation have substantially increased its funding? There is no way of knowing because the record does not show any request was ever made for added funding to fully support the facility.[30] According to a 1975 press account, Henry Dudley, a foundation official asserted that "the U.S. economic situation is indirectly responsible for keeping Mar-A-Lago closed."[31]

Apparently little or nothing was done about Mar-A-Lago during the directorship of Ronald Walker, who succeeded Hartzog in 1973. As early as October of that year, the following language appeared in the *Palm Beach Daily News:* "Park Service officials have said they aren't completely pleased with getting the 115-room mansion and grounds because of an agreement . . . restricting the mansion's use."[32]

Nevertheless, by January 1975 Walker had been succeeded by Gary Everhardt as director, and a now three-way agreement between NPS, the local historical society, and the Eastern National Park and Monument Association was then about to be signed, following long negotiations involving both field and Washington Office staff. Interestingly, the foundation was not a party to the proposed agreement.

On what was described by one of the principals as the very day before the agreement was to be signed early in 1975, Director Everhardt sent "word down to hold off on the agreement until he could study it." The meeting was canceled and, for reasons neither in the record nor remembered by former director Everhardt, was never rescheduled.[33] Planning and negotiations stopped until reopened informally some two years later. In retrospect, former Director Everhardt recalled that he opposed divestiture of the site because of the precedent it would set for other units of the national park system.[34]

In 1976, discussions with the Palm Beach County Historical Society were reopened with the Society's former president, Circuit Judge James R. Knott. Judge Knott said the society was definitely interested in operating the tours. A formal agreement to that effect was never signed, however, and legislation calling for divestiture surfaced again in 1978. A report of the appropriations subcommittee recommended "that the National Park Service return Mar-A-Lago and the endowment to the Post estate as expeditiously as possible." The committee disallowed a federal appropriation of $48,000 and two positions in support of the site, referring to the law and legislative history that asserted no federal funds would be required.

On March 24, 1978, NPS Director William J. Whalen, who had succeeded Everhardt, gave his official support to the legislation calling for abolition of the site. Interestingly, Director Whalen expressly considered, but did not support, an amendment to authorize the use of appropriated funds to care for Mar-A-Lago. No reasons were given. By 1978 whatever interest the Palm Beach County Historical Society had in administering the site had vanished, or at least so thought Director Whalen. On July 27, 1979, the Town of Palm Beach declared Mar-A-Lago a landmark property, giving it the protection of local preservation laws.

Between 1978 and 1980, the National Park Service focused the limited funds available from the foundation on preserving the main house. Features on the grounds were "allowed to deteriorate. . . . [However, w]e believed that all the bypassed items could be recovered later on."[35] By 1980 accounts in the press, mostly because of statements by Congressman Dan Mica and others supporting the divestiture legislation, asserted that the estate was "falling apart" and had been the object of vandalism and theft—all attributable to the failure of the Park Service to afford adequate maintenance and protection. The official position of the Park Service was that the site was only mothballed, awaiting a final determination on the status of the site. Site manager Griffin remembers no on-site vandalism or theft during those times.[36] However, by that time NPS had shown its official support for divesting.

Chairman Phillip Burton of the House Subcommittee on National Parks and Recreation continued to oppose deauthorization of the site. Whether he saw divesting as an undesirable precedent is not known, but he said publicly several times that he opposed abolition of the site because he felt it merited inclusion in the national park system. He visited Mar-A-Lago at least once while chairman and was therefore aware of what was necessary to maintain the property.

Appropriations Subcommittee Chairman Sidney Yates, however, had visited Mar-A-Lago on two or more occasions. Whether those visits reinforced his view that the site should be returned to the foundation or whether his opposition related more narrowly to the authorizing legislation is not revealed by the record. However, by early 1980 Chairman Yates had reversed his earlier position and in February he urged that "the Congress should reassert its role of maintaining Mar-A-Lago. . . ."[37]

On December 4, 1980, Congressman Dan Mica, took a lesson from Congressman Rogers' 1975 experience and in the process pulled off a major legislative coup. He bypassed Chairman Burton's subcommittee and had his divestiture bill tacked onto legislation already passed by the House, but then being considered in the Senate. Through action attributed in one press account to Arkansas Senator Dale Bumpers (D),[38] Congressman Mica's bill was attached as a rider to a bill that Chairman Burton wanted badly—one that was critical to the conservation of Lake Tahoe in Burton's home state. Though the Lake Tahoe legislation was debated and amended on the floor of the Senate, no senator spoke to the Mar-A-Lago rider added to the end of the bill. In 1980 Florida's two senators were Lawton Chiles and Richard Stone, both Democrats.

It can only be assumed that Congressman Mica had done his homework by obtaining agreement in advance that neither of the Florida senators would object and that no objection would be raised by other senators familiar with national park system legislation. The vote taken on the Lake Tahoe Bill did not record individual senator's votes. Senator Lawton Chiles knew of the Mar-A-Lago controversy but had taken no recent public position on it. Senatorial courtesies can account for the silence, but it is impossible to confirm any agreement that might have been reached.

The bill passed the Senate on December 4 and came back to the House the next day on the Consent Calendar, an arrangement by which measures are passed automatically if no member of Congress objects. No amendments are allowed. Chairman Burton was trapped. To squash the Mar-A-Lago divestiture he would have to object to his own bill, sending it back to the committee, where it faced an uncertain future as adjournment approached. The bill was characterized as one that Chairman Burton had spent years negotiating.

The Lake Tahoe Bill was complicated and of major significance, but Congressman Keith Sebelius (Kans.), ranking minority member on the Subcommittee on National Parks and Insular Affairs rose to speak:

> Mr. Speaker . . . I lend my very reluctant support to the adoption of the . . . bill to provide increased protection for Lake Tahoe . . . due to the fact that the Senate amendments include a . . . provision which will divest from our National Park System one of its very precious components—the Mar-A-Lago National Historic Site. . . . I absolutely deplore this action. . . . I . . . have long defended the retention of this magnificent mansion as a unit of our National Park System. The best interests of the citizens of the United States, and of future generations of Americans yet to come, will suffer a needless and shameful loss as a result of this provision. I am most sorry about it.[39]

Chairman Burton added for the record that he agreed with Congressman Sebelius, and that "it is one of the lamentable aspects of this session that we are confronted with this absolutely insoluble dilemma with reference to the Mar-A-Lago situation. . . . I just wish that this amendment had been attached to some other item." The Lake Tahoe legislation controlled the procedural strategy and, without objection, the divestiture passed and was signed by the president on December 23, 1980.[40] The law ordered return of the property to the Marjorie Meriweather Post Foundation along with any monies remaining from those donated to the government. The law also delisted the site as a National Historic Site and redesignated it "Mar-A-Lago National Historic Landmark." Although the new category retained some measure of national recognition for the estate, it gave the estate no substantial legal protection.

In 1981 the property was returned to the Marjorie Meriweather Post Foundation and was promptly put on the market for sale at an asking price of $20 million, a record at the time for a residential property. The estate was twice under contract to developers who failed to consummate the deal. Finally, in 1985 the property was sold to real estate financier Donald Trump for a total of $10 million: $5 million for the house, $2 million for the beach front property,[41] and $3 million for the furnishings.

The history and controversies surrounding Mar-A-Lago after its return to the Marjorie Meriweather Post Foundation are beyond the scope of this book. In 1994 the estate remains in the news in response to proposals by Mr. Trump to subdivide the estate and sell off eight lots (about twelve acres). The city rejected the subdivision, and Trump substituted a plan to convert the property to a private club. The proposed club is legal within the present zoning envelope. The arrangement would retain the exterior of the building—the only feature legally reachable by the city's landmark preservation ordinance. Trump has voluntarily agreed to retain part of the interior. One local official privately characterized the outcome as "the best we can hope for, for the foreseeable future."

The major policy issues raised by the Mar-A-Lago experience have no easy resolution. While many supporters of the national park system would argue vigorously in favor of making it essentially impossible for any unit to be divested, many of those same people argue that some existing units are unworthy or beneath national park system standards. Some would support a one-time purge of perceived mistakes, but would vigorously oppose periodic revision of the system or fluctuating standards responsive to short-term fads or crises.

If there were to be some sort of one-time or periodic review of membership in the national park system, it is very likely that various industry groups and others having an ideological agenda would campaign vigorously for major changes to the system. If such a review were done once, it is easy to project arguments for doing it again later.

Had Mar-A-Lago NHS remained in the national park system, it is likely that it would have been a relatively costly site to operate when compared to annual visitation. It would not, however, have been the most costly site in the system or even in the most costly group. Some sense of variations in costs-per-visitor are available in Appendix 7-1, where it is seen that such costs vary from a mere $0.17 per visit to sums over $100 and as high as $486. It is important to point out, however, that cost-per-visit data can be easily misused or misinterpreted. Seasonality, accessibility, and the nature of the resource must be considered in evaluating the significance of such data. In addition, comparisons using raw budget numbers may be comparing the proverbial apples and oranges, because some park level budgets used in this analysis contain certain park-specific funding not comparable to another park. Nevertheless, the data in Appendix 7-1 contain anomalies suggesting further study.

The absence of any official planning for Mar-A-Lago, failure to assign uniformed on-site supervision for the property concurrent with assuming responsibility for it, failure to carry through with documents negotiated with local representatives in good faith, failure to address the problems of financing proper care for the site—all reflect serious failure of the support systems that attend the national park system. And while there is no evidence to suggest some sort of conspiracy to divest the site, there were powerful forces working in that direction as early as four months after the site was originally authorized. For a new site to be on a senior Park Service official's hit list at all is bad news for the integrity of the normal support process that should be set in motion.

Interestingly, the National Park Service has no documented, consistent, activation process for new park system areas. Each is handled in its own way. Things can and do fall between the cracks, although the Service often relies on the same people to handle initial park activations. Experience is a good teacher, but a disciplined, written, consistent activation process and schedule would go a long way toward assuring that at least some of the problems that led to Mar-A-Lago's demise will not happen again.

In any case, Congress should never authorize a park system unit without retaining oversight of its care and financing. Advisory Commissions should be appointed early. Missing nominations from some recommending authority should not impede the process. Meetings by a body that ought to contain additional representation can be powerful levers to get the needed nominations. Likewise, the preparation of planning documents according to well-established procedures and policies should begin early and stay on a reasonable schedule. Public involvement should not be delayed. In Mar-A-Lago's case the absence of public involvement in an ongoing planning process gave potent support for the forces opposed to the site as a unit of the national park system.

The National Park Service needs to find constructive mechanisms for developing new and innovative approaches to site management problems. The problems attending traffic, parking, and other problems perceived by Palm Beach citizens and governing officials needed to be addressed. Fears needed to be acknowledged and dealt with. The National Park Service has done all these things on many occasions elsewhere. The reasons for the failures of the system at Mar-A-Lago are not, however, trivial. Even if the national park system is not materially damaged by the loss of this one site, the landmark may not survive. Precedents have been set that can be repeated elsewhere when circumstances again fall into the right order.

The National Park Service has never revisited the demise of Mar-A-Lago as a failure of the system. It should. There are important lessons to be learned, including a new level of understanding about what it can mean when personal opinions and idiosyncratic professional judgments are allowed to override the responsibilities for care and custody of a site spelled out in law and tradition. The integrity of the National Park Service ought not allow such deviations from the greatness of which it is capable.

NOTES

1. From a 1969 description by Nettie Leitch Major in files of the Historical Society of Palm Beach, West Palm Beach, Fla.

2. On the order of $60 million in 1990 dollars.

3. "Briefing Paper on Mar-A-Lago National Historic Site," National Park Service, Southeast Region, Jan. 9, 1979.

4. House Rept. 92-1541, Oct. 5, 1972, on H.R. 13067: 4.

5. House Rept. 92-1541: 4.

6. *Palm Beach Life* (Sept./Oct. 1976). In 1976 Mrs. Post had a staff of forty-six, including twenty to thirty who moved with her from each of her three residences during the year. The permanent staff at Mar-A-Lago was probably around twenty.

7. P.L. 92-527, approved Oct. 21, 1972 (86 STAT. 1049).

8. House. Rept. 92-1541: 5.

9. *Palm Beach Daily News*, Sept. 9, 1972.

10. Letter to the author from Melvin E. Laska, U.S. Secret Service, Washington, D.C., Oct. 3, 1991, in response to a formal freedom of information request.

11. House Rept. 92-1541: 4–5 and language in Section (b) of P.L. 92-527.

12. Advisory boards or commissions are common in the national park system. While their functions are only advisory in nature, they can exercise substantial powers of persuasion on occasion. They are typically as useful and influential as the superintendent wants them to be. Some superintendents use an advisory Board or commission in very creative and aggressive ways to build public awareness and consensus on new or controversial issues. Some commissioners have powerful roots in their communities and serve as important communicators of information to and from the Park Service and its constituencies. Other superintendents appear threatened by an advisory commission and may only rarely give the body real issues to work on or important decisions with which to wrestle.

13. Mr. James Griffin came to Mar-A-Lago with his parents in 1926 when he was six months old. His father was a contractor on the site and was asked

by Mrs. Post to remain as superintendent. He accepted and served in that capacity until 1955 when he was succeeded by his son James. Mr. James Griffin was still superintendent in 1994, but was training a successor in anticipation of retirement "someday."

14. Letter to the author from L. Boyd Finch, May 24, 1991.

15. Horace Albright reported that President Hoover spent $25,000 of his own money to develop the camp. He later donated the property to Shenandoah NP.

16. In late 1991 the press raised a fuss again about VIP housing and accommodations in the parks. In response to that bad publicity, Secretary of the Interior Lujan asked the Park Service to furnish him a report on VIP housing in the parks. In February 1992, over Park Service objections, the secretary closed four VIP facilities and ordered that they be converted to official uses only. Whether the secretary's action represents a formal policy change applicable Servicewide and for the future is unclear.

17. Numerous examples are cited in Albright, *Birth of the National Park Service,* 24–27, 39–40. See also George Hartzog's description of how he arranged for donations in support of annual "Show Me" tours for members of Congress in the Washington, D.C., area in *Battling for the National Parks,* 119–20.

18. Government employees living in on-site quarters are required to pay fair market value for their housing. In this instance, the value of accommodations within the site would be well beyond the salaries paid government employees.

19. "Mar-A-Lago National Historic Site: Alternative Management Options," Southeast Region, NPS, May 1976: 41.

20. Letter from Michael V. Gannon, chairman, Southeast Region Advisory Board, to L. Boyd Finch representing the NPS Southeast Regional Office, Mar. 26, 1976. The letter summarized meetings held locally with eleven area residents, and recommended that the Service "proceed with its plans for this estate."

21. Letter from Chairman Roy A. Taylor to Director Gary E. Everhardt, Jan. 21, 1976.

22. See *Planning Process Guideline* (NPS-2), published by NPS.

23. "Mar-A-Lago National Historic Site: Alternative Management Options," Southeast Region, NPS, May 1976: 15.

24. Vizcaya, the Miami (Fla.) home of John Deering, is owned and operated by the Metro Dade Park and Recreation Department. The adult admission fee in 1992 was $8.00. Visitation in 1991 was some 350,000. Also on the site are a restaurant and gift shop.

The Biltmore Estate in Asheville, N.C., remains in Vanderbilt family ownership, but is used exclusively as a historic house museum. The property draws revenues from entrance fees, two restaurants, three retail shops, an operating winery that produces some 40,000 cases a year, and the sale of trees and plant materials. The 1992 adult admission fee was $21.95, $16.50 for students and children ten to fifteen. The Biltmore Estate, including the 250-room house and 8,000 acres, employs a full-time staff of 450 and is said to be the largest employer in western North Carolina. Visitation in 1991 was 718,000, the first year since visitation began in 1952 that the property was completely self-sustaining. The estate would not release data on its operating budgets.

The Hearst Castle (San Simeon, or La Cuesta Encantada, the home of newspaper magnate William Randolph Hearst) is owned and operated by the state of California. The main house, Casa Grande, has 115 rooms, 3 guest houses, indoor and outdoor swimming pools, gardens, and a zoo. The present grounds are 137 acres; it was once a ranch of some 250,000 acres, about halfway between Los Angeles and San Francisco. Hearst San Simeon State Historical Monument is part of the state park system. It is visited by about 1 million people a year who pay entrance fees of $14 for an adult, $8 for children. All visitation is by guided tour. Daily tour capacities are often sold out in advance. Entrance fees are deposited to the state treasury. The annual operating budget is about $8 million. The site employs 175 to 325 people, depending on the season. Only one national park system historic site has a budget over $8 million: Independence NHP (Pa.). Only thirteen parks systemwide have budgets over $8 million.

25. House Rept. 92-1541: 5.

26. *Palm Beach Times,* June 2, 1976.

27. According to L. Boyd Finch a planning reconnaissance was done shortly after NPS took over the site. In addition, a detailed inventory of the personal property was made. Several discussions were also held with selected local people and with Mrs. Post's daughter, Dina Merrill. Information developed during these meetings helped in writing the management options document.

28. Memorandum to the associate director, Professional Services, from the director, Office of Archeology and Historic Preservation, Subject: Scope of the National Park System, File H30-PH, Mar. 3, 1973.

29. *Palm Beach Post-Times,* Dec. 8, 1974.

30. In a conversation with the author on April 1, 1992, Mar-A-Lago Superintendent James Griffin recollected his understanding that foundation funding was always intended to be only temporary until regular appropriations were made. Mr. Griffin indicated he knew nothing of a statutory bar to such funding.

31. *Palm Beach Daily News,* Sept. 22, 1974.

32. Ibid., Oct. 14, 1973.

33. In a conversation with the author on April 1, 1992, Superintendent James Griffin recalled the telephone call he received from Director Everhardt instructing him to "send the regional office folks home," because the agreement would not be signed. Griffin said he believes the agreement fell apart because of direct intervention in Washington, D.C., by local Palm Beach persons who opposed federal ownership of the property.

34. Conversation with the author, June 10, 1991.

35. Letter from L. Boyd Finch, May 24, 1991. Mr. Finch was in 1978 NPS associate regional director of the Southeast region in Atlanta and was the principal official responsible for Mar-A-Lago, which at that time had no superin-

tendent. A plan to detail an employee from another site to provide a uniformed presence at the estate was another casualty of the order to hold up signing the agreement in 1974.

36. Conversation with the author, Apr. 1, 1992.
37. *Miami Herald,* Febr. 25, 1980.
38. *Palm Beach Post-Times,* Dec. 26, 1980.
39. *Congressional Record,* Dec. 5, 1980: H12135.
40. P.L. 96-586, approved Dec. 23, 1980. (94 STAT.3386)
41. The beach was a separate transaction, not involving the foundation. For the financial aspects of Trump's purchase of the property, see Wayne Barrett *Trump: The Deals and the Downfall* (New York: HarperCollins, 1992), 330–40.

SIX

Planning for the National Park System

There is no plan or planning process for the whole national park system. All planning is park or site specific. The central element of national park system planning is the General Management Plan or GMP. The present General Management Plan and the processes by which it is developed and used, are about two generations away from "Master Plans" done for the parks by the first federal cadre of professional landscape architects beginning in 1926.

The first master plans were site plans, on which were shown the location of roads, buildings, landscaping, and other manmade and natural features. Plans sometimes showed construction phases and dates and an accompanying schedule may have estimated costs. Master plans were often, but not always, covered by a narrative explanation. Over the years master plans became more graphic and the narratives became longer, particularly in the context of controversial proposals or expensive undertakings.

Early park planning, though documented by landscape architects, was the product of park management amateurs. Indeed, no park management profession existed in the early years of the National Park Service. The ranks of superintendents were dominated by civil engineers, a profession whose imprint on the bureau and system is still tangible.

As William C. Everhart points out in his book about the National Park Service, "Many of the national parks contain examples of spectacularly bad planning, but in most cases the pattern was set early by park administrators who could not possibly have foreseen that visitors would one day come in automobiles and be counted in the millions. Given the difficulty of stagecoach travel and the limited funds available, it is understandable that tourist facilities were clustered near the popular features and that support facilities were added near the popular complex."[1]

All early park planning was an internal exercise, at least until an approved plan could be given out to an interested public. The release of planning proposals often sparked instant controversies and on many occasions plans were scrapped or redone. Public participation in the processes of government was, however, virtually unheard of. Then, in major part because of new planning requirements associated with the National Environmental Policy Act of 1969 (NEPA)[2] a new planning structure was developed to take account of innovative federal requirements for public involvement in the planning processes and for the consideration of management alternatives *before* major decisions on federal projects were made.

As a result of the consideration of alternatives in a public forum, combined with the application of multidisciplinary planning skills, park plans were more sophisticated and more controversial. Environmental issues were routinely exposed to the scrutiny of people outside the Service, including technical and legal experts, affected individuals and interests, and organizations acting in the capacity of watchdogs on matters of principle or policy.

Thus the concept and content of park plans were significantly changed. The modern General Management Plan is intended to be a comprehensive document to elaborate management objectives and issues, to develop alternative strategies for carrying out those objectives, and to identify the preferred means to address goals and issues. The plan also includes an implementation strategy, cost estimates, and timetables.

General Management Plans are developed within the context of each park's regional setting, taking into account the relationship of the park to adjoining lands, resources, and institutions. Though National Park Service jurisdiction normally stops at the park boundary, the Service is acutely aware that parks are often the object of events and forces beyond park boundaries whose effects can be anything from benign to fatal. The park also creates impacts outside its boundaries, such as increased traffic, expanded needs for local law enforcement or emergency services, and business opportunities that range from overnight accommodations and food service to rental cars and sports instruction. To help planning in a regional context, local agencies and institutions, both public and private, are brought directly into the planning process through meetings, discussions, questionnaires, and other engagement techniques. Public involvement ranges from one or two public meetings on a proposed plan to multiple public workshops, printed draft plans, polls and questionnaires, and both formal and informal consultations with other federal and non-federal public agencies, private organizations, and landowners.

Public participation in park planning is a classic double-edged sword. It can stir up controversy where none existed before. Yet it can also help resolve controversies through negotiation and through the crafting of compromises and by exposing radical or self-serving positions to public scrutiny. Not all public participation is successful as measured by Park Service professionals whose preferred proposals or actions may not stand the test of public debate or may be simply overwhelmed by the decibel level of opposition.

Public participation in park planning is also sometimes buttressed by the direct involvement of a park advisory board or commission. Such bodies, made up of people appointed by the secretary of the Interior from nominations normally generated at the local and state level, may be assigned a lead role in the development of a General Management Plan or in a plan revision or supplement. Because advisory boards and commissions are appointed by the secretary of the Interior, their membership inevitably has something of a partisan political slant in the direction of the administration in office. The remarkable fact is that many very intelligent, informed, and dedicated people are appointed and serve with distinction.

Though bureaucracies of all sorts would rather conduct their affairs without public involvement, Park Service experience during the twenty-five years since passage of the National Environmental Policy Act certainly suggests the wisdom of an involved constituency. Today there is no lawful alternative. On rare occasions the level of controversy surrounding a proposed park plan becomes so intense and positions so rigid or nonnegotiable that planning stops. A few plans languish unapproved for years. Though inaction sometimes reflects a lack of courage on the part of someone to take responsibility for something, inaction normally assures that whatever might have caused the problem is *not* going on. Once in awhile time heals such controversies; sometimes new participants find new accommodations; sometimes new information or technology resolves an issue. Occasionally old adversaries retire or die.

General Management Plans are developed by a cadre of specialists at the Denver Service Center, a consolidated Servicewide staff of people who handle construction and planning of all types—buildings, roads, utilities, and so forth. The staff who work on GMPs travel to the parks for which plans are being done. If the plan is a large undertaking they may be moved temporarily. The GMP planners are organized in teams, usually made up of selected appropriate disciplines under the leadership of a planning generalist. Teams may be as small as three or four people or as large as a dozen, some of whom may only participate on an as-needed basis. Technical specialists, also normally employees of the Denver Service Center or, for interpretive services the Harper's Ferry Center in West Virginia, may be called upon to deal with specific problems or topics, such as an expert on toxic waste disposal or an expert on Native American artifacts.

Nearly all national park system planning is done by National Park Service employees. In rare or specialized circumstances the Park Service may contract some planning tasks to outside firms or individuals. Such contract planning is usually limited to buildings, roads, or other physical features—almost never general site planning or planning at the level of the General Management Plan. There have, of course, been exceptions. The reasons for keeping things in-house are essentially twofold: it is generally less expensive, and it keeps the NPS staff employed. Funding available for planning has a habit of going up and down, injecting frequent instability in both workloads and output. In lean budget years the Denver Service Center staff may shrink by as much as 10 to 15 percent. Contract work by architectural and engineering firms is sometimes done to even out the highs and eliminate the need for reductions in force associated with reduced budgets. Planning at the strategic level, however, is almost universally done in-house.

General Management Plans are centrally financed from an appropriation made specifically for that purpose. In fiscal year 1995 the Park Service budget included some $6.6 million for general management planning. That level of effort would involve sixty-three full-time equivalents (FTEs), would continue work on forty-three plans already underway and would initiate nine new starts, including GMPs for four newly authorized units.[3]

Planning for many units is done entirely on-site. The amount and degree of involvement in the actual planning by the superintendents and their staffs vary widely from park to park. Some superintendents exhibit little interest in the plan. They are too busy with day-to-day management matters in the park, or they have other sorts of scheduling conflicts. Some superintendents regard GMPs as "an exercise," poorly related to the real problems in the park and something that only results in a document that will be put on a shelf somewhere and forgotten. Some superintendents are overtly hostile to the Denver team, treating them as outsiders and "only planners," untutored in and uncaring for the real problems in the park. On no small number of occasions Denver's planners are reminded aloud, sometimes in public, that they are "only planners who have no experience running a park." Some superintendents never do connect with the plan or its substance.

Other superintendents are engaged in the planning process in degrees from only-a-little to all-the-way. My experience suggests that the correlation between superintendents and park plans has something to do with length of service: those with the longest tenure are the least involved. Again, there are exceptions here too. Many older superintendents remember fondly the good old days when the parks were run with much larger measures of autonomy. Money was obtained largely through informal contacts with someone in Washington, D.C. Intuition and tradition were even stronger elements of park administration. What the superintendent wanted, he got.[4]

Other factors that probably influence participation by the superintendents include the amount of known or probable controversies surrounding the park, the degree to which local interests have established agendas they wish to press on the planning process, the length of time the superintendent expects to remain at the park, and so forth. Involvement by the superintendents may vary from merely reviewing and commenting on draft planning documents to personal participation in planning sessions, conducting public meetings and workshops, making public appearances on behalf of the planning effort in support of elements he or she thinks important. Superintendents do normally sign off on General Management Plans, but they are not the formal approval authority. That rests with the regional director. Involvement in planning by the regional director is almost universally less than that of park-level officials. Occasionally the director or one of his staff has been involved, sometimes to resolve a major dispute or to ratify a proposal that is likely or known to be controversial.

With plans for Yosemite NP, Everglades NP, Gateway and Golden Gate NRAs, and several others, one or more elements of the General Management Plan have been subject to prior review by secretarial-level officials. Upper echelon review is done partly as a courtesy to political appointees who will be the probable recipients of the heat generated by those who disagree, in part to avoid surprises that come from reading it in the paper, and also as a means to share some level of responsibility in the bureaucracy.

However, there is a more profound reason for involvement of the director and secretarial level officials in General Management Plans. All plans involve political decisions. Many choices embedded in the

planning process involve decisions with large social or economic consequences that may affect the lives of many people. The long-term
effects of many development and environmental decisions may be
virtually irreversible, and involve choices of exquisite difficulty.

Planning proposals and their associated actions are often not merely the apolitical findings of nonjudgmental professionals. Professionals in any field reflect learned values and bring those values to their
work. The practice of politics in a representative democracy is the
process by which decision makers of all sorts can in some measure
be held accountable for their judgments. Commonly the interface
between politics and the national park system professional is the director of the National Park Service. Former Director George B. Hartzog, Jr., summed it up this way: "Many people contend that the position of the director is—or should be—nonpolitical. This is ludicrous.
It is the command post on the fireline where politics meets parks. . . .
Mather and Albright's living legacy is not the myth that they removed
the director's job from politics, but that they took the politics out of
the parks and put it into the director's job. The politics stopped
there."[5]

Varying levels of involvement by park superintendents in General Management Plan activities mean that after the plans are completed and approved they experience similarly variable levels of support
from those superintendents. Many plans are put on an office shelf
to gather dust. Almost none is used as an active part of a superintendent's strategic planning or annual budgeting. There is nothing
in Park Service policy or tradition to require or explicitly encourage
such uses of General Management Plans.

Though some superintendents complain from time to time about
cookie cutter planning—too many look-alike features shared with
other plans—plans tend to be very site specific in their orientation.
They and others have also complained about insufficient standardization of certain common structures and facilities and too much
customizing of buildings and other construction elements. Visitor
centers are a special problem in that regard.

The visitor center is often the central public facility in a park. It
is the place to which all visitors are invited to come, to learn what
the park offers, to obtain orientation on its features, and to learn the
variety of means by which it can be experienced. Some visitor centers have small museums and exhibit artifacts associated with the site.
Many visitor centers have auditoriums or other places for audiovisual presentations, ranger talks, demonstrations, and other interpretive
services. All visitor centers furnish rest rooms and many also provide

snacks or food service and an outlet for the sale of film, books, and other interpretive aids by one of the cooperating associations.

Because they are such a pivotal park facility, they have both internal and external significance far beyond their physical features. For many visitors (too many, to be sure) the visitor center is the only park feature they will personally experience. Everything else, if anything else, will be experienced through the windshield or windows of an automobile or bus. Superintendents often behave as if they regard the visitor center as critical not only to the success of the park but also as a necessary symbol of their own professional success. Though as much can sometimes be said of all constructed facilities, the visitor center has special meaning. They are often the most expensive single thing visible in the park.

A consequence is that visitor centers are afforded a level of significance higher than they naturally deserve, though they are typically something that will cost a million dollars or more. They are also often larger than they need to be and are often sited in bad locations only because someone wants them to be more visible.[6] Substantial premiums are often paid for unique designs or for the use of special materials or construction technology. The construction and designs of visitor centers often reflect the direct interest of influential persons or organizations outside the Park Service, up to and including a member of Congress. Visitor center designs and other park features have occasionally used contract services and on several occasions design competitions, for example, the arch at Jefferson National Expansion Memorial in St. Louis (Mo.), designed by Eero Saarinen, and the Vietnam Veterans Memorial (D.C.), designed by Maya Ying Lin.

Federal buildings of all types, from post offices to high-rise office buildings anywhere in the United States, draw a mixture of plaudits and scorn for their architectural merit. It is a difficult balance between architecture that appears to waste public funds and that which insults a community and the sensibilities of its residents. The same can be said of National Park Service visitor centers and other park buildings and facilities. While many people would argue that structures should be carefully sited and designed to complement the park environment, others are offended by siting that is too out of the way or structures whose design is "too far out." Others object to structures deemed too primitive and rustic to the point of discomfort. Thus exists a balancing act for Park Service employees and supervisors. Virtually any decision can be depended on to offend some group either before or after the fact.

The most expensive planning elements are likely to be totally invisible to the public: water and sewage treatment systems, of which there are some 300 currently in the park system. In other locations the National Park Service is merely hooked into the local utility systems. Major investments are induced by two essentially irresistible forces: increasingly rigorous enforcement of clean water standards and aging systems that cannot meet those requirements. Another major planning component is roads, of which there are over 8,000 miles in the park system. Several roadways—the four parkways in particular—are the principal visitor use feature. One parkway, Natchez Trace, between Nashville, Tennessee; and Natchez, Mississippi, is the most costly funded project in the national park system. Some 400 miles out of a total of 445 are now completed. Proposed fiscal year 1995 funding for that project amounted to $4 million—second only to work in the District of Columbia—out of a total highway construction program of $54.7 million.[7]

Other plan components may include trails, campgrounds, landscaping, employee housing, internal transportation, parking, safety and informational signs, maintenance facilities, and other infrastructure. Historic sites and parks having historic structures may include rehabilitation, restoration, or fix-up activities. A few have involved replication of a lost structure, although formal NPS policies strongly discourage such things.

A key feature of every General Management Plan, and often of other plans as well, is the examination of alternative proposals to solve a problem or meet a foreseen need. The alternatives in a plan vary widely in both their quantity and their quality. Sometimes there are, indeed, several different approaches to a problem, any one of which is logical and cost-effective. Sometimes differing approaches reflect different judgments about the value of certain resources or about the merit of certain forms of recreation. Sometimes alternatives are developed and articulated in planning documents to satisfy a constituency that may be pressing for something it wants. Sometimes alternatives are simply a front, designed to deflect interest or discussion or to mask the reality that no really viable option exists to a single proposal. Park Service plans evidence all varieties of alternatives, once in awhile in a single planning effort. As a practical matter, it is often very difficult for a planning team (or any other group) to come up with a credible, realistic alternative to that which they "know" is the best or probable outcome. Some people, including the author on occasion, have argued that alternative plans can and should be drawn up by alternative planners. It may be the only way for real alternatives to be plausibly put on the table.

Another vital function of planning at the GMP level is the assessment of environmental effects and impacts. Ever since passage of the National Environmental Policy Act in 1969 all federal agencies have been required to consider the environmental impacts of their actions and proposals. Though it may seem surprising to those who assume everything the National Park Service would propose must necessarily be good for the environment, NEPA forced the Park Service to vastly different understandings of its developmental proposals. It also put a legal and procedural spotlight on proposals that made many of them controversial and caused much rethinking of park plans. Roads, employee housing, and visitor center siting are principal cases in point.

Many of the Park Service's strongest supporters are among its severest critics when it comes to developmental planning. The disagreements stem in part from differing agendas, in part from deeply held philosophical differences, and additionally because the Park Service has shown a strong bias in favor of "more." More facilities mean more visitors which means the need for more facilities, and so forth. The issue relates to the whole set of problems relating to visitation and the numbers game. More affects the civil service grades of the staff, from superintendents on down. More is synonymous with prestige and peer appraisals. For all of that, it is enormously useful to have friends who care enough to raise cain when more becomes too much.

GMPs often lay the groundwork for further detailed data collection, analysis, and studies, especially those that would tie a developmental proposal to the outcome of such studies. For much of its history General Management Planning has dealt primarily with physical features—things, resources, structures. The software side of park management has not been given equal time and attention. Such things as interpretation, visitor services, in-park programming, education, resources management and monitoring, and basic research have not drawn major planning attention. Planning for the large urban parks, where programs and other noncapital investments are often of equal importance with capital investments, has helped planning elsewhere to focus more attention on such elements.

Virtually every General Management Plan identifies large data needs, on past and present resource conditions, on trends, and for future projections that might guide present actions. Some of this data collection and analysis are characterized as research, a term that all too often spells budgetary defeat. For many years Park Service budgets have attempted to gain congressional support for research in the parks, largely without success. The dilemma was characterized by former Director George B. Hartzog, Jr., who once told the story that he "went to see Congressman Michael J. Kirwan, the chairman of the Interior Department Appropriations Subcommittee, to discuss funds to beef up our natural science research effort. Flat-out he bombed the idea. 'Research is a function of NIH [the National Institutes of Health] not the park service.' Research was dead—so be it. So I changed the name from research to resource studies."[8]

The Park Service is itself ambivalent about the role of science and research in the management of the national park system. Many NPS professionals view basic research in the parks as irrelevant, needs being limited to the results of applied research as it helps day-to-day management decisions in the parks. Thus, Representative Kirwan's opinion about research in the national park system has been shared not only by most of his successors, but also by other officials in the Department of the Interior and at the Office of Management and Budget.

One school of thought asserts that if only all national park system planning and management decisions were based on scientific principles, many problems and their attendant controversies would be resolved. Some observers see a fundamental conflict between "scientific" resource management and "traditional" park management. This perspective generally ignores the sharp disagreements often found among scientists about causes and effects and for whom clear-cut answers seldom exist. It also ignores many lessons learned by even the most traditional of park managers. However, the rather short list of science-related professionals in the past and present ranks of the Park Service lends considerable support for those who bemoan the absence of scientific justification for various decisions.[9]

In perspective, however, science has never done very well in federal budgeting. Though there are long-established scientific and research elements in the federal establishment, ranging from the old Bureau of Standards to the National Institutes of Health, the largest share of scientific research and data collection has been an offshoot of the military budget, or, in the 1960s particularly, the budget for the National Aeronautical and Space Administration (NASA). Today's newspapers carry many stories about needs for expanded federal funding for research on AIDS, cancer, alternative energy sources, prenatal care, and literally hundreds of other topics. Even subjects in the social sciences—welfare dependency, recidivism among criminals, drug abuse, and many others are listed among subjects needing federal funding support. The competition for funding is fierce.

Federally funded research has suffered from the image created by stories of projects funded on topics whose subject matter is deemed trivial, humorous, or even obscene. Studies on various topics related to reproduction, whether human or in the animal or vegetable kingdoms, draw sharp critical barbs and, recently, serve as one of the primary justifications for a so-called line-item veto, by which the president can kill individual budget items in a larger appropriation. Though trivial or obscure projects may be only a minor part of the total federal research budget, public and press attitudes paint them with a very broad brush. Former Wisconsin Senator William Proxmire (D) for years gave an annual "award" for federally funded projects he regarded as out of bounds. The image persists, with enough new evidence produced every year to assure its survival.

General Management Plans, and occasionally the more detailed Development Concept Plans (DCP) that follow them, have a mixed record of relevance and success. They do serve, however, to put the public on notice about what can ultimately be expected from the National Park Service at the affected park. The process by which they are created affords a vitally important opportunity for community input and dialogue with NPS and its people and institutions. They resolve many controversies and occasionally create new ones. But, mostly they are oil on any troubled waters, by explicitly dealing in constructive ways with concerns and issues raised during the planning process.

Critics of Park Service planning typically argue that the Service does not listen enough to the criticism it receives. Professional opinions are often viewed as a form of bureaucratic arrogance. Often a particular park constituency has a well-defined agenda or set of requirements, some or all of which cannot for some reason be accommodated by the plan. Sometimes local residents or nearby landowners suggest (or demand) features or developments clearly intended to restrict uses or keep certain uses or users away. The not-in-my-backyard syndrome is present in park planning in the same way as in other public planning.

Other critics base their objections on broader policy grounds, such as general opposition to all forms of recreation at certain historic sites. Some critics object to in-park visitor facilities of all types, asserting that each park should be experienced exclusively on its own terms, without embellishment by any unrelated facilities or services.[10] Many forms of outdoor recreation that require substantial capital investments, sometimes with visible impacts on the landscape, such as downhill skiing or marinas, are particularly controversial when proposed. Occasionally they have been controversial even after they exist—for example, when the Park Service inherits such a facility in a new park.

Many people see the development-versus-nondevelopment dichotomy as *the* principal policy dilemma in the national park system.
Some people see it as a political issue, sometimes even a partisan
matter. While still others see the subject as an either-or controversy
requiring definite resolution once and for all. For many the countless matters it raises are not negotiable. There are either winners or
losers. Period.

The reality, however, is that the dichotomy is essentially unresolv-
able in any context other than the political give and take of competing forces in a democratic society. Language in the National Park
Service Organic Act contains the essence of the dichotomy: "to conserve the scenery and natural and historic objects and the wildlife
therein and to provide for the enjoyment of the same in such manner and by such means as will leave them unimpaired for the enjoyment of future generations."[11] Some artful wordsmiths, of course, can
manage to find in this language support for no development whatever, usually by leaning heavily on the word "unimpaired." The argument then devolves on examination of that word and disagreements about whether something is an impairment. Formal NPS policy
favors preservation over development.

The early history of the national park system does not give much
support for nondevelopment options. Development in the form of
roads, new visitor accommodations, and more and more visitation—
all were prominent and persistent features of park policy during the
early decades of the National Park Service. Directors Stephen Mather
and Horace Albright saw the railroads, hoteliers, and tourist industry as major allies in their efforts to gain broader national support
for the existence and expansion of the national park system.

Focus on developments within the national park system did not
end with Mather's and Albright's successes. MISSION 66, a ten-year
park development program undertaken during the administration of
Director Conrad Wirth, was a major developmental effort, designed
to play catch up in visitor facilities and accommodations following
the lean years of the Great Depression and World War II. It involved
both new construction and the rehabilitation of older facilities.

Sensitivity to many environmental and aesthetic consequences of
park development has evolved over a period of some three decades—
much of it *after* MISSION 66. Predators are no longer eliminated.[12]
Now efforts are occasionally made to reintroduce predator species
where they have once been obliterated. Wild fire is no longer routinely controlled. Natural fires are understood to be a part of the natural ecosystem. Present national park system policies no longer sup-

port increased overnight visitor accommodations in the parks. Developmental activities are questioned and evaluated in terms of their environmental impacts and aesthetic qualities—albeit imperfectly and not always successfully. Only recently, the Park Service assented to additions to the stock of overnight facilities in Yosemite NP—in spite of earlier planning that clearly did not support such action.

General Management Plans are intended to be cyclic, revised and updated every ten years or so to keep them abreast of needs, trends in visitor use or expectations, new technologies or research data, and other factors. In practice though not all plans are updated regularly.[13] A few seem never to get out of the planning process, always trying again to find a planning solution for whatever is driving the process. One reason is money. Full-scale GMPs are expensive, especially for the larger or complex sites. Some Superintendents also simply prefer not to get involved in the process of revising a GMP. They can be inconvenient if a new plan could radically change the current way of managing the park.

At present there is no institutional linkage between park planning and budgeting, either operating or capital. Annual budgets are prepared by a different staff, are reviewed by different people, and are only rarely cross referenced beyond the experience and memories of principal park staff. It is not essential that budgeted capital developments be first identified in an approved GMP, although in all probability construction items large enough to warrant inclusion in the line-item construction budget are contained in a plan. They may not, however, appear in the plan in a sequence or phase originally identified in the plan. Because linkage between the plan and budgets is weak, there is very little incentive and no reward or punishment for failures of planning and budgeting to appear in sync. Similarly, there is no assurance that a planned activity, either capital or programmatic, will appear in a budget proposal.

One other factor influences the weak linkage between plans and capital development budgets: congressional add-ons. An add-on is an item that was not included in the formal budget of the president but is added during the appropriation process during consideration of the budget by Congress. Some superintendents know in advance that an add-on will be proposed; they may therefore omit it from their request and opt for something else as their share of the budget.

The NPS construction program is the only part of the budget that has explicit, programmed multiyear dimensions. All other parts of the budget are essentially one-year elements, though that description has something of a flaw in it for this reason: like substantially all federal budgeting, the sums included each year begin from a "base" that normally slides forward from year to year without explicit rejustification or reexamination. The principal focus of budget reviews, analysis, and scrutiny is on the increments above the base. For obvious reasons, a major objective of many justifications is to get them into a new higher base, by that effectively eliminating the need for annual reexamination of the item.

The National Park Service has recently evidenced an interest in strategic planning. In this context strategic planning is conceived to be a means for identifying and analyzing trends and events likely to influence the future of the agency or its resources over an extended period. The scope of a strategic planning function would include changing demographics of both the National Park Service work force and visitors to the parks; economic trends that influence travel, vacations, and visitor expectations; consumer product changes that may affect the parks; trends in technology; and so forth. Strategic planning also typically includes processes for evaluating the effectiveness of operations, as measured against a set of goal- or output-related criteria.

Former Director Ridenour created a small office responsible for strategic planning. The action was in part an outgrowth of a recommendation to that effect made by an internal task force several years ago and a reinforcing recommendation coming out of a Seventy-fifth Anniversary symposium at Vail, Colorado. Such an office can be an important new dimension in National Park Service decision making. Realistically, it will take several years for its role and activities to be thoroughly effective, and only then if Park Service managers are successful in integrating the output of that staff into appropriate processes and actions. The new office, however, is a valuable step in the right direction, though it and its work will almost inevitably be controversial, particularly because of its Denver, not Washington headquarters, location.[14]

Planners and their work do not enjoy the best of reputations in the National Park Service. Inevitably, both catch a lot of flak internally and externally. Few managers relish being told that an idea they have is inconsistent with a plan or with the planning schedule. Many superintendents regard formal plans as confining and inconsistent with the flexibility needed to meet new conditions or circumstances. Planning often exposes ideas regarded as meritorious by their author to levels of controversy totally unpredicted. Public participation in park planning can be full of tension, vociferous disagreements, name calling, table pounding, and fist waving.

Many people feel strongly about the very nature of plans. For everyone in favor of a proposal it is very probable there will be someone strenuously opposed. Few plans escape all controversy. Park Service planners have some special handicaps. They are geographically isolated from park management. They do not report to the person responsible for the resource for which they are doing the planning. They often come and go in what seems inadequate time to become appropriately familiar with the resource(s) and all of its nuances. They do not have to live with the plan they develop. Park planners rarely have park level operating experience. They may come from a discipline or background that would really not qualify them for a job as a ranger or superintendent.

A lot more could be done to improve the credibility of park planners: field level details and training programs, temporary assignments in a park, or lateral transfers into and out of the planning field. In a similar vein, more could be done to improve park management's understanding of the complexities with which planning must deal. Every superintendent should be required to sign on to the plan for the park he or she directs. If there is something wrong with the plan, the superintendent should take on the responsibility to change it, amend it, or otherwise bring it into consistency with his or her view—then live with it or change their mind and conform to it.

Plans need more institutional support. They need to be dusted off at least annually, because every dollar included in an annual budget request should be consistent with the park plan, including its timing and phasing. No plan, no money, no project. Every budget request should contain a formal certification by the affected superintendent that it is consistent with the park's plan. One of the major complaints about plans is that they are unrealistic—too grandiose or too expensive or too ambitious. If they had to be consistent with both the thinking of the superintendent and with the budget, realism would be much more common.

Present National Park Service delegations place the formal responsibility for plan approvals at the regional directors' level. One effect of that delegation is to give superintendents the opportunity to say, "Well, it's not my plan, it's the regional director's." The delegation should necessarily be reviewed and the superintendent made the responsible officer. Plans need to be reviewed by someone higher up the organizational ladder. If plans are not reviewed higher up, there is too much opportunity for nonsense. The problem can be helped to some extent by more Regional Office (if not regional director) involvement in plan preparation on a real-time basis—while it is being put together. Substantive intervention can happen then as things are being decided in draft. It would also be helpful if the Park Service tried to fashion more servicewide standards and guidelines for things that ought to be the same or similar in all parks.

I favor the review of plans by upper levels both in the Park Service and in the Department of the Interior, including, on occasion, the secretary personally. Such reviews can be an important part of Park Service accountability. They can also expose political officers and others to the real problems and opportunities that parks evoke. Higher levels will only meddle if involvement is nothing more than mere rubber stamping. Involvement should be not only real but also realistic. It can thereby educate and inform and, ultimately, inspire commitment and the willingness to be a part of the translation of a plan into performance. If involvement cannot succeed at these objectives, the higher levels will probably not be very helpful anyway. Review of park plans by authorities higher than the superintendent need not undercut a formal delegation of authority for plan approval to the superintendent, who still needs to be satisfied and committed to the substance of the plan.

Park planning and planners are not often instruments of change in the national park system. Their judgments and products tend to reflect prior successes. Yesterday's successful proposal may soften tomorrow's potential controversy. Nevertheless, many new things do emerge in plans. The problem is they end up having little transferability or replication elsewhere. Plans are not widely read or reviewed by other parks, and although they seldom educate park management beyond park boundaries, they certainly could. The park planning process could be a major instrument for making and binding the 365-plus units managed by the National Park Service into a truly national *system*.

The park planning process is a potentially useful means by which directors of the National Park Service can influence park management. Few directors though have done that except on a park-specific or issue-specific basis. Some directors have not brought to their job any clear park management philosophies or objectives. Unfortunately some directors would rather micro-manage the agency. But that is another topic for another book.

NOTES

1. Everhart, *National Park Service,* 57.
2. 42 USC 4321.
3. *Budget Justifications, F.Y. 1995:* NPS-295 to NPS-300.

4. The use of the gender word "he" in this context is about 85 percent accurate. Though there were a few women site managers and superintendents in the early days—the first was in 1940—the number is not large even today (under 15 percent). All directors since the early 1970s have publicly supported goals to increase the share of superintendencies held by women (and minorities), but progress has been slow. Critics blame it on "The Old Boy Network." The Old Boys blame it on a shortage of qualified candidates. Both arguments are credible, but the Old Boys are the only group that can change the reality any time soon.

5. Hartzog, *Battling for the National Parks*, 273.

6. MISSION 66, a large-scale development program discussed in a later chapter, led to the development of several visitor centers on prime historical sites at Gettysburg, Antietam, Vicksburg, and elsewhere. Passage of the Historic Preservation Act of 1966 and special requirements to consider the effects of such actions on the historic scene did much to reverse the trend.

7. *Budget Justifications, F.Y. 1995:* NPS-187, NPS-288.

8. Hartzog, *Battling for the National Parks*, 103. Actually, the U.S. Forest Service and the U.S. Fish and Wildlife Service have large, long-standing natural resource research functions.

9. See, for example, Appendix 8. For an interesting history of the attempted integration of science into park management during early years of the Park Service, see Richard West Sellars, "The Rise and Decline of Ecological Attitudes in National Park Management, 1929–1940, Parts I, II, and III" in *George Wright Forum* vol. 10, nos. 1, 2, and 3 (1993).

10. For a discussion of many of these issues see Sax, *Mountains without Handrails*.

11. 16 U.S.C. 1.

12. Though the statement is true as a matter of NPS policy, predator control is exquisitely complicated and full of unknowns and inconsistencies. For a discussion of some of those issues see Chase, *Playing God in Yellowstone*. The inconsistencies are spelled out in a recent article in which Chase asserts that the return of wolves and other predators "is not all good news. Their comeback signals other ecological changes that could have devastating effects." (Alston Chase, "Wilderness in the Balance: As Endangered Species Rebound Our Parks Pay the Price," in *Conde Nast Traveler* June 1993: 28).

13. NPS reports that 125 parks have GMPs 15 years old or no plan at all (*Budget Justifications, F.Y. 1995:* NPS-297).

14. National planning has only been tried once in U.S. history. In the depths of the Great Depression of the 1930s, President Franklin D. Roosevelt created the National Resources Planning Board (NRPB). NRPB made and sponsored studies of resource use and development including the field of parks and recreation. Many NRPB studies remain as seminal attempts to guide development in regions of the United States. NRPB was always in a precarious position, however, because of strong political objections to "state planning" in any form, regarded by many people as something associated with socialism. Though NRPB had no real powers, the effects of its research and pub-

lished studies were powerfully influential in many parts of the country, notably with respect to water and power development in the Tennessee River Valley and in the States of Washington, Oregon, and California. NRPB was abolished in 1945, and nothing comparable has existed since.

Hot Springs National Park was much visited by early NPS directors, who used the Arkansas park for their own recreation and as a place to lobby members of Congress and other influential people. The scene shows the Fordyce bathhouse dating to 1914. (NPS photo by Mike Kelley.)

Yosemite National Park receives a majority of its visitors from metropolitan Los Angeles and San Francisco. No one would argue, however, about the national significance of this unique resource. (NPS photo by Richard Frear.)

Abraham Lincoln Birthplace was established as a National Park in 1916, re-named a National Historical Park in 1939, and renamed a National Historic Site in 1959. The site was administered by the War Department until 1933. (NPS photo by Allan Rinehart.)

Denali National Park has as its centerpiece Mt. McKinley, the name of which remains unchanged even after that of the park was changed to adopt the ancient Alaska native name. (NPS photo by M. Woodbridge Williams.)

Shenandoah National Park was an early addition to the national park system east of the Mississippi, and consisted of cut-over and burned-over lands whose character hardly qualified them for National Park status. Today parts of this much-visited park are of wilderness quality. (NPS photo by Richard Frear.)

Little Bighorn Battlefield National Monument was known as Custer Battlefield National Monument from 1946 until its name was changed in 1991. The name change reflects what many people regard as a more balanced memorialization of the epic battle that took place here in 1876 between the Seventh U.S. Cavalry and the Sioux and Northern Cheyenne Indians. (NPS photo.)

Isle Royale National Park provides wilderness recreation and research opportunities in a roadless park accessible only by boat or float plane. The park's remoteness and relatively low annual visitation inflate the per-visitor costs at this site. (NPS photo by Richard Frear.)

Jefferson National Expansion Memorial, now graced by the spectacular arch that has become the symbol of St. Louis, Missouri, is a memorial to Thomas Jefferson and westward expansion. The arch design by Eero Saarinen was the result of a national competition. (NPS photo.)

Gettysburg National Military Park, site of the Civil War battle that marked the beginning of the end of the Confederacy, provides a guided ranger history lesson with the recreation of a bike tour. (NPS photo by Richard Frear.)

Eugene O'Neill National Historic Site marked a new departure in the designation of sites commemorating noted writers and others in the world of ideas. The site's location in a residential area near Danville, California, and its theme militate against large annual visitation. (NPS photo.)

San Francisco Maritime National Historical Park includes the National Maritime Museum and a growing number of vessels afloat. For years some NPS officials voiced discomfort with this non-site related resource. (NPS photo by Tim Campbell.)

Mar-A-Lago, landmark home of the late Marjorie Meriweather Post, was part of the national park system for eight years, but was returned to private ownership in response to strong local opposition and resistance by some NPS officials. (Photo courtesy of the Historical Society of Palm Beach County, Fla.)

Blue Ridge Parkway's Linn Cove viaduct made use of novel construction technology to avoid damage to the slopes of Grandfather Mountain. Begun as an employment program in the 1930s, the 470-mile parkway is the most-used facility in the national park system, counting over 17 million visitors annually. (NPS photo by Hugh Morton.)

General Grant National Memorial on a bluff above the Hudson River in New York City is typical of memorials whose site gains national significance solely by virtue of the memorial itself. (NPS photo by Richard Frear.)

The National Park Service ranger in the early days needed to be "of good character, sound physique, and tactful in handling people ... possess a common-school education, be able to ride and care for horses, have experience in outdoor life, be a good shot with rifle and pistol, and have knowledge of trail construction and fighting forest fires." (NPS photo from the historical collection.)

Modern park rangers combine a wide assortment of duties, continuing a pattern dating back to the earliest days of the national park system. Many rangers are law enforcement trained and carry sidearms. (NPS photo by Mike Floyd.)

Gateway National Recreation Area includes Floyd Bennett Field, New York City's first commercial airport. The large hangers have been put out to bid for private redevelopment for recreational uses, while preserving the historic structures. (NPS photo by Brian Feeney.)

Acadia National Park along Maine's rugged coast began as the consequence of private land donations that led to a presidential proclamation as Sieur de Monts National Monument in 1916. It was renamed Lafayette National Park in 1919, and given its present name in 1929. Donations of land to the park have continued to present times. (NPS photo by Richard Frear.)

SEVEN

The Institutional Setting

The National Parks are being loved to death. Recent studies show the National Park Service has a backlog of over $2 billion in unmet rehabilitation and construction needs. Many parks are in "intensive care." Some parks or parts of some parks may have to be closed. More than fifteen hundred bridges need maintenance now. New park areas are forcing reductions at old parks to pay for unwanted new responsibilities. Personnel and programs are being cut. Resources are suffering. The parks are neglected and in need of critical care. Some park budgets have not even kept pace with the effects of inflation.

External to the parks, a wide variety of developments and forces are endangering park resources, even harming them irretrievably. Acid rain, the preemption of water, nonnative plant and animal species, and toxic wastes threaten resources in both acute and imperceptible, but inexorable, ways.[1] Things are both better and worse than they appear: better because the parks have really done quite well in a long period of hostile economic and environmental policy making, worse because the institutional capacity to plan for and obtain the funding and staffing needed for long-term care of the national park system is not apparent. Uncritical clamoring for larger budgets by outside interest groups, however well intentioned, may succeed in only applying band aids when the need is for major surgery. It may also take new blood.

Proposed solutions to this litany of actual and potential disasters range from more money to total divorce of the National Park Service from the Department of the Interior and a new life beyond the reach of politics. We cannot here document the truth or extent of all the ills said to afflict the national park system. That aim is the function of advocacy groups and National Park Service budgets. Our purpose is to examine the institutional setting within which long-term commitments to the units of the national park system are identified and executed. It is useful, however, to consider the national setting for current conclusions about the national park system and some of its perceived problems.

The deterioration of the park system infrastructure must be considered along with the status of the entire public works infrastructure in the United States: roads, bridges, public buildings, airports and aircraft operations support systems, and similar elements. Federal, state, and local governments have not made the necessary capital investments to repair and replace worn out and obsolete public works systems throughout the country. It would, indeed, have been a remarkable event for the national park system to have avoided that condition. A relevant question is: can this issue be effectively dealt with in isolation and without companion efforts in other public facilities? It seems very unlikely.

In regard to the Park Service budget, a similar issue arises. In these years of large federal budget deficits and large unmet needs in medical care, education, child care, law enforcement, and other public services, is it realistic to expect the Park Service budget to now or in the future meet the needs of inanimate resources and the expectations of people whose national park experience is for many others an unreachable luxury?

The answer to both questions is likely to be a direct function of the importance attached to the national park system as a feature of national life. If parks are important they should receive the resources necessary for their proper care and custody. Certainly, people whose lives are intimately associated with the national park system—those who work in it, those whose jobs are to defend it, those who use it with regularity—can be expected to evidence great concern over its perceived problems and financial shortcomings. Current articles, books, and other evidence of such concerns abound. There is concern—much of it. Some of it puts great urgency on the needs. According to the National Parks and Conservation Association, "The issues and problems facing . . . our National Park System, are leading to another in the long list of American tragedies that have plagued the nation during the last decade. Literally, we are in a race against time."[2]

A recent poll sponsored by Citibank Mastercard and Visa, in cooperation with the National Park Foundation, suggests that experience with the national park system is wider and deeper than many people have formerly believed. The poll shows that 68 percent of all Americans have visited one of more units of the national park system and some 82 percent said they are likely to visit one in the next few years. Fully 70 percent of the respondents suggested they would be willing to designate $5 a year of their federal income tax specifically to help pay for the national parks. However, earmarking part of present taxes for a specific purpose is different from supporting additional taxes for that purpose and only 46 percent indicated "strongly" that "it is up to the American people to provide *greater financial support* so the parks will not have to turn to commercialism for needed funds" (emphasis added).[3] In their analysis of another question, however, the pollsters concluded that 67 percent "want more money to go into preserving and maintaining the National Parks."[4]

Such inconsistencies, especially when it comes to taxes and the allocation of public monies, are hardly unique. Poll after poll shows public support for increased funding for public services of almost every stripe, but little or no support for any tax increases, except those targeted specifically toward reduction of the federal budget deficit. There are also strong forces supporting reductions in federal discretionary spending.

Of the respondents 62 percent said that the federal government should remain financially responsible for the national park system in the future. A total of 18 percent thought the states should assume that role; 17 percent would devolve it to the corporate world. Surprisingly, almost 40 percent of those polled thought the federal government should *not* be responsible for the national park system.

The National Park Service and the national park system do enjoy a wide measure of affection and respect. For many years, polls have listed the National Park Service as among the most respected of all federal agencies.[5] The Service clearly has an enviable image with the public, caveats and complaints by experts and unsympathetic antagonists apart. It is that image and support that the National Park Service and its constituencies hope to turn into the engine capable of delivering the resources required to meet the present and future needs of the system.

From its inception in 1916 the National Park Service has struggled for funding. In its founding year Congress appropriated only about $500,000 (about $3 million in 1991 dollars) for the national park system, which then included some thirty-six units. Funding was always behind needs, and in those early years, Director Stephen T. Mather, a wealthy person, contributed the equivalent of a small fortune to the national park system in support of land acquisition, buildings, supplies, and expensive lobbying of congressional leaders and others. In those same early years there were no land acquisition costs associated with new units because they were donated or carved out of the public domain, lands already in federal ownership. That principle was extended even into states east of the Mississippi by the passage of legislation requiring that the lands to make up a new park either be donated or purchased with private funds.

The beginnings of the Park Service saw the new agency classified as a "major bureau," a classification placing the Service on the lowest rung on the federal office hierarchical ladder. In 1923 Horace Albright sought to have the bureau's status elevated to that of one of the "largest and most important" bureaus, by that, offering grade and pay raises and increased prestige to NPS employees. However, even by modern standards, the National Park Service is a small federal bureau, with a full-time staff of under nineteen thousand people, spread over more than 350 locations in forty-nine states, the District of Columbia, and four overseas territories. Though individual parks are big business in many rural areas, the NPS budget is on the smallish side of the federal ledger—approximately one-tenth of 1 percent. While 138 parks have budgets over $1 million, 107 have budgets under $500,000. Though Government agencies do not have such a classification, even unofficially, most units of the national park system would be generally regarded as small businesses in terms of employment and gross economic activity.

The economic significance of the parks is, however, substantial when measured locally. NPS is probably the largest employer in more than one hundred counties, particularly in the West. Parks generate income to local businesses and others from tourism and various recreational activities that are very important to many communities. At one time, NPS planners routinely included predictions of such economic benefits in new area studies. A small office of professional economists in Denver made many such studies, usually as a way of pumping up a proposal the Park Service supported. The economics expertise is mostly gone today, and the Park Service has great reservations about touting predicted economic benefits. Many NPS professionals feel economic goals have been too successful a rationale for new park areas—to the detriment of other qualitative criteria by which a new area's merits should be measured. Economic goals have sometimes overshadowed preservation objectives, causing unwarranted exploitation of historic resources. Or economic considerations have even led to the inclusion of new units in the national park system having lesser intrinsic significance—all in the name of local economic development. So the arguments run.

The National Parks and Conservation Association has waged a campaign to remove the National Park Service from the Department of the Interior and give it independent status. One of the arguments made in support of that proposal is that NPS is buried in the Interior Department where it cannot effectively compete for the federal budget. Independence, the argument goes, would make competition easier. Similar arguments have supported making the Social Security Administration independent of the Department of Health and Human Services. On the other hand, independence may instead make competition more difficult, given that its budget might then be handled by appropriations committees of the Congress totally unfamiliar with the national park system. Competition would be principally with regulatory agencies whose agendas, requirements, and reasons for existence are far afield of the national park system. Many existing independent agencies are regulatory in nature, made independent because of quasi-judicial functions that they perform. NPS has no analogous role.

Other reasoning behind proposals to move NPS out of the Interior Department relates to what is perceived as the politicalization of the Park Service in recent years. Complaints are made that in the early years the director of the National Park Service reported directly to the secretary of the Interior, but now the director must report through an assistant secretary and through persons who are mere staff assistants to such persons. It is essentially true.

Part of that reality reflects that the Government is much more complicated than it was sixty or seventy years ago. It may also be true that there is unnecessary layering between the director of the Park Service and the secretary. The present structure has been in place, however, without significant change since the early 1960s. NPS has reported to an assistant secretary (as opposed to the secretary) since World War II.

A major part of the problem with the Park Service's organizational setting and competitiveness is the fact that the director of the bureau is a secretarial appointment not subject to Senate confirmation, one of only two such bureaus in the Department of the Interior.[6] That fact pushes the director into a position that is neither fish nor fowl, neither career nor political. The director is not necessarily "on the President's team," although many of the same criteria may have been used in that person's selection. The director is not necessarily even part of the secretary's own team, in part because there is a strong tradition to try to insulate the Park Service and its programs from politics.

It is difficult to understand the logic behind proposals to reorganize the National Park Service as an independent agency to make the bureau less political. Such a change would in no way alter the political character of decisions made either by the Park Service or those decisions made affecting it. No qualitative change would result. Appointments to the new agency would similarly be political in character, perhaps more so than they now are. Any such appointment, like all existing independent agencies, would most probably require Senate confirmation. If the term of the director were separated from that of the president, it would be possible for the director and the president to be from different parties or of very different political persuasions. Such a situation might exacerbate the problem of competitiveness.

Some proposals would have the bureau run by a board of directors through a chief operating officer, after the fashion of a corporate model. The U.S. Postal Service, partly governmental and partly private might be used as an example. While such an arrangement might have merit as an administrative apparatus, it does not seem to address in any direct way the issue of competitiveness or problems of intergovernmental coordination. Problems between the Park Service and the Forest Service or the Bureau of Land Management would not change in any structural way and could only then be negotiated by the Office of Management and Budget, the president's management arm. Making every major interagency conflict one requiring OMB intervention could only lead to very unhappy circumstances. There is no assurance whatever that the NPS batting average would improve. Absent the pleading of a cabinet officer it might be worse.

Hartzog and others, albeit mostly officials at levels below that of bureau chief, have expressed a great deal of displeasure and frustration with present arrangements, by which secretarial underlings, sometimes the starched young "Assistants to the Assistants" (both male and female), can intervene in bureau operations in very specific and petty ways. The system gives many junior political types, so-called schedule "C" appointees, a measure of power that is easily and too-often abused. Cabinet officers and secretarial level officials down to the level of assistant secretaries are busy enough or preoccupied with their political duties enough to be willing to delegate, often without anything in writing, substantial authority to their junior assistants. The reality has been around a long time, but probably is more widespread now, simply because the trend has been in place so long.

The formal system is made even worse when personalities conflict, and, at least in the hierarchy between the director of the National Park Service and the secretary of the Interior, such personality conflicts have been virtually a standing rule for the better part of thirty years. This is not to say that secretaries or assistant secretaries have been universally hostile to the National Park Service. They have not. Though conventional wisdom places President Reagan's first secretary of the Interior, James Watt, as anathema to Park Service interests, the reality is that in a variety of ways, NPS fared rather well under Secretary Watt, especially with its budget, which did not experience the cutbacks handed other agencies and programs. Watt supported a $1 billion park and recreation improvement program (PRIP) a decade ago in an attempt to deal with the same deficit phenomenon said to exist today. However, a long list of program decisions were not made to the liking of the Park Service, reflecting the very conservative tone of the Reagan administration. Examples would be the virtual suspension of all land acquisition and a no-new-parks policy. Those policies did not significantly change when Watt left and was replaced by Donald Hodel.

A strong case can be made for changing the director's job to one requiring Senate confirmation. It would be another important piece of evidence that the National Park Service is one of the "largest and most important" bureaus in the Department of the Interior and the federal government. Also, it would increase the director's prestige and renew access to other political officers in an administration. Senate confirmation hearings could be a valuable means of illuminating a potential director's vision of the national park system and their principal agenda while in that position.[7] Though confirmation hearings are a heavily orchestrated event in today's world, with detailed programming of both responses and nonresponses by handlers and sponsors, they are a chance to lay out in public not only the qualifications and agenda of the president's nominee, but also for Congress to share its agenda and concerns with the candidate.

Some, perhaps most, National Park Service professionals would oppose Senate confirmation because it would appear to make the director's job more political than many NPS staff would hope for. However, the Association of National Park Rangers strongly supported Senate confirmation in 1989 and again in 1990.[8] That support was subject to the condition that the Park Service director be a career parks person with governmental experience and that the term of the director coincide with that of the president.

Some careerists would see Senate confirmation as making it more unlikely, if not impossible, for a career NPS employee to become director. Whether such aspiration is realistic at present is uncertain at best. Four of the last seven directors, including the last three, have come from outside the Service.[9] Though persons within the service could certainly qualify for the position and probably be fine directors, the nonpolitical nature of all principal jobs in the Park Service, realities aside, leaves many potential candidates outside the processes by which directors are chosen. In recent times only President Jimmy Carter and Secretary of the Interior Cecil Andrus deliberately sought a director from within the ranks of the Service, interviewing close to a dozen candidates and selecting one of them.[10] It could, of course, happen again, depending on the president and the secretary of the Interior.

Senate confirmation for the director might also have the effect of making it more likely that the deputy director, the number two officer in the bureau, would be a career person selected from within the Service. However, that is not a certainty. The most likely source of candidates for director from within the Service is a person in the Senior Executive Service (SES). SES positions are nominally career jobs, but the secretary enjoys considerable discretion in both their appointment and in their assignments. Twenty-one positions in the National Park Service are now SES jobs.[11] In SES they are subject to reassignment either within the Park Service or elsewhere within the department for almost any reason. SES persons have been moved for training, or to broaden their experience. Many such moves are seen as means of making personnel changes, period.

There are no active proposals to make the director's job subject to Senate confirmation.[12] Most probably, the subject will arise only in response to a major public brouhaha over some proposed (or actual) appointee, in which case the initiative may come from the Congress. There are no obvious reasons why an administration would propose it, if for no other reason than that there is some exposure for a president. His designee could fail of confirmation or the nominee's confirmation hearing could expose personal or policy weaknesses or rifts that can simply be avoided by direct appointments without confirmation.[13]

Attempts on the Hill to divorce the National Park Service from the Department of the Interior have received recent attention and support. Talking about it publicly sometimes does have the effect of bringing attention to problems or personalities or policies on which there are acute differences. Perhaps the lingering threat is useful. The setting within the Department of the Interior is similar to dozens of other federal bureaus: a bureau reporting to an assistant secretary, in turn reporting to the secretary. In the Park Service's case the bureau shares the assistant secretary with one other bureau, the U.S. Fish and

Wildlife Service. Though the Park Service and the Fish and Wildlife Service have occasional differences, particularly where their lands adjoin, both bureaus have much in common. Both are uniformed career services. Both manage sites having many "natural" characteristics. Both provide substantial volumes of public recreation. Both are committed to long-term land management objectives on behalf of their agency's mission. And both are relatively small (the Fish and Wildlife Service is the smaller, with some six thousand employees and a budget of about $600 million).

Assistant secretaries have rather inconsistently "represented" the bureaus. More assistant secretaries have come to that office from the fish and game field than from a background identified with the national park system. One of the latter group of assistant secretaries, Nathaniel Reed of Florida, was a strong conservation-preservation minded person. Ironically, it was Reed's abiding interest in the national park system in the 1970s that led him to "meddle" with the detailed management of the Park Service. He introduced a management style that has persisted with his successors and that has developed into a widely perceived problem.

The role of an assistant secretary is by its nature a difficult balance between policy representation and program interference. The more interest an assistant secretary evidences, the less likely bureau officials are to like it. Any form of uninvited micro-management of bureau programs is taboo. Secretarial officers can and should exert strong leadership. Not only should they reflect the policies of the president and secretary, they can be a vital means of encouraging the good works and initiatives emerging in the bureaus. Also, assistant secretaries ought to be vigorous communicators, not only up to the secretary and the president but also down to the bureau and its workers. Such leadership and communication roles are vital, activist, responsible, and not inherently intrusive meddling. They do require great skill and wisdom if they are to be done effectively.[14]

Other institutional actors in the care and custody of national park system units include numerous departmental functionaries and offices: budget, personnel, equal opportunity, law (the Office of the Solicitor provides legal services for all bureaus in the department, each of which has no legal staff of its own), congressional liaison, and, on occasion, the Office of the Inspector General. Departmental staff offices perform two primary functions: standard setting and functional reviews.

The standard setting function is something of a misnomer, because the word standard implies a measure of uniformity that does not exist in practice, even in such things as budget formats and accounting. Federal bureaus have been created and have grown in different environments. Though more uniformity exists today than ten or twenty years ago in some specific matters, any student of government must be impressed by the diversity of approaches to every element of the administrative process from bureau to bureau. Standardization is the exception.

This same principle applies with equal force within bureaus, where suborganizations retain discrete identities, processes, terminology, and, often, policies. Former Director George B. Hartzog, Jr., has gone as far as to characterize the Park Service as not one bureau but ten, with each region operating with substantial autonomy.[15] In modern times the separateness and distinctive character of each *park* has become a virtue and a quality to be preserved from the effects of standardization or uniformity.

The review function of departmental staff offices and functionaries ranges from perfunctory oversight of deadlines, processes, and formats to substantive intervention in decision making, legislative proposals and reports, budgets, regulatory issuances, legal interpretation, Congressional relations, publications, and informational activities. Departmental reviews are made to assure consistency with the programs and policies of the administration in office, to ensure legal consistency or conformance to the official legal position of the administration, and to obtain conformance with White House programs and budgets. Such reviews are often intrusive in nature, at least until the "message gets through" and the bureaus comply with the president's program.

Disagreement often arises between the bureau and a departmental officer. Sometimes those differences are negotiable, sometimes not. There are often no right answers, only truths that are right for a particular time. Of course, bureau officials wish most such intrusions would go away. However, the involvement of departmental officials in many of these matters is an important part of the checks and balances within the Executive Branch. They are a necessary means of assuring a responsive bureaucracy and accountability to the elected president.[16] The style by which such reviews are accomplished and the manner by which compliance is sought therefore make a large difference in the measure of enthusiasm or resignation with which they are received. In the Reagan and Bush administrations the level of tension between the National Park Service and departmental officials rarely gave much satisfaction to the Service.

Though some people argue for organizational realignment of one form or another, the matter is actually more related to personalities than institutional arrangements. Reorganizations almost never solve personality-based problems, though that avenue of relief is a heavily trafficked route. This comes about because it is easy to be seen as "doing something" or because it is simply easier than dealing with a difficult personality. Persons outside the government are prone to recommend reorganizations because they have no means of either defining problems as personality-based or of resolving such issues. Public attacks on individual personalities sometimes make for spicy conversation over coffee, but they seldom resolve significant policy or institutional problems. Reorganizations are the only remedy easily amenable to public presentation and discussion.

Another vital part of the institutional setting by which the parks are cared for are the ten National Park Service regional offices.[17] These are the units that former Director Hartzog called minibureaus, operating with substantial independence and subject to direct manipulation by secretarial level officials and members of Congress on park level decisions. The regional office structure in 1994 was largely the product of a 1974 governmentwide reorganization action taken by President Nixon to standardize regional boundaries throughout the federal government. Though NPS boundaries and regional offices do not conform exactly with those governmentwide standards, the ten present offices reflect that effort.[18]

The rationale for regional offices is twofold: to reduce the span of control from the director's office and to consolidate various common services and functions on an aggregate level that gains efficiency thereby. Each of the regional offices has technical specialists whose replication at the park level would be prohibitive in terms of positions and funding. Land acquisition specialists, certain planning specialties, and various administrative functionaries prevail. In addition, the Park Service has a central planning, design, and construction staff in Denver and a specialized center handling exhibits, audiovisual materials, publications, and interpretive planning in Harpers Ferry, West Virginia. Those offices serve all parks.

The regional offices are intended to behave like all such offices: collect and consolidate information and data from field offices for transmission to central headquarters, with or without analysis and commentary. They are also supposed to do the same thing in reverse, elaborating on communications they have received from headquarters as necessary. The regional offices, and the regional directors in particular, also function as political and public relations buffers, between parks and the Washington, D.C., headquarters and

with the outside world. They are often lightning rods for controversy and complaints.

The regions manage several fund sources, such as cyclic maintenance and several named "initiatives," in which sums are apportioned
to each region for reallocation to individual parks. The concept per-
mits funds to be targeted toward emergencies or consolidated to meet
special needs. The regional offices also serve in various watchdog
roles, overseeing quality controls on reports, statistical compilations,
administrative activities, financial controls, personnel management
practices, and so forth. They also conduct periodic program audits
and evaluations. The regional directors are also responsible for both
performance standards and annual performance evaluations for all
superintendents under their jurisdiction. The regional directors themselves are evaluated by the director, based on agreed upon performance standards set each year.

On many occasions superintendents will bounce a particularly
troublesome decision up to the regional office, either for advice or
as a way to run it by a higher level and see if it will fly. Such shared
decision making is one way of avoiding responsibility for a decision
that may later be unpopular. It is also a way of keeping higher headquarters informed on matters that can draw flak. Superintendents are
regularly admonished to avoid causing surprises for their supervisors
and others up the line. Superintendents often find it much safer to
pass a not-quite-made decision up the ladder to see what happens.
If there is no response, the action may go ahead. If it does draw attention, it is often not too late to change someone's mind, modify
the decision, or withdraw it.

On many occasions the regional offices and regional directors
themselves push an issue higher up the organizational ladder for the
same reason and purpose. The director or one of the director's staff
may do the same with the department. When abused, however, the
system can reflect weakness at the field level. It can also be much
unappreciated at higher levels, when officers are only reluctantly responsible for an unpopular action. The willing assumption of accountability for political decisions is not a universal quality of political appointees.

In practice the roles of the regional offices in the Park Service reflect a high degree of individuality based on the personality and administrative style of the regional director. Some regional directors
hold many park-level decisions close; others delegate or otherwise
allow superintendents wide latitude for action. Some regional directors are inveterate travelers, spending large portions of their time in

the parks. Some visits are made to inspect something, others to review a set of circumstances first hand either before they make a decision or before giving the superintendent the go-ahead to decide. Comparative evaluations of park performance, however, are *not* one of their activities. Beyond the individual judgment of each regional director, no interpark comparative performance standards or cost-effectiveness criteria exist.

Few regional directors have strong personal agendas. Some see their role as buffering the parks from overly demanding staff at Washington headquarters. Not infrequently the regional director, to accomodate special circumstances thought to prevail in that region, will seek to have reversed a certain action from the Washington office. Regional directors may conveniently bury or forget to pass along some Washington office request or issuance. The Park Service does not have a strong tradition of administrative discipline, and issuances of many types, important and less important, are often simply ignored by both the regions and parks. There are seldom sanctions or other disciplinary effects of such actions.

As discussed in the chapter on the crown jewels, the Service's sense of hierarchy extends to the regions as well as the parks. Though in theory all of the regions have equal organizational status, in practice they do not. The National Capital Region (NCR), for example, with its responsibilities largely limited to sites and activities in the Washington, D.C., metropolitan area, sits well outside the mainstream of the regional offices. It is urban, program (not site) oriented, and thoroughly preoccupied with congressional inventions and interventions. The United States Park Police, attached to the National Capital Region for "rations and quarters" but reporting more practically to the director, is a constant source of issues and actions. No other region has a comparable set of programs and pressures. NCR's budget reflects the special attention its sites and clients receive. The Midwest Regional Office in Omaha is widely regarded as an unneeded concession to the politics of federal offices. The North Atlantic Regional Office in Boston and that of the Southwest region in Santa Fe are similarly regarded as probably unnecessary from an administrative point of view. However, from time to time almost all of the regional offices are regarded as unneeded, depending on the speaker's agenda.

The third component of the institutional setting within which the Service cares for the units of the national park system is the headquarters office in Washington, D.C. (WASO). Every bureau of the government has a Washington office, even those that are most far flung and decentralized. The size, functions, and operations of Washington offices do vary. An example may give some perspective on where the National Park Service comes down.

The Forest Service, a bureau in the U.S. Department of Agriculture, is a land management agency nearly three times the size of the National Park Service in personnel, with some 42,200 FTEs. Its annual budget is over $4.5 billion. (NPS's budget is about $1.3 billion.) It has over 900 field offices of one type or another, located in 44 states, Puerto Rico and the Virgin Islands. (NPS has some 370 offices in 49 states, Puerto Rico, the Virgin Islands, American Samoa, and Guam.) Its Washington office has a staff of 857. (NPS has about 420.)

The Forest Service is a highly decentralized organization, with major responsibilities and authority resting with forest supervisors. The Forest Service also has regional offices (nine, compared to NPS's ten) between the National Forests and Washington, and subunits, called districts, within the National Forests. There are 156 National Forests and 617 Ranger Districts. Sometimes Ranger Districts might effectively be compared to units of the national park system in size, complexity, and even budgets. The Forest Service also administers sixteen National Recreation Areas and one National Scenic Area.[19]

There is, however, a major distinction between the roles played by the Forest Service's Washington office and that of the National Park Service. Oversimplified, that distinction is that the Forest Service central office is essentially a standard setter, a source of rules and guidelines, and an enforcer of administrative homogeneity within and among the field offices. Within an elaborate structure of manuals and standards, Forest Service field supervisors have considerable authority to act. Few decisions are elevated to Washington headquarters for resolution.[20]

The Park Service Washington office, on the other hand, issues relatively few how-tos and must-dos. NPS has no counterpart to the Forest Service five-foot shelf of administrative and program manuals. Such detailed manuals that the Park Service once had were thrown out by Director Hartzog in the late 1960s. He believed strongly that such manuals were straitjackets that inhibited thoughtful and responsible administration by the superintendents and others. That general sense prevails today as a tenet of Park Service faith, though NPS now has its own one-foot shelf of guidelines and other documentation. The "Management Policies" book of some 122 pages provides a general framework for park planning, facilities development, cultural and natural resources management, and operations.

The NPS Washington office is the object of much complaining and grousing in the Park Service.

They do not understand anything about park problems.
WASO does nothing to support the parks.
They're always asking for more stupid reports on totally useless things.

And on and on, sometimes in "language that would make a sailor blush."

According to former Director Hartzog nine out of ten WASO employees have never held field level jobs—a statement that has considerable shock value. The reverse is probably equally true, and field employees cannot reasonably understand the WASO perspective from their positions. Park superintendents can often be heard making similar statements about the regional offices.

Tension between field and headquarters staffs is endemic. It has been present in every resource management organization in which I have had experience or with which I worked. Most probably it is inevitable. What does seem important, however, is that the headquarters office role be clearly defined and that it then rigorously operates within that definition. The Park Service has never really resolved the issue of roles. WASO sometimes behaves like a standard setter and guideline writer and then without even a thought will intervene on the level of micro-management at the level of an individual park. Almost every director I have known has not only spent much of his time in the field, he has spent it reviewing and being party to particular decisions or actions that are, at least on paper, the prerogative of the superintendent. Some superintendents deliberately bring the director in on particular matters they have reason to think will be controversial, much less to forewarn the director of a possible issue than to share (or "reverse delegate") responsibility for the decision up front.

Even with the existence of written guidelines and policies and the image of a uniformed service, the Park Service is a remarkably undisciplined career organization. Failed orders, ignored guidelines, and even overt insubordination seldom raise more than eyebrows. The strongest discipline is likely to be a transfer to another post. The discipline associated with a uniformed service is far more for external projection than for internal control. The absence of strong institutional discipline leaves uncommon leeway for policy and management variations associated with individual personalities and idiosyncrasies.

WASO takes flak from all sides: from NPS field offices and from other offices and institutions in Washington, D.C.; from departmental functions and functionaries; from Congress (both staff and members); and from the D.C. representatives of several dozen interest groups and organizations that ply their stock in trade with WASO officials. Field offices are largely unaware of the volume or importance of the external operations of the Washington office staff and officials. That is true even though it is not at all unusual for certain Park superintendents to have a separate communications link into various Washington institutions—Congress, conservation organizations, and other groups having an interest in a particular issue or site.[21]

The largest consistent complaint from the field is that the Washington office is forever requiring new reports and new reporting on all sorts of items large and small. The complaint is entirely accurate in that paperwork in the Park Service has grown in about the same way as every other institution in and out of government. Superintendents notice the requirements more than might otherwise be the case because for decades they operated as largely independent organizations, reporting very little and infrequently in any systematic way. Park Service field officials regard much of the paperwork as unnecessary and trivial, keeping them away from more important matters to which they would rather be attending. Just what those important matters are is not always made clear, because superintendents are paid to be managers, not face-to-face greeters and guides. It is a fact that many superintendents would rather be doing the sorts of field duties that were typical of their fathers and colleagues in the early days.[22]

Because planning is such an important part of the process of decision making on essentially all capital investments made in and for the national park system, the one item most likely to end up on the desk of a WASO official is a draft planning document. In times past WASO review of all or parts of planning documents was very common. It has become less routine in recent years, but still happens with considerable regularity. Reviews are often substantive, and will address the essence of a plan or one of its components. Sometimes such reviews are held formally. Field staff, including the superintendent and regional director, may be present to make a formal presentation to WASO office representatives. The director or deputy director may be present, depending on the park or the potential significance of the planning decisions.

WASO comments, especially those from the director and his top assistants, are usually taken seriously and plans may be changed or alternative methodologies adopted. Sometimes the director or someone acting for him may veto a proposed planning action. A building may be relocated, a design modified, phasing rearranged, or a potentially controversial element dropped entirely. Sometimes planning reviews surface new ideas or novel approaches to a problem, though such results are more often likely to happen earlier in the development of the planning document. By the time things come to Washington, they may be rather far along—or they may have generated controversy intense enough to warrant rethinking something in the plan. As is the case of many staff functions, the success of most WASO officials rests in their capacity to persuade and educate those in the field who hear or read their comments. It also matters whether those field officials see the particular office or person as helpful and a facilitator or as a roadblock and obstructionist. The reality is tied to personalities in a large measure.

Another set of official players on the national park system scene are the special interest groups who count the system as an object of their attention. There are many such groups, beginning with the National Parks and Conservation Association, whose primary focus is on the National Park Service and the national park system. NPCA has almost half a million members, a Washington, D.C., office and professional staff, and a cadre of field representatives whose job it is to monitor local and regional developments and activities affecting the interests of the association. NPCA carries weight on Capitol Hill and with Park Service officials, both for the quality of the homework it does and because it has shown the capacity to grow with the system. Its position taking is reasoned and reasonable, though it can be very tough minded, especially when it is dealing with its "friends" in NPS.

In addition to NPCA, other highly influential membership organizations whose interests include the national park system are the Sierra Club, the Wilderness Society, the Audubon Society, the Nature Conservancy, the National Recreation and Park Association, the National Trust for Historic Preservation, the National Geographic Society, and others. Each of these organizations has as its principal mission some set of goals or perspectives either larger or smaller than the national park system. However, all of them are engaged in national park system issues and outcomes either on a continuing or case-by-case basis.

A number of other membership organizations reflect interests that sometimes parallel—but sometimes conflict with—national park system goals, programs, and policies: the Izaak Walton League, the National Wildlife Federation, Ducks Unlimited, and various other groups whose focus is on sport hunting. Also, several nonmembership institutions engage national park system issues from time to time: the Conservation Foundation, Resources for the Future, the Natural Resources Defense Council, the International Union for the Conservation of Nature, and others.

The ranks of organizations and institutions that often engage the national park system or the National Park Service also include a generously long list of hostile or sometimes-hostile groups: the American Land Rights Association; the National Rifle Association; and various groups promoting motorized biking, snowmobiling, motor home camping, and so forth. In addition, literally hundreds of organizations and institutions—at the regional, state, and local level, friend and adversary alike—work to make their views known on park specific matters large and small or issues important to their constituencies.

One of the central features of all these external players on the national park system scene is that they almost all universally voice their support for the system and assert their only disagreements are with specific policies, programs, or actions taken or proposed by the National Park Service. Even the most ardent supporters of the system—NPCA, for example—are often sharp and persistent critics of something-in-particular. They can very often make truth of the old expression about not needing enemies when you have such unfriendly friends. The role of friendly critic is, however, one of the most constructive functions performed by these organizations—bringing to bear citizen pressures and institutional muscle to affect change or to prevent an action that it is believed would be inimical to the long-term interests of the national park system.

The give and take of interest groups whose perspectives are often at odds with each other and with the Park Service, is an important part of the checks and balances that characterize our governmental structure and system. It is modern conventional wisdom to bad mouth so-called special interest groups, on grounds that their activities somehow distort the political process, particularly through their contributions toward political campaign financing. Such problems and realities aside, interest groups are a vital part of the American governmental structure, and represent one of the few means available to individuals and groups by which they can express their opinions and values in the political process. They are an important and often effective check on the tendencies of all bureaucracies, both public and private, to see themselves as infallibly correct in all matters within their domain.

With two major exceptions, the National Park Service has no formal structure or process by which it relates to outside organizations: no designated liaison, no central point of contact. One exception is the travel and tourism industry. NPS has a full-time paid senior staff member whose job is to serve as liaison with that industry. The other is the Park Service staff relating to the business firms and individuals who own and operate an array of visitor accommodations and facilities and services in the parks through concession contracts.

Some federal agencies do maintain liaison offices or functionaries by which they maintain relationships with outside organizations and institutions and by which they attempt to control contacts or responses. One effect of not having any central point of contact is that outside groups and individuals can deal directly with the people or offices they believe are most likely to turn a favorable ear to their pleading. It would, of course, be exceedingly difficult to try to begin such an arrangement in NPS today. The decentralized character of present contacts is powerfully institutionalized.

A study of National Park Service relationships with its various constituencies is well beyond the scope of this book—albeit one that would merit careful study. However, on balance I believe the Service has done remarkably well in keeping such contacts relatively open and free of embarrassment, although the subject of national park system concession policies and practices sometimes teeters on the brink of scandal. The subject merits objective study and analysis, both internal and by others.

In the context of interest groups it is worth remarking that the ultimate power and potential influence of even a single person motivated to press a point or lead a cause can be enormous. One person has more than a few times sparked the equivalent of a revolution, caused a new park to be created, stopped or started a major activity or development, or stimulated an unmoving bureaucracy to action. The pivotal role of Florida's Marjorie Stoneman Douglas in the life of Everglades NP is a case in point. The list of similar champions for the parks is long, and without such persistent and often financially generous help the national park system of today would be much the poorer.

Since 1935 a secretarial level advisory board has served as a consultant resource on proposed additions to the national park system and on other policy issues. The National Park System Advisory Board has enlisted the volunteer talent and support of numerous nationally recognized experts in science and history and other interested lay persons. The board's role has varied from administration to administration, but in the Reagan-Bush years its role was largely muted by highly political appointments and by presidential policies to oppose virtually all expansion of the national park system. Legal authority for the board expires in 1995, and there seems to be little support in the Service or Congress for renewing its charter.

The sixth and final set of players on which the care and custody of the national park system depends is the Congress and the committees that oversee the National Park Service and system. Although a full examination of the workings of Congress is well beyond the scope of this book, it is a subject that merits study because it is the beginning and the end of the processes by which the United States government does or does not keep the democratic faith with the American people. It represents them, and in that role is the principal means by which and through which the people can both influence and draw accountability for the resources that make up the national park system.

Four committees of Congress have primary jurisdiction over the national park system: one each in the House of Representatives and the Senate responsible for the substance of the system, and one each in the House and Senate responsible for the appropriations that finance everything that happens.[23] While this division of labor may sound clear and distinct, the reality is that the substantive and appropriations committees' jurisdictions inevitably overlap, and not always happily. Legislation creating new park units and legislation affecting the policies and programs of the National Park Service normally arise in and are under the jurisdiction of the substantive committees. Because it is almost impossible to separate the money used to do something from what is done or how it is done, the appropriations committees are inevitably involved in program and policy decisions of major substance and effect.

On one recent occasion the appropriations committee created a new unit of the national park system through an appropriation act. No hearings were ever held and no report written by the substantive committee. Parks have been created by the legislation approved by the substantive committee, only to have its financing fail time and again before the appropriations committee. Such intercommittee jurisdictional overlaps and squabbles are not, however, the everyday rule. The business of the Congress follows generally predictable paths, even if not always toward predictable destinations.

An important aspect of the congressional committee process is the committee's oversight role—a watchdog function that only may or may not be related to a specific piece of legislation. The oversight function of committees is very much a function of the chairman.

Oversight hearings are not required by law, nor is there a strong tradition favoring some regular pattern of when they will be held or what subjects may be their objects. At some times in the past, notably during the directorship of George B. Hartzog, Jr., oversight hearings before the House subcommittee were done with regularity. They were an opportunity for Director Hartzog to "tell it like he saw it" and to respond to members' questions in ways that did an effective end run on the normal congressional reporting processes. Oversight hearings were largely nonconfrontational, often friendly and supportive, even when there were more than ample issues on the table to suggest otherwise. Hartzog is widely regarded as uniquely skillful in using the oversight hearing process as a way to get his point of view across to members of Congress and as a means to illuminate the needs of the Service to the members. No other director since Stephen Mather has had such a close and supportive relationship with the Congress.

In recent years the tone of executive-congressional relationships has militated strongly against the development of similar candor and effectiveness between the director and subcommittee or committee chairmen. Bureau chiefs throughout the federal government have operated under White House instructions that have severely limited all contacts with Congress. On many occasions even informal one-on-one meetings with members have been monitored by administration representatives whose acknowledged function is to make certain that bureau chiefs and their minions do not waver from established administration policy. Such practices have largely succeeded in their desired effect, resulting in vastly reduced dialogue between bureau officials and the Congress.

Some observers blame divided government for the phenomenon. With the White House dominated by one party and the Congress another, there has been a perpetual state of tension between the two. Some would characterize it as a state of perpetual political war. Whether the Clinton administration will develop a more cordial and symbiotic relationship with the committees of Congress and their members is unknown at this writing, though the popular notion is that congressional deadlock is (for a time) over.

Divided government has been only part of the reason. It is also a function of how the role of government is perceived in our society as a whole. For the lion's share of twenty years, the federal government has been described as "the problem" by successive presidents, their cabinet officers and appointees, and by many members of Congress and the media.[24] An entire generation of the public has grown up with what the Brookings Institution has characterized as "stereotypes of civil servants as faceless bureaucrats—overpaid, underworked, marching in lockstep, and enjoying tenure guarantees that remove any incentive for excellence."[25] This stereotype exists both as a perception of the career service held by the public, and of vastly more significance, it has infiltrated the career service's perception of itself. A major effect of this reality is a widespread lowering of expectations: lower expectations *of* government, and lower expectations *by* the government itself.

If people, adults or children, are told long enough and with enough conviction that they are the problem—that the things they do have no value, that they are part of a bloated bureaucracy whose works are without merit—they will in time adopt that self image as their own. They will live down to the expectations of others and themselves. How many athletes or sports teams do well while showing low self-esteem? These effects are well documented in the literature of child and adult psychology and in studies of self-esteem and motivation. It is a modern miracle that the Park Service is fortunate to have within the ranks of its committees in both Houses of the Congress members whose sympathies, yes love, of the national park system overshadows the politics of our time. Costs have been paid, however. The loss of effective dialogue regarding new park areas is serious, and in the end opportunities will be lost, perhaps forever.

Will constructive change occur? Probably only when it changes for the nation as a whole. It seems highly improbable that the national park system will somehow be treated in a way qualitatively different from other valued services of the federal government. Constructive change cannot occur until the American people, acting through their votes and as expressed through the institutions in our society that reflect their will, determine it will happen. That seems only probable with some new kind and quality of leadership or a national crisis of catastrophic proportions—at least equal to the Great Depression of the 1930s or a galvanizing event of equal impact.

Another important aspect of Congress's role relates to the need for Congress and the Executive Branch to be much more disciplined about the ways and terms under which units are added to the national park system. We have argued for a clear and strict accounting—agreement—between Congress and NPS about what is in the national park system and what is not. We have suggested the units be numbered so that it is clear when the next one is added. Coming to such an agreement ultimately requires a cooperative approach between Congress and the administration—on at least that item. There is, unfortunately, great reluctance on the part of any administration to take the initiative in a matter such as this. It implies some defect, some sloppiness, some inattention in the process. That is hard to admit or deal with politically.

While no one seriously believes the larger integrity of the national park system is in danger—now—there should be in place established processes that give to the system the measure of permanence and integrity it deserves. The experience with Mar-A-Lago NHS and some of the other divestitures ought never happen again under any foreseeable circumstances. Similarly, NPS and the Congress need assurance that the processes by which areas are added to the system have believable and supportable integrity of their own. The national park system does not need the sort of badmouthing that has attended Steamtown NHS, arguments for and against aside. It is the system itself that is hurt. Only after many years will Steamtown NHS be able to live down its image as a piece of unwarranted legislative pork. Both the resource and the career rangers and other employees who work there now and in the future will suffer. Such should not happen.

NPS is not likely to lay aside its myopia regarding many recent additions to the system (and some not so recent) unless it can develop a new level of faith in the process. It must, of course, be a part of that process at appropriate times in appropriate ways. NPS must mature enough to understand that it will not always get its own way. Congress will not always agree that something-in-particular is as good or as bad as some NPS professionals think it is. Some decisions are just too important to be left to professionals whose agendas are often much too self-serving and resistant to change. Sometimes jarring mutations are essential if a species is to survive.

The overall organization of the Service and of each park also impacts decisions regarding the allocation of funds, professional assignments, staffing levels, and so forth. There is considerable opportunity to standardize the organization of individual parks. Perhaps three to five models based on the size or principal resource of the park would be sufficient. Organizational standardization would allow more realistic comparisons of performance, simplify interunit transfers, permit the development of career ladders, and make comparative cost analyses more feasible. Organizational standardization would not be readily appreciated because it flies in the face of deeply perceived notions that every park is unique. The core of truth in the statement overlooks the fact that the policies, processes, skills, and tools used to provide care and custody for the resource are basically the same from park to park. That similarity of resources and the need to treat each resource element with the same care and attention was a fundamental reason for abolishing the old three-tiered management policies. Nevertheless, the concept prevails that "today, there is not a single National Park Service. It varies from region to region and park to park. . . . Successful leadership at each site requires unique adaptation of general NPS policies to idiosyncratic local circumstances."[26]

Park organizations much more similar—and it is only a matter of degree, because considerable similarity exists already, and the long-term trend is toward similitude—would also facilitate other forms of linkage in personnel systems, financial management, vehicle fleet management, equipment utilization, and so forth. There is, of course, some danger in standardization. It can lead to types of homogeneity that are neither desirable nor defensible. Parks are unique in the resources they shelter and in their individual message. It is very possible for sameness to creep into interpretive programs, architecture and design, and other park elements that few people would really want. Therefore, the issue of standardization in the context of something in particular, rather than something in general, must necessarily be addressed.

Gauging the quality of performance by National Park Service organizations and people is an art form barely explored. While comparisons are only rarely made between and among parks, many comparisons are assuredly possible. The listings and analyses contained in Appendixes 6 and 7 suggest a few possibilities. The larger problem of "Whither the Public Service?" is vastly more troubling. Public attitudes, from recent presidents of the United States to every citizen, are sorely infected with elements of disrespect and hopelessness that defy easy or quick solutions. It has, after all, taken more than a generation to move from John F. Kennedy's call to "let the public service be a proud and lively career" in his first State of the Union address to where we are now. The move to some new set of understandings about our government, some new compact between those who serve and those who are served, and some new level of self-esteem for those in the public service, is a move only the people can take and only leadership define.

NOTES

1. Perceptions similar to those in the preceding paragraphs have been around at least since the publication in 1968 of Robert Cahn's Pulitzer Prize winning series of articles in the *Christian Science Monitor*, "Will Success Spoil the National Parks?"

2. *A Race against Time, A Report by the National Parks and Conservation Association,* Washington, D.C., Aug. 20, 1991.

3. From "The 1991 Citibank Mastercard and Visa Report on Our National Parks: Preserving a Priceless Heritage, Executive Summary, a National Survey Conducted by Research & Forecasts, Inc.," June 1991: 10.

4. Ibid., 11.

5. Each year the Roper Organization, Inc., a national public opinion research service, includes in the "Annual Roper Report" a question to rate various federal agencies. The Park Service has consistently ranked at or near the top of such lists, garnering a "moderately favorable" or "highly favorable" rating from about 80 percent of those polled.

6. The other bureau whose director is a secretarial appointee is the Minerals Management Service.

7. Though a historical examination of the thirteen men who have served as directors of the National Park Service is well beyond the scope of this book, only a handful of past directors have conceived and pushed a personal concept or agenda for the national park system. Directors have tended to be pragmatic practitioners, not visionaries. Several former directors have written books about the National Park Service, all of them valuable sources of insights into the workings of a federal agency. They are books listed in the bibliography by Albright, Wirth, and Hartzog; Albright, Dickenson, and Mott also collaborated on a book.

8. Letter to the author from Richard T. Gale, president of the Association of National Park Rangers, Mar. 25, 1992.

9. Though the late William Penn Mott, Jr., was regarded by many people as a Park Service insider, his exposure to NPS was as a landscape architect in the 1930s. His major career was with the East Bay Regional Park District in Oakland, California, and with the state, where he served as director of the state park system.

10. They selected Russell E. Dickenson, then Pacific Northwest Regional director and a former deputy director.

11. The director, deputy director, ten regional directors, six associate directors; and three special assistants. SES salaries at the beginning of 1994 ranged from $96,830 to $120,594.

12. Former Director Hartzog has suggested the director should be a ten-year term appointment, without renewal. Former Director Conrad Wirth told the author in a conversation September 27, 1991, that he supported Senate confirmation for the director.

13. Senate confirmation hearings have a very uneven history of effect and value. Many have the effect of a rubber stamp; others appear as love feasts among persons all known to each other through prior or present associations. Some, such as the hearing on Judge Clarence Thomas for the Supreme Court, are difficult, divisive political battles. By no means would every president and senator relish increased confirmation activities. It is, however, a constitutional responsibility that is a vital ingredient in this nation's processes for accountability.

14. From 1963 to 1966, I served as staff assistant to the then under secre-

tary of the Interior, John A. Carver, Jr. Carver had moved to that post from that of assistant secretary for public land management, in which job he supervised the National Park Service, the Bureau of Land Management, and the Office of Territories. Carver once clashed in what is often characterized as historic proportions with the Park Service leadership. In a speech to Park Service superintendents and professionals Carver accused NPS of self-centeredness, inertia, and bureaucratic inflexibility. Not only has Carver, who went on to become a member of the Federal Power Commission and a law professor at the University of Colorado, never been forgiven his candor, the event is told and retold within NPS as evidence of unfair political and personal intrusion. However, no small number of people, even within the Park Service, applauded (and continue to applaud) Carver's remarks as honest and right on target.

15. Hartzog, *Battling for the National Parks,* 269–70.

16. One of the most compelling and intrusive interventions by departmental officials in the last two decades has been in the hiring of minorities and women, all part of governmentwide efforts. Even with vigorous departmental intercession, however, the effects of affirmative action within the Park Service have not caused revolutionary change. This reality is heavily influenced by Park Service practice to almost always hire at the bottom of the career ladder. Real change takes many years to work its way up the organizational ladder.

17. Located in Boston, Mass.; Philadelphia, Pa.; Washington, D.C.; Atlanta, Ga.; Omaha, Nebr.; Denver, Colo.; Santa Fe, N.Mex.; San Francisco, Calif.; Seattle, Wash.; and Anchorage, Alaska.

18. The first NPS regional offices were created in 1937, when there were five such offices. Interestingly, in 1924 a proposal was advanced within the Service to consolidate the management of all the national monuments under a field headquarters to be run by much-respected Frank Pinkley. Pinkley was the long-time keeper of Casa Grande Ruins NM (Ariz.) and supervisor of up to twenty-one southwestern NMs, many of which were cared for by volunteers and $1-per-month custodians. The idea died because Mather did not want to lose central control of the monuments.

19. Letter to the author, Mar. 4, 1992, from Bernard E. Akin, chief, work force management, productivity & systems branch, Forest Service, Washington, D.C.

20. For a classic study of Forest Service organization and institutional cohesion, see Kaufman, *The Forest Ranger.*

21. Many superintendents make it a point to get to know and attempt to stay on friendly terms with the representative in whose district the park lies and with one or both senators from that state. They may also have direct access to a member of the appropriations subcommittee or to the substantive committee handling national park system legislation. Sometimes those contacts are with the members directly, sometimes through one of the member's staff. Park Service and departmental officials are rather inconsistent in their approach to such relationships. On most occasions the official position

is that contacts with Congress should be handled through channels, which means through the director and the secretary. On the other hand, the regional directors and often individual park superintendents are brought to Washington, D.C., to participate in both appropriation hearings and those on other park-related legislation. On other occasions the initial contacts are initiated by the member or staff person. Either party may keep the relationship active. In practice such working relationships are tolerated, even encouraged, as long as they are working in ways that go smoothly and without bad public relations for the incumbent administration.

22. In his autobiographical account as chief ranger at Yellowstone NP, Dan Sholly mentions that he normally has about three hours of paperwork daily—work he accomplishes *before* normal working hours! He also noted, "I am very much a ranger with his heart in the outdoors, not just another paper-pushing bureaucrat" (*Guardians of Yellowstone,* 59). The quotation would be unabashedly seconded by many supervisory level park rangers and superintendents.

23. The reality is more complicated. On infrequent occasions the Park Service director may testify before a committee that normally has little relationship with the park system. For example, the Armed Services Committees may consider legislation on surplus military lands destined to become part of the national park system—for example, the Presidio of San Francisco. Laws on environmental quality, hazardous wastes, the civil service, worker safety, and dozens of other topics impinge on Park Service management.

24. Author John Kenneth Galbraith has suggested that current negative attitudes toward public servants and their work are part of a much larger phenomenon associated with a "culture of contentment," by which a large majority of the population disdain those parts of the government that are not perceived as directly supportive of their personal status quo. See Galbraith, *The Culture of Contentment,* 70–77, 175–77.

25. DiIulio et al., *Improving Government Performance,* 29.

26. From the "Draft Reports of the Working Groups on Our National Parks: Challenges and Strategies for the 21st Century," a publication for consideration by a working congress on national park management, Vail, Colo., Oct. 7–10, 1991: 18, 16.

EIGHT

The People Who Make the Difference

The care and custody of the resources of the national park system are large tasks of great complexity. They require skilled technicians and generalists, money, authority, and a myriad of tools ranging from undersea diving gear to aircraft and from scientific instrumentation to snow plows. An inventory of the things owned by the National Park Service that it uses to do its job would be impressive for its scope. The inventory at one park of its accountable personal property—the things valuable enough to keep track of in a systematic way—contained hundreds of separate items: from acid to zoysia.

However, none of the things in the Park Service inventory move or accomplish their role without one or more operators—the people who staff the parks and offices that manage the national park system. There are far fewer people than things, so few in fact that many of them must be the proverbial jack-of-all-trades. And therein lies a problem we will shortly explore.

In December 1991 the National Park Service had approximately 19,700 employees, of which about 14,200 were full-time permanent staff. Less than a thousand of those totals were seasonal employees subject to furlough.[1] The largest single occupational category was that of park management, which included the park ranger group of some 3,281 employees, representing about a quarter of the total Park Service permanent labor force. There were an additional 2,105 non-full-time permanent people in the ranger force.[2] The second largest occupational category was maintenance employees with 1,558 full-time permanent employees and 496 other than full-time permanent. The third and fourth largest occupational groups were secretaries and the U.S. Park Police, with 681 and 619 full-time people respectively.

As of the beginning of 1992, the National Park Service employed people in 288 separate occupational classifications. They are listed in Appendix 8. In the listing, occupational groups called "specialists" involve higher graded jobs in the same field as those labeled "technicians." The list of systemwide occupations is interesting for what it documents about the organization and programs of the Service. Several important characteristics are evident in the list:

1. The list confirms the absence of parallel organizational arrangements from park to park and from region to region. Forty-one occupational groups were represented by only one person. One hundred sixty-five occupations were represented by fewer than ten people systemwide—less than one per NPS Region.
2. Many technical resource management professions were represented by only a handful of persons. There were only three professional foresters, three sociologists, two range conservationists, two plant pathologists, only six botanists, a dozen horticulturists, and twenty-four geologists.
3. The largest group of professional resource-related employees was "general" biologists (345). The next largest resource-related group was historians (130). There were, however, more landscape architects (176) and architects (153). Both of the latter two groups would, of course, often treat historic and cultural resources.
4. The occupational pattern suggests that defined career ladders or other progression within an occupation may be difficult or impossible to achieve. The only route up the ladder is through wide spectrum occupations having numerous general points of entry. Many technical and professional specialties appear to be dead ends, absent a shift to an occupational classification outside the specialty.

Some Park Service critics have used evidence such as the data in Appendix 8 to show that NPS has inadequate depth of professional resource-related professionals. The perception is that a list of NPS staff should show a cadre of persons clearly having the professional credentials to evaluate and manage the full range of natural and cultural resources of the national park system. The existence of such a cadre of professional skills is not obvious in the list of 1992 Park Service occupations in Appendix 8.

The list, however, does not tell the whole story, because the formal occupational classifications to which employees are assigned only reflects in part the reality of their skills and the work they do. In order for a job to be classified according to one of the occupational listings discussed above, the job has to essentially be a full-time do-almost-nothing-else sort of thing. The fisheries biologist must be doing that line of work predominantly, not merely part time or in addition to other unrelated duties. The effect of this requirement is to understate in a potentially significant way the real professional capabilities and duties of several hundreds of National Park Service employees whose jobs are classified under any of several generalist occupational groups: park management, environmental protection specialist, program management, and others. Furthermore, occupational categorization says nothing about the education or experience of the incumbents.

About 75 percent of all park rangers hold at least a bachelor's degree; about 50 percent of that number have degrees related to natural or cultural resources.[3] Of course, not all those rangers are doing work related to natural or cultural resources. Further, it is also true that about 25 percent of the ranger force do *not* have college degrees, a situation that does seem unusual in a resource management organization whose labor force has more than doubled in the last generation.

The list of occupational titles is also interesting for the incidence of the words "miscellaneous" and "general" in their titles, again reflecting the fact that the tasks performed are less specialized, less definitive. A critical issue for the Park Service is whether such generalized positions and competencies do not significantly compromise the level of expertise or the attention specific resource management activities really need. It is certainly something people outside the organization cannot make easy judgments about. However, it may be equally difficult for those directly involved to objectively consider the subject and its implications.

The problem has deep roots, beginning with the first men employed in the earliest units of the national park system. According to former Director Horace Albright, in the primal days of the Park Service[4] "applicants for ranger positions had to be between twenty-one and forty years of age, of good character, sound physique, and tactful in handling people. They were required to possess a common-school education, be able to ride and care for horses, have experience in outdoor life, be a good shot with rifle and pistol, and have knowledge of trail construction and fighting forest fires."

A few years later the following description of the park ranger's job was spelled out in the first formal civil service announcement for ranger positions in 1926. The job paid $1,680 a year, open to men and women, ages 21 to 45.[5] Rangers paid for their own uniforms and food. The announcement said the ranger's "duties involve knowledge of methods of fighting forest and prairie fires; packing horses and mules; habits of animals; ability to ride and handle horses; construction of fire lines and trails; reading of topographic maps and com-

pass; tact in handling people; cooking; use of firearms; driving motor cars and motorcycles; and in those parks where needed, skill on
snow shoes and skis; incidental clerical and information work."

At the time this recruiting material was released, then Acting Director Albright added his own stern admonition.[6]

A ranger's job is no place for a nervous, quick-tempered man, nor for a
laggard, nor for one who is unaccustomed to hard work. If you cannot
work hard ten or twelve hours a day, and always with patience and a
smile on your face, don't fill out the attached blank. . . . The ranger's
job is especially hard. There will not be more than twenty ranger's jobs
in next year's force of rangers and there is really very little chance of
your being considered unless you possess *all* of the qualifications mentioned herein.

And apply they did—and do today.

Many initial National Park Service rangers came from the army,
reflecting the fact that it was the military that had responsibility for
several parks for many of their earliest years. Then came engineers
(largely civil engineers), then a mix of all sorts of professional disciplines including the social sciences. Many early employees had no
college degree, and Albright was moved to observe that "there was a
natural resistance on the part of the traditional rangers when the
college-trained people began to come in on a permanent basis, but
the old timers soon learned that a college education didn't make this
'new breed' so different after all. They got the same starting salaries
as other rangers."[7]

It is of interest to note that while the National Park Service was
building a ranger force of generalists from a wide and disparate pot-
pourri of disciplines and backgrounds, the Forest Service in the U.S.
Department of Agriculture, created in 1905, was building a staff made
up largely of college-trained foresters. The first chief of the Forest Service, Gifford Pinchot, was a European-educated professional forester.

The Forest Service emphasis and focus on the professional forester and a companion tradition of bureau chiefs always appointed from
within the ranks of the organization, has meant that no chief has
ever been appointed to head the Forest Service who was not first a
trained forester. The tradition has stuck, even in administrations that
would have devoutly wished to have appointed someone from the
timber or lumber industry or someone more beholden to the administration elected to office.[8] Forest Service chiefs have evidenced remarkable political longevity.

Over the years, the Park Service propensity to treat the ranger profession as a polymorph, the conscious embodiment of the jack-of-all-trades, has become deeply institutionalized. It is relished by the ranger force to the point that as a body they have vigorously resisted any change that would further professionalize the ranger occupation at the expense of what is regarded as the core of what makes the ranger's job interesting and rewarding. The problem is not that rangers are happy with their present lot, but that they seek to have the work of rangers redefined solely on their terms. The president of the Association of National Park Rangers reported that at its 1991 annual business meeting the association "clarified that its intent was to define the ranger profession *as we see it,* then go to OPM to work out a solution" (emphasis added).[9]

The Office of Personnel Management (OPM) has not in the past regarded the work of a park ranger as professional in character. To be such, the job would have to require that incumbents possess a definable body of knowledge and skills associated with a specific educational degree. Substitution of generalized work experience, which has been acceptable, undercuts a professional classification. It has also affected the self-image of rangers and others with whom they work.

The rangers' view of the ranger job is very close today to what Albright described in 1923. A 1991 flyer titled "What is a ranger?" distributed on the occasion of the Seventy-fifth anniversary of the National Park Service, reads in part:

> In the seventy-five years since the National Park Service was established, the demands placed on park rangers have grown dramatically. Today when there are medical emergencies in remote areas, rangers certified as emergency medical technicians or as paramedics are often flown to the scene. But the traditional skills remain important. What if a fierce thunderstorm prevents aircraft from flying? Then rangers must respond the fastest way possible: by foot, by four-wheel drive vehicle, or, perhaps . . . on horseback.

The issue not only relates to the historic park ranger, but also affects the ranger interpreter, the ranger whose specific job is at the interface of the park experience and the visitor. The identity confusion and frustration were articulated in an article by Rob Fudge, an interpretive ranger at National Capital Parks. He wrote that

> depending on who you talk with, you can get a wide range of opinions on what interpreters are and what they should aspire to be. Some have visions of them as scholars, while some see them as creative and charismatic orators and writers. . . . And some in position classification

see them as "guides" or "information receptionists." . . . The confusion over what we are stems in part from ambiguity over what types of training it takes to become a good interpreter. . . . we continually claim that we can train people to be interpreters in two weeks or less.[10]

Federal personnel systems base the grade and pay of civil service employees on a variety of factors, including the measure of important decisions embodied in the job, their complexity and potential effects, and the type and extent of education and training necessary to meet the job's requirements. It also matters whether the complex decisions are made without close and continuous supervision and whether they are a regular, continuing part of the everyday experience or if they are only occasional or even rare. Civil service personnel standards have not given much credit for the fact that jobs involve multiple, disparate tasks and responsibilities. The resulting problems are extraordinarily important and extraordinarily difficult.

A long-standing effect of the nonprofessional characterization of the ranger's job has been to place a ceiling on the Park Service grade structure. Some Park Service employees are not as well paid as their counterparts, for example, in the Forest Service.[11] For a long time, the problem was masked, even hidden, behind a rapidly expanding park system and a long waiting list of young people who were willing to take temporary, seasonal, and part-time Park Service jobs in the expectation that eventually they would be converted to full-time permanent positions. The average seasonal ranger was a powerfully motivated person. Seasonal Park Service jobs were over subscribed by factors as high as (and even exceeding) a hundred applicants for each job. Competition was so fierce among applicants who were essentially equally qualified that summer jobs were offered on the basis of a lottery.

Some people waited five years and more to become full-career employees, often then beginning at the bottom of the career ladder in Grades GS-3 or GS-4.[12] Many jobs have paid salaries so low that these federal employees and their families qualified for food stamps! Over the last decade the situation has gotten incrementally worse. In a release issued in August 1991, the National Parks and Conservation Association asserted that

Rangers are leaving the Park Service for better pay and career opportunities. . . . Due to the diverse job skills National Park Service rangers generally possess, after working a few years in a park, they are attractive candidates for better pay with other federal land management agencies or the private and civic sectors . . .

It is not uncommon for rangers to remain at the GS-05 or GS-07 grade level, with roughly the same duties and pay, for 5–10 years. . . . there is only a one in 15 chance that a Park Ranger hired in 1991 will reach a GS-09 level in 15 years.[13]

Park Service employees themselves write about the status of morale in the organization. In an article in the Fall 1991 issue of *Courier, Newsmagazine of the National Park Service,* a monthly journal directed to employees and alumni, John Reynolds, named deputy NPS director in the Clinton-Kennedy administration, summarized his impression of employee morale in the Park Service, "Well, my morale is pretty good, but the morale of the organization isn't."

Grades and salaries are only two of a long list of issues and topics that Park Service employees mention. Others include housing, opportunities for promotion and career development, jobs and careers for both spouses (and sometimes children living at home), the quality of supervision, the availability of continuing education and training, and the need for "an overarching, unifying, agreed-upon direction for the future."[14]

Formal documentation of employee concerns has existed since the mid-1980s, when the Park Service conducted a full-scale employee survey under the direction of professional sociologists at the University of Washington. The survey was conducted using standard survey techniques and its results were shared with all employees and Park Service management. Many problems documented in the employee survey were issues over which the director of the National Park Service had no jurisdiction or powers, for example, salaries and benefits. One persistent problem identified was the absence of health insurance among the temporary and part-time staff—that large group of employees waiting on the sidelines for conversion to the career federal service. Efforts were made to find a private insurance carrier who could offer those employees medical insurance (at no cost to the government). In 1992 coverage finally became available through a program sponsored by the Association of National Park Rangers.[15]

The director attempted to follow up on those issues over which he could exercise some influence and several changes were begun, not the least of which was the continuing major financial investments being made to improve employee housing. As suggested by Reynolds' call for an "overarching, unifying . . . direction for the future," the problems begin at very fundamental institutional levels. The Association of National Park Rangers has also asserted that "we need a plan which defines the Service's role in preserving and interpreting the country's heritage."[16] This book has asked the question earlier whether there should be a grand design for the national park system. As difficult as such an undertaking may be, striving for it can be all as important as the finished product, particularly when that effort engages the intellect and energy of employees.

Professionalizing the ranger force is a very tender subject. Whatever steps may be taken holds the potential for bringing many people in the existing labor force to a crisis of identity. If the rangers of the future will be degree-qualified specialists in biology, archeology, forestry, wildlife biology, and similar fields, what will happen to the existing ranger staff? Competition between them and the new breed of rangers may be even more destructive of morale and performance than the present situation. Is the Service prepared to develop and pay for the costs of reeducating its present staff? The scale of such an undertaking is monumental. However, this dilemma is in no qualitative way different from what must be done with large and growing segments of the American labor force in a myriad of other fields— atomic weapons, the defense industry, aircraft production, the airlines industry, and literally hundreds more.

By no means is all the news bad. As evidenced by polls and surveys of recent vintage, National Park Service employees are among the most admired people in our society. The national park system is by all measures one of the most revered constructions of our culture. Political attacks from the far right and self-serving assaults from anywhere else notwithstanding, the national park system and the National Park Service are institutions in no serious danger of destruction from without. Their friends have power, and they would use it if defense were necessary.

NPS has by any measure one of the most dedicated and highly motivated staffs of any organization, anywhere. Even without the opportunities that rapid growth provides, there are many young people who would "give their eye teeth" to work for the National Park Service. In an economy where opportunities in many other fields are similarly limited or nonexistent, the Park Service is in a buyer's market for talent. That modern reality places a special burden and urgency on Park Service management to understand the problems at hand and craft the vehicles and means to address them. That element of change must start at the top, because the people standing at the bottom of the ladder have no means to cause needed change when those at the top may not hear or understand or if they cannot or do not act.

In any organization, institutional change is one of the most diffi-

cult things to effect. Many changes only occur as a result of a catastrophic event. In the private sector it may be a buy-out, merger, near
bankruptcy, or a change of leadership, typically from the outside.
Institutional change in the National Park Service is made even more
difficult by the nature of the agency's mission—to conserve, to keep
things as they were or are, to resist the forces from outside that would
harm or destroy the resources as they are understood to exist. However, changes will take place, if for no other reason than the fact that
present agency managers will eventually be replaced by younger men
and women whose experience base and orientation are different.

Rather than beginning and ending with today's self-image of the
ranger's occupation, it may be useful to begin with a clearer understanding of what the ranger of the future should bring to the task. A
much clearer understanding of what that future might be could help.
Then the job would be to fashion the means and timetable for a transition from present reality to whatever the future is perceived to require. Given the long history of the Office of Personnel Management's
failure to bend Civil Service classification standards to fit the best
wishes of the NPS ranger staff, the more productive approach is likely to be one that would gradually move the Service toward some new
understanding of itself.

Beginning in 1993, the Service began several pilot programs to re-
allocate work and positions to qualify new positions for higher grades.
The results are described as encouraging. The approach may have the
effect of reducing the size of the "old" ranger force, while building a
new group of professional resource specialists in new patterns of work
and jobs. I hope the effort will be reinforced by training and reedu-
cation programs on a comparable scale.

New understandings of the interrelationships of natural and manmade systems are calling for new skills and new professional qualifications among virtually every segment of the labor force. New demographics of the visitor population make new requirements on
rangers, interpreters, and other staff who have regular or occasional
contacts with the visiting public.

NPS does not now have any systemwide means of identifying or
dealing with such changes. While training is an important part of
the Park Service management style, substantially all such training has
been indoctrinational in character. It was designed to teach people
how and why things are done the way they are *now*, not how they
might be changed or reoriented to some new understanding. The recent training programs for resources management may be a useful
exception. In that instance people have been selected for such train-

ing as a new departure and much of the curriculum for that effort was new, even speculative.

Training and retraining on a large scale is expensive, and it is likely funding will be very limited, as it has been for many years. An alternative seldom used in the National Park Service is to look outside the Service for skilled people. Almost no one enters the National Park Service above entry level positions. Except for the large influx of people coming to the Service at the time of the NPS-HCRS merger in 1981, no significant infusion of outside talent has come into the Service since World War II. The Service's experience with HCRS would assuredly militate against considering large-scale outside recruiting, although such recruiting could be specifically focused on documented skills needs or professional specialties in short supply. Persons already having such qualifications could not, however, be hired at entry level grades and salaries. For many people in the Service that would be a major problem.

New professional blood could help the Park Service leap frog its way up the learning curve. In computer and communications technology, in resources management specialties, and in other professional disciplines underrepresented in NPS, the Service could gain an entire generation by selective, but generous, outside recruiting of already-skilled professionals. However, outside recruiting in a time of job retrenchment may be politically impossible on any scale worth the effort.

A further option is for the Service to collaborate directly with selected colleges and universities to produce curricula finely tailored to help fill professional gaps. This approach does not gain time, but it can be done without large in-house training investments and can avoid double training or retraining persons already employed. NPS has entrée into several universities through already established cooperative research units. While there are several dozen professional park management curricula at U.S. colleges and universities, none is specifically tailored to jobs in the National Park Service. That linkage has previously been almost exclusively with state park agencies and local government park and recreation departments.

The Smokey Bear hat is a symbol a thousand organizations would give a bundle to own.[17] There are no doubt countless children who grow up saying they want someday to be a park ranger and wear that distinctive hat and uniform. Of course, only a relative handful will actually do it, but it must certainly be in the same league as being a fireman or a police officer or a doctor or nurse. It is no longer limited to boys and men.

For an entire generation and more the Park Service has been a passive recruiter. People did not need to be encouraged to apply for Park Service jobs. Many view this fact as absolute proof that all is well on the input side of the equation. It may not be so. By relying virtually 100 percent on selecting people who have knocked on the Park Service door and said, "Hire me," the Service has left its later choices to a self-defined employment market that only may or may not include the skills the Service most needs for now and the future. Because NPS does not hire from the outside on any regular or systematic basis, its only options are to find needed (new) skills from within. Perhaps even worse, because NPS does no outside recruiting, it has no real incentive to look ahead and figure out what new skills it needs or will require in the future. It is unfortunately a vicious circle.

Turnover in the National Park Service is something on the order of 3 percent annually—a very low number by any standard. While many organizations would be very glad to reduce their own turnover rates, when that rate reaches such a low level, new problems emerge. Few vacancies are created into which others may be promoted or rotated. In years of tight budgets (and there have been many) relocation that is not combined with a grade promotion is unwelcome by almost all employees.

The National Park Service does have personnel problems that merit the attention of management, the secretary of the Interior, and the Congress. Some of those problems are beyond NPS control, even beyond the control of the president. Some problems will not be addressed by Congress except in the context of larger national dimensions. The director and other NPS leadership, however, need to delineate clearly areas they can address and do something about and then set goals and timetables to work in the proper direction. A real fix may take a working generation.

NOTES

1. From a computer printout from the Park Service PAY/PERS record system, Jan. 3, 1992, Program-ID: PQP016.

2. Included in the previous two totals are 237 seasonals, most of them permanent employees, subject to furlough. When the season is over or if funds run short, they may be furloughed. Some furloughs last only days or weeks; some last months. The insecurity of such jobs and the known and imagined hardships such employment causes were a major consideration in the 1980s to convert seasonal jobs to full time permanent.

3. Robert Clay Cunningham, "National Parks, Rangers and the Next 25 Years," *Courier* vol. 36, no. 3 (Fall 1991): 11.

4. From *Birth of the National Park Service,* 139–40. At about the same time, the U.S. Forest Service was also recruiting its own rangers. Norman Maclean has written about those days, during which time he worked summers for the Forest Service as a lookout, fire fighter, and trail builder. His memory indicates not every new Forest Service ranger was college educated. Maclean observed, "Nowadays you can scarcely be a lookout without a uniform and a college degree, but in 1919 not a man in our outfit, least of all the ranger himself, had been to college. They still picked rangers for the Forest Service by picking the toughest guy in town" (*A River Runs through It,* 138–39).

5. The entrance level salary was the equivalent of about $7,600 in 1990 dollars; the top salary, about $10,100.

6. Albright, *Birth of the National Park Service,* 145.

7. Ibid., 143.

8. This tradition was fractured by the Clinton administration with appointment of a professional biologist to that position, albeit one who was a longtime employee of the Forest Service.

9. From *Ranger* vol. 8, no. 1 (Winter 1991/92): 15.

10. From "Interpretation and Position Management: Definitions for the Future," *Ranger* vol. 7, no. 2 (Spring 1991): 18. The reference to classifying ranger interpreters as guides is a particularly sore point with many rangers. Fudge used the word "pejorative" as its effect. As shown in Appendix 8, there were only three positions in NPS formally having that title.

11. The term "counterpart" used here reflects the perception held by many NPS employees that essentially all persons having the title "ranger" involve comparable responsibilities, specifically forest rangers in the U.S. Forest Service. Such comparisons are also often made with various state and federal law enforcement officers, state foresters, firemen, and teachers. For an example of the uses made of these comparisons, in this case as evidence of inadequate salaries, see "Report on Ranger Economic Hardship," *Ranger* vol. 5, no. 3 (Summer 1989): 7–15, 23.

12. Temporary employees have an average of eight years employment with NPS (*Budget Justifications, F.Y. 1995:* NPS-99).

13. *A Race against Time,* a report of the National Parks and Conservation Association, Washington, D.C., Aug. 20, 1991: 22.

14. *Courier* vol. 36, no. 3 (Fall 1991): 7.

15. In 1995 NPS intends to create 2,600 new permanent positions (equal to 2,200 FTEs) in order to provide long-time temporary staff with health and life insurance, retirement, and other benefits. *Budget Justifications, F.Y. 1995:* NPS-99.

16. Letter by ANPR President Rick Gale to the chairmen and ranking minority members of the authorizing committees of the House and Senate, in *Ranger* vol. 7, no. 4 (Fall 1991): 9.

17. The reference to Smokey Bear's hat contains a paradox of interest. The hat is, indeed, the one worn by National Park rangers. Smokey the Bear, however, was a creation and public relations mascot of the U.S. Forest Service, Department of Agriculture. The Forest Service ranger hat is a conventional

felt Stetson with a pinched front crown and moderately narrow brim. Smokey's campaign hat belonged to the Park Service. The paradox surfaced early and was never corrected, in part because the Forest Service was always very generous in loaning Smokey to others in its annual fire prevention program put on through the Advertising Council. Smokey was a real bear, found as a cub in a New Mexico forest, having been orphaned by a forest fire. Under the deft tutelage of Forest Service Information Chief Clint Davis, the idea of the fire-preventing bear has lived to educate and inspire three generations of children and adults.

NINE

The Money to Work With

Any National Park Service employee—from the director on down—*knows* that many of the Service's current and future problems could be solved with more money. More money can mean more people or more supplies and equipment, or more research or data collection, more contractual authority, more care and attention to the resources that make up the national park system. Many of the things said about the current status of the national park system speak to the inadequacy of funding. Many complaints about new units added to the system in recent years relate to the perception that as new units have come into the system staff and funds have been scavenged from existing park budgets to staff up and operate the new parks. If new areas came into the system with their own staff and funding, it is likely many present attitudes about new additions would be softened and perhaps that problem would mostly go away.

But new areas do not come with their own staff and funding. New areas are typically added through the work of one set of congressional committees, and the funding and staffing come through another channel. Sometimes the second channel is overtly hostile to the first, as if to hold a new park hostage to the satisfaction of some slight or abused jurisdiction. Over the course of time some new areas have waited a long time for their first official appropriation, sometimes because the administration in power did not ask for needed money to get things started and sometimes because the Congress, in its wisdom, offered none, requested or not.

The current financial predicament in which the national park system finds itself can be looked at in at least three ways: (1) Have appropriations over the last decade or more kept pace with the effects of inflation? (2) Have appropriations grown to reflect new responsibilities added to the system? (3) Are the real needs of the parks being met?

None of these questions is easy to answer and any statistical indicator used to understand the issue is only a crude measure at best. In addition, a substantial gap exists between conclusions that may be drawn from various financial analyses and the conclusions felt by National Park Service officials. Perceptions and intuition play a very large part in how superintendents feel about the adequacy of budgets and staff. This reality holds special effect when there are no systemwide indicators or standards or comparative analyses to gauge relative needs and the degree to which they are satisfied.

Has the Park Service budget kept pace with inflation? The answer appears to be: "Yes, and substantially more so, on a systemwide basis." This conclusion is based in part on a study done by Denis P. Galvin, former deputy director and currently associate director for Planning and Development. Galvin's study was done park-by-park. He based his study on data for 1980 and 1988, using the Consumer Price Index to adjust budget data to a comparable base. He then concluded that on an overall basis, park operating budgets more than kept pace with inflation.[1]

However, below the level of national and regional aggregates, not all parks did so well. Nearly one-third of the parks, mostly small units and mostly in the East, failed to keep pace with the Consumer Price Index. Golden Gate NRA (Calif.) showed a net increase in available budget of some 4.7 percent above and beyond the effects of inflation. Gateway NRA (N.Y., N.J.), however, showed a net loss to inflation of some 12.7 percent. Yellowstone NP showed an increase of 10.3 percent, while the George Washington Memorial Parkway (Md., D.C., Va.) lost 6.3 percent. Patterns were uneven. Acadia NP (Maine) increased 15.7 percent; Federal Hall NMem (N.Y.) lost 17.5 percent. Zion NP gained 21.3 percent; Yosemite was down by 5.6 percent.

Among the largest gainers were:

Allegheny Portage Railroad NHS (Pa.)	+ 98.1 percent
Bering Land Bridge NPres (Alaska)	+132.1 percent
Big South Fork NR & RA (Tenn., Ky.)	+115.4 percent
Channel Islands NP (Calif.)	+139.9 percent
Ellis Island (N.Y.)	+487.5 percent
Glen Canyon NRA (Utah, Ariz.)	+102.4 percent
Lowell NHP (Mass.)	+ 60.8 percent
USS Arizona Memorial (Hawaii)	+200.2 percent

Among those units that lost the most to inflation were:

General Grant NMem (N.Y.)	− 29.6 percent
Kings Mountain NBP (S.C.)	− 15.9 percent

Lassen Volcanic NP (Calif.)	− 8.8 percent
Moores Creek NB (N.C.)	− 22.2 percent
Obed WSR (Tenn.)	− 57.9 percent
Rainbow Bridge NM (Utah)	− 97.6 percent
Yucca House NM (Colo.)	− 33.8 percent

Some percentage gains and losses were spectacular, but the percentages may mask their relative significance, because at smaller sites with smaller budgets even small percentage changes can have dramatic effects on what happens locally. For example, the budget for Yucca House NM (the smallest site budget in the system) was very small—only $1,000 in 1980, the same in 1988, and only $1,100 in 1991.[2] Inflation had eroded the original $1,000 to barely half that sum during the 1980s. The same principle applies to the smallish budgets of other sites showing significant losses to inflation.

Based on Galvin's analysis and the importuning of many small site superintendents, the National Park Service included a special "over target" sum in the 1991 fiscal year budget with which to play partial catch up (at the parks whose budgets have slipped behind the inflationary curve). The Service requested an additional $10 million for that purpose. According to the director's justification, money to catch up the small parks with the effects of inflation and other uncontrollable costs "was the most frequently requested item in the NPS FY 1991 budget call, with requests totaling over $43 million for around 1,750 increases."[3] The request said that the $10 million requested "could address approximately 225–75 requests, or nearly every small and medium-sized park."

Figure 1 displays three trend lines: operating funds, units, and total visitation. Though there is substantial departure from the trend line as far as operating funds are concerned, reflecting wide swings in the amounts available from year to year for construction, it is evident that funding has increased significantly. The trend lines fit the data in Appendix 5 and are based on appropriations adjusted to take account of inflation.

Another important conclusion drawn by Galvin from his study of NPS budgets for 1980 and 1988 was that "growth at the park level was much slower than total growth. As a result the park portion of the operations appropriation declined from 68 percent to 51 percent ... [reflecting growth in] general administration and the nonpark portion of park management."[4]

The numbers are distorted, however, by the fact that general administration did not exist as a separate activity in 1980, but by 1988 it was individually identified. Comparisons are, therefore, difficult.

Figure 1. National Park System Trends, 1916–94 (in constant 1990 dollars).

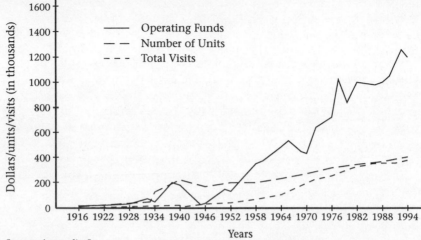

Source: Appendix 5.

It does, however, seem clear that activities funded through the regional offices and WASO increased faster during the decade of the 1980s than did individual park budgets. While this conclusion fits a popular perception about the general growth of overhead in federal agencies, it also reflects a conscious policy decision by the National Park Service to fund a variety of (particularly) maintenance activities through regional, rather than park, accounts. NPS believes this affords increased flexibility to move money to where the urgent problems are and to concentrate available funding to solve problems that cannot be effectively dealt with in small pieces. The natural tendency of decision makers to spread money around so that everybody gets at least a little bit ignores the reality that solving problems often means concentrating resources at a single point to get the job done.

Many superintendents believe, however, that regional financing of maintenance programs and other activities allows or even reinforces informal allocation systems based on personal networks or the pleading of people on particularly friendly terms with the regional director or someone on the regional office staff who is in position to influence the allocation of funds. Whether such opinions are actually based on fact, wishful thinking, or mere rationalizations cannot be determined. There is no Servicewide systematic allocation process or criteria of comparative need or productivity measures to serve as a basis for the distribution of money or personnel.

Nevertheless, many superintendents believe they have suffered because of regional funding for various activities. They would rather see the money at the park level, arguments for pointed concentrations aside. The superintendent's opinion obviously depends on the total size of the park budget and whether "a little bit of funding" is regarded as a meaningful addition.

To judge whether NPS overhead has grown in any inordinate manner would be difficult. Many people believe so, but evidence to support the conclusion is largely speculative. WASO is not materially larger today than it was ten years ago; certainly it has not grown in any functional way or in a manner congruent with overall budget increases for the Park Service as a whole. The real operating budget of the Park Service has increased by more than 34 percent over the last decade.[5] No other indicator has increased proportionately: not staffing (+7 percent), not areas (+7 percent), and not visitation (+22 percent).

Such a conclusion does not, of course, account for the fact that the nature of the job of managing units of the national park system is also changing year by year. Management demands increase every year in ways that are not measured by visitation or the size of the park or its staff. New concerns have emerged for hazardous wastes, new specifications for occupational safety and working conditions, new scientific requirements in species management, new construction requirements that afford additional protection for environmental qualities or to provide access for people with physical disabilities. These all—and more—simply cost more to accomplish now than they did a decade ago. Typically they were not on anyone's agenda ten years ago.

Feelings about the growth of overhead are also influenced by the general growth of paperwork. More paperwork must mean there are more people at the other end asking for it or doing something with it when it is completed. The proposition may contain partial truth, but staff sizes have by no means grown exponentially as paperwork has. Computers have helped, to be sure. But it is also probable that those who manage the paper have shown some increased productivity. There has not been any systematic study of the subject in the Park Service to confirm or deny the proposition that paper managers are doing somewhat better today than they did a decade ago. The statement of the hypothesis would alone generate howls of disagreement or support, depending on which end of the process a person is on.

It seems substantially true that the Park Service budget has displayed significant growth over the last decade, above and beyond the effects of inflation. Whether the budget has grown enough to cover everything that ought to be done is a separate issue, well beyond the scope of this book. We will, however, further explore the budget in light of the other two questions: Have appropriations grown to reflect new units added to the system? Are the real needs of the parks being met?

Former National Park Service Director James Ridenour made his position clear when he was director: he believed that new areas added to the system in recent years were in danger of "thinning the blood," and may have caused neglect of the so-called crown jewels and other existing units. Many people, both in and outside the Service, shared this opinion, including the Association of National Park Rangers and the National Parks and Conservation Association. It is more than an opinion; it in fact is a conviction deeply embedded in Park Service understandings of what is really true. It is, however, almost impossible to prove or disprove in any dispassionate way whether appropriations have kept pace with the addition of new areas. New park system areas do not come with new staff and new budgets attached. Perhaps they should, but absent an entirely new approach to decision making in and by the U.S. Congress it is very unlikely to happen.

The responsibility for funding new park areas rests first with the director of the National Park Service, whose responsibility it is to examine NPS needs in the normal process of preparing the annual budget. If the current year included a new area that is to be staffed and administered in the budget year now under consideration, then the director should include the funds he believes necessary to accomplish that end in his budget request. The reality is that directors do not always do that. A director may determine that all of the system's current areas will consume all of the potential budget he can request. He may not wish to make hard choices between existing areas and a new unit, especially facing the reality that the new area may not be one many of his professional colleagues hold in esteem. They may, indeed, not like it at all. So he may leave it "swinging in the wind," in the belief that someone somewhere will add money to the budget if the area has sufficient constituent support to warrant the addition. Steamtown NHS (Pa.) was relegated to the status of an affiliated area with precisely that effect. That tactic often works, because when the budget gets to the Hill, the affected member of Congress will negotiate a congressional add-on sufficient to get the park started. Again, Steamtown NHS is a classic case in point.

An examination of the 1995 NPS budget shows all but three of the recent new areas included in the regular appropriations request.[6] Whether the existing or prospective superintendents would agree the requests made for other new units are adequate is a separate issue; they were at least included. There is no minimum or standard appropriations package that might represent a new park's start-up costs. Each new area does, however, need certain minimum resources to become a functioning unit: a superintendent, a headquarters office or other facility, office equipment, supplies, telephone, and so forth. Most new parks start with several initial staff, usually in the form of persons detailed to the site from an existing park. Often the first people on site are people who have started a new park operating at least once before, so they have some experience in getting things off the ground. If land acquisition is involved, that activity may be particularly controversial. The Service may then send in a person with established negotiating skills or someone who has earlier experience that can be transplanted in some form. Often the person starting up a new park will do so on a detail used as a probationary period. If the person works out, the job becomes permanent, sometimes, but not always, with a promotion to sweeten the move.

Before a new park receives its first congressional appropriation, NPS sometimes bootlegs minimal financing from other uncommitted funds to get someone on site and working. Whether that sort of advance work is done may depend on the status of land acquisition, the physical state of a building or other objects on the site, some immediate threat (such as an approaching winter or a visitor season about to begin), or it may simply depend on whose congressional district in which the new park happens to be found.

Part of the problem in handling new park areas is the way in which new activities and new or temporary programs are treated in the budget process. They all start as an addition to whatever is the existing base funding. Congress or OMB is likely to put great pressure on the Park Service to rearrange existing funding levels to accommodate the new site from within the existing base. To whatever extent such pressures are explicit or result in reallocations within a region, such actions reinforce the perception that the Service is having to "rob Peter to pay Paul." Occasionally it may also be true, at least in the short term. It is also difficult sometimes to distinguish between something that has caused a real cut in another budget or is merely a reduction in a proposed or anticipated increase. Sometimes the latter causes about as much pain as the former, and the "cut" is easily characterized in ways that convey the impression it really did reduce the original base. This phenomenon often typifies perceptions regarding the overall federal budget, in which cuts come from projected increases, not from the previous year base.

In an attempt to find some reasonably objective means of discovering whether new monies have followed new areas, I attempted a linear correlation between the budget and the number of new areas, from 1916 to 1994. The results of that correlation are shown in figure 1. Although the results are not definitive, they do not appear to support the notion that new areas have resulted in money being stolen from old parks. Funding levels increased much faster than the number of new areas. No other conclusion seems possible with this method, as much as there is no meaningful way of indexing the effect of adding a new area to the system.[7]

I also did a standard correlation analysis of the number of areas in the system and appropriated funds (in constant dollars). The results of that analysis similarly show a very high positive correlation between appropriations and the number of units in the system.[8] Again, that correlation does not account for the type or size of areas in the system or the type or size of areas added from time to time. However, this correlation also clearly does not support the proposition that appropriations have lagged behind the addition of new areas.

The strongest argument I discovered to support the notion of "thinning the blood" is the fact that more than one-third of all sites' budgets did not keep pace with inflation over the years 1980–88. This discovery can be interpreted as evidence someone was "robbing" some parks to keep other parks whole and to afford substantial increases to some others. However, the list of winners and losers does not appear to support the notion that the "Peters" were being short changed to finance newly created parks. The "Pauls" were other parks that had been in the system some time.

Given the lack of supporting evidence, then, it becomes clear that NPS decision makers did not explicitly undertake such a step. Indeed, that so many parks did not stay abreast of inflation was not even discovered until mid-1989, coincident with the study by Denis P. Galvin. As is shown in the discussion relating to the third question, there is some evidence to support the conclusion that small sites in general have been consistently underfunded for quite a while. It seems highly probable that the inflation shortfall is attributable to something other than the addition of new areas.

It is unlikely that any statistical measure can demonstrate, except negatively, that new money has consistently been given to new areas. On the personnel side of the equation, the reality is even less susceptible to meaningful analysis. The Service's work force, as measured by full-time equivalents has gone up somewhat in the last decade, from 17,237 in 1982 to 18,423 in 1991 and to a proposed 18,882 in fiscal year 1995—an increase of approximately 9.5 percent. During the same period the amount of full-time permanent employment increased from 10,806 (1982) to 13,185 (1991) and is projected to increase by an additional 2,600 in fiscal year 1995, a 46 percent increase. This growth occurred because the Service has been converting part time and seasonal employment to permanent full time. This conversion has happened in every region, but mostly at the park level—not in regional or other nonpark offices. A large number of formerly seasonal rangers and interpretive staff have been converted.

This action follows a long period during the 1970s when overall NPS employment was not growing in any significant way. As a result, many people who joined the Service right out of college were hired as temporary, part-time employees. Many of them stayed in that status for as long as five to eight years, sometimes even when they were married, had families, and were thoroughly committed to a lifetime career with the National Park Service. The waiting period was a severe hardship on many people, forcing them to seek second and third jobs during the year and sometimes even concurrent with their seasonal NPS job. Temporary and part-time employees are not eligible for normal federal benefits, such as health and life insurance. They cannot be promoted. It is also difficult for experience in such jobs to count toward later jobs and promotions even if they are later converted.

This situation created a major problem for seasonal workers and superintendents alike. Therefore, many superintendents took the flexibility afforded by FTE accounting and converted temporary FTEs to permanent employment,[9] sometimes resulting in one new permanent employee displacing three or even four temporary staff. Various interpretive programs have been cut back, ranger walks discontinued, and other services cut.

The exchange made is often visible to park visitors, who assume it reflects employment cuts made by either Congress or the president. Many NPS people, including superintendents who know better, say nothing to dispel that understanding, in hopes that visible losses will stimulate some visitors to complain to their congressman or senator, or otherwise try to stimulate additional FTEs for the park.[10] Taking up more and more of the FTE pool in permanent, full-time positions also reduced significantly the possibility of more creative use of the flexibility the FTE concept affords, such as part-time employment for spouses or working-age children. If the FTEs are not available, alternative work formats may not be possible, at a time when more and more agencies and institutions are experimenting with less than full-time employment as a means of improving both work performance and employee morale.[11]

Caught in this squeeze, it is very probable that staffing for new areas has resulted in direct losses from parks then already staffed. The FTEs needed would be (mostly) year-round permanent. New staff for new parks would, therefore, place added strain on the availability of FTEs from the pool. The existing parks may lose under such realities. No detailed analysis of annually available FTEs and their utilization by old and new parks has been made. Such an analysis would need to be made on a park specific basis for at least the last ten years. The results could, perhaps, help the Service in making a case for additional FTEs needed to staff new areas. As long as the Service makes those accommodations every year—and goes well beyond new area needs to convert seasonals to permanents at older established parks— it is unlikely OMB and Congress will be very sympathetic to more than very modest FTE increases.

It is also a fact that not everyone in the Service agrees that parks are understaffed. Some are, maybe, but by no means even a majority. Ever since a number of parks benefited from having persons formerly with the Heritage Conservation and Recreation Service assigned to them, some of them have said aloud that their FTE allotment was fully adequate—the problem was in the mix of skills or grades or both.

In 1981 Secretary of the Interior James Watt abolished the Heritage Conservation and Recreation Service (formerly the Bureau of Outdoor Recreation) and transferred its budget, programs, and staff to the National Park Service. The transfer was done with the explicit understanding that no one would be "RIF'd."[12] The reorganization resulted in a substantial surplus of relatively high graded, longtime career employees whose occupational specialties did not always fit Park Service patterns or needs. Many affected employees were in their late forties, with fifteen and more years of service.

The reorganization was for a time much resented by both NPS and those formerly with HCRS. Some HCRS employees had no meaningful jobs to do. Some never found real jobs. In time, NPS tried to reassign as many HCRS employees as possible to field jobs. New assistant superintendent and assistant to the superintendent positions were created for administrative generalists who formerly worked for HCRS. Sometimes the HCRS person involved did so at a grade level inconsistent with the prior organizational structure at the park. On many occasions the new employee (who did not have a long NPS background) closed off promotion opportunities for long-time Park Service employees. Many people on both sides of the equation were left embittered and angry. For many of those people the only long-term solution was (or is) retirement.

The largest mistake in the matter was in Secretary Watt's failure to understand the near and long-term consequences of the no-RIF policy. Though initially structured to be humanitarian, in the long run it was a major disservice to both NPS and HCRS and to both groups of employees. Even those who would have lost their jobs would likely have been better off in the end. Alternative jobs in the public sector and in private industry were far easier to find in 1981 than in 1994.

All of the negative effects on people and parks aside, the HCRS-NPS merger was a constructive action on Secretary Watt's part. First, it broadened the clientele base of the Park Service by adding the Land and Water Conservation Fund and programs in historic preservation external to the activities of the National Park Service. Second, it gave the Park Service serious reason to engage people and institutions outside the Service, though comfort with those externalities has been slow to arrive. And, third, it also infused the Service with a significant number of highly talented people, some of whom have gone on to become park superintendents and at least one regional director. The benefits of Watt's merger continue to this day.

A further consequence of the shift in FTE use—from temporary to permanent—is that it has now masked and made enormously difficult judgments about whether the parks are adequately staffed to accomplish their everyday mission. Again, there are no standards or convertible measures that allow park-to-park comparisons of staffing and productivity.

The analysis of visitors-per-FTE sampled in Appendix 7-3 suggests that productivity vis-à-vis visitation varies widely within the system, from a group of nine sites where the annual staff-to-visitor ratio is under 1:1,000 to a group of eighteen sites where the ratio is over 1:50,000, of which four have a ratio in excess of 1:100,000.[13] The first group includes four National Parks and both groups include National Historic Sites. While all of the first group have small visitation levels, four of the second group serve more than a million visitors a year. Yellowstone NP is the most-visited park with the lowest (best?) annual visitor-to-staff ratio, 1:6,256. The most-visited park with the highest (worst?) visitor-to-staff ratio is Muir Woods NM (Calif.) with a ratio of 1 FTE for every 217,286 visitors.

Assuming (for example) that the 217,286 visitors to Muir Woods

NM were evenly distributed over a 2,080-hour work year, each staff person related to them would have an average of 104 people an hour yearlong. It is hard to imagine that very many visitors have any contact whatever with a Park Service employee under such circumstances. These ratios seem extraordinary, though there are no standards or productivity indicators by which *any* staff-to-visitor ratio may be judged.[14] The range and groupings within these extremes are interesting for their regularity. Similar patterns exist regarding costs-per-FTE, showing variations that are inexplicable in magnitude and inconsistent by park type, size, or location (see Appendix 7-2).

Is it, then, possible to know whether NPS staffing has been sufficient to staff the new parks added to the system in the last decade or whether the blood is being thinned and parks are losing ground as new parks are added? It is not possible to really know with any certainty. Staff levels have increased. There has also been a shift away from temporary and seasonal to permanent full time. Overall numbers do not, in aggregate, clearly support a staffing shortfall at new parks or real losses at old ones. Individual parks may be able to document another pattern, however.

The most serious reason for not being able to really know the answer to the question with certainty is the complete absence of any form of organizational standards or productivity measures. Given the very wide ratios that exist, it seems almost inevitable that there may be serious overstaffing at some locations and serious understaffing at others. Of much more significance in the data shown in all three parts of Appendix 7 than the absolute values is the range of values that exist. At a minimum differences from park to park should be capable of being explained in some rational way.

Finally, we ask the question: Are appropriations adequate? The short answer for every program of every agency of every government is "No." The longer answer is "No, by a long way." That is the nature of bureaucracy, at least most of the time. It goes with all organizations. Not surprisingly, growth of programs, budgets, staffs, jurisdictions, and so forth is the very measure of corporate success. But when it comes to public services and government, almost everyone regardless of political persuasion expresses dismay when growth occurs. It does not matter whether growth results from the effects of monetary inflation or from an enlarged service clientele or new program mandates. The public, the press, elected officials—almost everyone—expresses their dismay at the reality.

Of course, government has grown enormously over the years. From an institution that consumed less than 10 percent of the Gross National Product before the Great Depression, the federal government today accounts for about 23 percent. The largest single area of growth has been in programs and activities paying for past, present, or future wars, including debt service, much of it also war or defense related.

As shown in Appendix 5 and figure 1, appropriations for the national park system have also increased, and they have done so at a rate that outraces both inflation and growth of the system. Even many people who believe most strongly that present resources are inadequate would agree that the total level of funding available has increased over the years. Many of those people believe very sincerely that real needs have, however, so far outdistanced real appropriations that dangerously large gaps continue to exist and even grow. As a practical matter, it is very difficult to know where the truth lies. Truth in such matters lies very close to a person's knowledge and assumptions about the nature of the resources, their needs, and the costs of doing whatever it is that needs doing. The perceptions and answers are many. They usually involve more. They may all be right in their own way.

First, it must be said that there is no agreed upon agenda, standard, or benchmark against which to measure adequacy. Though many in and out of the Service speak of a backlog of unmet maintenance needs on the order of $2 billion and a land acquisition backlog of similar or somewhat larger magnitude, there is no plan or documented needs to prove that figure. It is a guess, although an informed one.

Several years ago the Park Service attempted to inventory "threats" to the parks. The resulting list has been a gold mine for people and groups seeking to demonstrate the need for added funding and more staff. Depending on one's perspective, the identified threats were serious, acute, and in need of emergency attention; others thought they were vague, unspecific, and endemic in character, needing attention but within the context of the long haul, not on a crash basis.

The Park Service has largely backed away from the list of threats, in part because it failed many tests of specificity and scientific accuracy. Its tone and trend were, however, thoroughly supportable, even within the scientific community and among those who would approach the problems in a more disciplined manner. The parks face many real problems from within, and from without still other forces affect the parks.

Yet the list, unfortunately, did not come with solutions or even guesstimates about what it would cost to grapple with the problems. Also, the list was too long to enable focus on problems that could be dealt with in reasonable time frames and realistic budgets. Nevertheless, NPS is often criticized for not having stuck by the list and having "done something about it."

Part of the problem stems from the NPS budget. Although the budget grew during the Reagan and Bush administrations, the growth was far too slow to accommodate major remedial initiatives beyond those defined in the annual budget. NPS has no inventory or program documenting long-range or period-defined needs. No long-range program has ever been done for the national park system.[15]

The Service did attempt an alternative approach in the early 1980s that merits examination, although, as will be explained, it was aborted before implementation and its results ignored. It began as essentially a defensive budget strategy by then Director Russell E. Dickenson. Dickenson was neither an expansionist nor an aggressive budget seeker. Rather, he saw his term as Park Service director as "a time of consolidation and a time of nurturing the growth of the last several years."[16]

In that spirit and because he saw agency after agency of the federal government facing severe budgetary cuts . . . Dickenson invented an exercise he called "Basic Operations," a takeoff on a zero-based budgeting approach.[17] He asked every park in the system to review its mission and its "basic" operational needs and to document those needs in a program-specific format. The results were to reflect core requirements, not pie-in-the-sky wish lists. They were to reflect minimums necessary to carry out the requirements of each park's enabling legislation and other laws affecting the unit. They were to justify both the first and last dollar, not merely increments that would be good to have.

The Basic Operations study was of near-monumental proportions in the agency. Superimposed on top of normal budget and financial management reporting and programs, the study sometimes used new people detailed to the undertaking, and sometimes it was treated as added work for existing staffs. All in all, it took over a year to accumulate all the data. Later, in response to a question asked by Secretary of the Interior James Watt's office, an estimate was made as to its cost: $8 million.[18] Unfortunately, Basic Operations was quite a wrench for the parks. A few superintendents did not take it seriously, delegating its production to others and puting very little into it themselves. However, most superintendents took it quite seriously, rightfully viewing the activity as a serious effort with Director Dickenson's personal interest and commitment. A (very) few saw it as a means to get monies they wanted for every conceivable pet project.

Dickenson made a major effort to structure the study in ways that would make it possible to aggregate the information systemwide when it was finished—a first in the bureau. Programs and subprograms were defined. Detailed instructions attempted a degree of program and activity interpark compatibility never before attempted. Having no computer network, much of the work was done manually. The results were then sent through the regional offices to Washington, D.C., where they were consolidated on a systemwide basis. The final Servicewide tabulations were computerized, and the results were by any measure astonishing.

The conclusions summarized below are taken from the preliminary draft report, a document never officially recognized by the Reagan administration and suppressed from public release or review. The principal findings and conclusions were as follows:

1. The Basic Operations Survey supports and confirms judgments reached in other contexts regarding the deterioration of the national park system infrastructure. Unfunded Basic Operations suggest the need for major investments in repair, rehabilitation, and cyclic maintenance, totaling about $150 million annually. Roads and water and sewer systems predominate.[19]

2. While the survey confirms that needs are large, it also suggests they are rather highly concentrated in much less than a majority of park system units. Only eight parks accounted for half the unfunded need.[20] Only 45 parks reported needs more than $1 million. Some 107 parks (34 percent) reported unfunded Basic Operations of $100,000 or less, of which 76 parks reported unfunded needs of $50,000 or less, and 28 parks reported needs of $10,000 or less.

3. The distribution of identified Basic Operations needs highlights the problem of resource allocation—to put present and future funds in the places they can be used most cost-effectively. At the same time the study identifies some of the tradeoffs available, and illuminates the classic management dilemma: to allocate funds in small amounts over a broad base of needs or to concentrate available resources where needs are the largest? The survey results suggest the need for developing cost-benefit indicators that might help in resolving that dilemma.

4. The Basic Operations Survey data contain subject matter aberrations that require more analysis to determine whether those differences are associated with the process of data collection, or are the result of some substantial difference in the nature of the resource involved, or whether there is a management problem that needs attention. Much of the needed analysis cannot be done without further examination of financial records or data collection not part of the Basic Operations Survey. The full cost of campgrounds is one example.

5. While the units and resources of the national park system are high-ly diverse as to geographic location, size, complexity, and intensity of use and management, there are strong common elements reflect-ed in the management tasks and activities performed. . . . the simi-larities appear much stronger than the differences.
6. The Basic Operations Survey identified a proportionally larger need for funds than it did for personnel. The largest financial needs were in the areas of repair and rehabilitation and cyclic maintenance; the largest personnel needs were for visitor services.

Additionally, the survey concluded that a new accounting system then being implemented needed to be coordinated with the program structure then evolving for the Basic Operations exercise in order better to reveal comparable operating costs, allowing correlations between and among park units.

In summary, the Basic Operations Survey concluded that overall NPS needs would require a 69 percent increase in funding, a 12 per-cent increase in full-time permanent employment (FTEs) and a 48 percent increase in part-time employment. (See table 1 for a summary by major program.)

Interestingly, the general program mix would remain much the same, though visitor services would increase, largely at the expense of overhead (program support). The survey concluded that "the avail-

Table 1. Survey Summary by Major Program

	Amount (millions)	Percent
Present Program (1980)		
Natural Resources Management	$ 39.4	11
Historic Preservation	47.8	13
Visitor Services	183.8	51
Program Support	91.7	25
Total	$363.0	100
Basic Operations		
Natural Resources Management	$ 72.7	12
Historic Preservation	83.8	14
Visitor Services	348.0	57
Program Support	107.8	18
Total	$612.3	100

ability of $1.0 million could eliminate all unfunded Basic Operations needs in 63 parks. With $5.0 million the unfunded needs could be met in a total of 117 parks." It is also interesting that forty-eight park units reported no unfunded Basic Operations.

When the study was completed and published in draft it was given to then Secretary of the Interior James Watt so he could study it before a meeting with NPS representatives on it. In the meeting, which I attended, without any discussion of the report or its substance, Secretary Watt summarily dismissed the survey as a joke with, "You've-got-to-be-kidding!" He ordered the study squashed.[21]

As a result, no action was ever taken on or with the survey results. It was dead. Perhaps surprisingly, no one in NPS leaked the report to the media or anyone in the myriad groups outside the Service that would have an interest in its substance. In a town in which the leak is a widely used strategy for both getting and giving information, it is remarkable that the Basic Operations Survey never surfaced in any contemporary public arena. No one ever requested it under the Freedom of Information Act, an action that would have immediately placed it in the public domain.

By killing the survey, Secretary Watt missed a golden opportunity. The product provided documentation for only a modest appropriation increase. For a very small sum the administration could have taken credit for solving the basic operating needs of many parks. The $5 million needed for 117 parks is almost extraordinary! The report was conservative in its focus and perhaps its strongest asset was that it had grown from the park up; it was completely defensible.

The survey is certainly no longer valid. Not only would the numbers change, but other realities will have also changed. In the intervening years neglected infrastructure would likely inflate needed funds by significant, although unknown, sums. Unfortunately, one of the casualties in the process was the credibility of centralized efforts of the sort represented by the Basic Operations Survey. A heap of honest effort went for nothing, and many people will remember that reality for a long time. It was also a failed undertaking by a director whose credentials for the effort were absolutely impeccable. Dickenson was the consummate park ranger and the epitome of the successful National Park Service employee, having served his agency for over forty years at the time of his retirement in 1985. The concept was part and parcel with Dickenson's temperament and style. He was widely respected for his cautious determination. If any director could have pulled it off, Dickenson was the one to do it. A similar undertaking will carry with it many memories of Basic Operations' failure. Nevertheless, Basic Operations' major lessons are important for the future.

Smallish sums strategically allocated in some rational manner can potentially resolve the problems in many parks. Such a strategy can succeed because in many circumstances (such as small parks) small needs can loom large in both professional and public perceptions. A few thousand dollars or a few tens of thousands can be very important to a park whose entire budget is only small multiples of that sum. But for such a strategy to be successful the Service needs to develop some sense of what is cost-effective—some indicators to help guide investment decisions. As difficult as comparative analysis of park needs is, more must be done to attempt it. Even the act of trying can shed light on compatibles and comparabilities. Explicit allocation processes (however crude their rationality) have a measure of credibility and life expectancy far beyond the best that old boy networks and similar mechanisms can deliver.

Another Basic Operations Survey, however titled, seems unlikely at present. Federal budget constraints militate against truth in budgeting. Secretary Watt's reaction was perhaps predictable. The best proof of large unmet needs is more unacceptable than the wildest speculations. The latter has the advantage that there is no political compulsion to take it seriously; not so the former, if it becomes public.

In recent years the Park Service and the Reagan and Bush administrations have taken an alternative tack. They have invented "Initiatives" with high sounding names to wrap around very modest program increases, capturing not only a small incremental change but the base as well in its hoopla. The 1991 National Park Service budget contained several:

- President Bush's Urban Recreation Initiative
- Secretary Lujan's STEWARDSHIP agenda
- The America the Beautiful Initiative
- Legacy 99
- The Columbus Quincentennial Celebration

The STEWARDSHIP Agenda was reflected in many individual line items in the budget; so also was the Legacy 99 initiative, which was defined broadly enough to catch most of the Park Service construction program.[22]

This approach was far from new. Naming programs has been popular since the demonstrated success of MISSION 66, which ended in 1966. Then came the Bicentennial Land Heritage Program (scaled to 1976). Secretary Watt ordered up the Park Restoration and Improvement Program (PRIP) as a major rehabilitation program that would remedy the then existing backlog of unmet needs. That effort, too, amounted to little more than sloganeering, since it ended up adding little new money to a construction program already funded.

Experience with each and all of these initiatives was similar. They do, in fact, generate new money for a year or two, then OMB and the administration stop putting in significant amounts of new money while leaving the program intact covering the base sums. The experience is analogous to that of many states with lotteries. Florida, for example, promised lottery receipts would be used to bolster and improve the state's educational systems. Soon after the lottery became successful, the state legislature forgot the incremental approach and began substituting the lottery for regular appropriations. The results have been near disaster for the school systems. NPS has not experienced any disaster, but the backlog of unmet needs largely remains intact.

Budget slogans and labels, such as those that embellished the 1991 and later National Park Service budgets, may be worse than a waste. They imply a real effort is being made to accomplish something on a scale that could actually make a difference. For the most part they do little more than provide a cover for ongoing efforts plus minor increases. Incremental additions may be trivial, and often are. In a year or two all the additions will probably disappear and the problem remains for someone else to tackle under a new banner.

The Park Service really does not have many options on this matter. The covering slogans and initiatives are crafted and labeled by people at the level of the secretary of the Interior and in the White House. It is part of the stage management of modern presidential and cabinet politics. In no way are the initiatives associated with the national park system any different from the war on drugs or the rhetoric supporting the image of the "Education President," and with about equal effect.

In spite of conservative budget requests, the National Park Service has done remarkably well before Congress. In the line-item construction program (which accounts for most of the construction undertaken by NPS), appropriations exceeded budget requests in seven of the ten years of the 1980s (see figure 2). In one year (fiscal year 1989) Congress appropriated $141.6 million when the administration had requested a mere $6.6 million. Yearly appropriation levels have, however, fluctuated widely, from a high of $300.2 million to a low of $28.4 million.[23] Such variations in workloads are an administrative nightmare. It is virtually impossible to keep a stable professional work

Figure 2. National Park Service Construction Program, 1980–95.

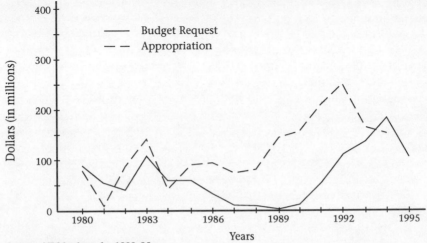

Source: NPS budgets for 1980–95

force under such circumstances. One effect is that much of the work is contracted out.

Congressional add-ons for construction have been a feature of Park Service life for decades. Much of the financing for the Natchez Trace Parkway (Miss., Ala., Tenn.) over a period of twenty years has come to the agency as unrequested money. Sometimes add-ons are the personal work of members of the appropriations committee, but many are not. Many are added in the normal course of legislative give-and-take during congressional consideration of the budget. Some are stimulated by informal, off-the-record relationships between individual park superintendents and the local representative or senator. Some superintendents may even believe the personal attention they gave a member of Congress or a committee staff person influenced a decision that resulted in an add-on. Such linkage cannot, of course, be documented, but as a former colleague remarked recently, "Superintendents don't roll out the red carpet for congressional and White House VIPs just for the fun of it. They *know* it pays off later."

In many dimensions, add-ons are insidious. They distort agency priority setting. Furthermore, they can easily overload the system and jeopardize the effectiveness of the add-on and other projects. They promote imbalance in the affected programs. Add-ons can also subtly (and perhaps not so subtly) undermine the budget process itself. If superintendents have reason to think a project they want will be the object of an add-on, it may be deliberately omitted from the regular program. It encourages playing games with the process. Such practices are, of course, endemic to the congressional appropriations process. There is very little remedy when it is so widespread throughout government. That fact is one of the most mentioned reasons for the so-called line-item veto. Under those proposals the president (read the Office of Management and Budget) could knock out individual projects included by Congress if they were "inconsistent with the program of the President."[24]

The add-on process is, by other reckoning, simply another part of the American political process. True, it violates the formal processes of the system, but the add-on is also part of the system. It remedies needs that may otherwise be overlooked or opportunities otherwise not taken. Its effects are as valid and worthy as anything else that comes out of the process. Add-ons are probably here to stay.

To summarize the money business: the National Park Service has experienced a growing budget over the last two decades and more, probably at a rate high enough to accommodate the effects of both inflation and the addition of new areas, though certainly not at a rate high enough to meet perceived needs. NPS has no means by which it can judge the effectiveness of its budget; no performance standards or interpark comparisons. The Service feels strongly that the backlog of needs is large and growing, though no disciplined systemwide studies support that conclusion. No process exists to allocate funds among competing needs based on their cost-effectiveness. As was shown in the Basic Operations Survey, relatively modest investments in some parks could solve or forestall problems that will only get worse if unattended.

In the short term NPS must compete in a market that includes a large array of also-worthy alternative places to put the limited federal budget dollars available. To do that, it must set priorities with care and justify them with persuasive data and arguments. In the long term, the Service must gain a solid handle on the extent of the needs and be prepared to tackle those needs in a sustained effort that is likely to take as long to remedy as it has taken to get to the present set of circumstances.

NOTES

1. Denis P. Galvin, "Trends in the Operations Budget of the National Park Service: 1980–1988," July 1989, 66 pages.

2. The budget for Yucca House NM was in subsequent years consolidated with that of Hovenweep NM.

3. Memorandum from the director, National Park Service, to the assistant

secretary for Fish and Wildlife and Parks, Subject: F.Y. 1991 Budget Request (File: F30(330)), May 22, 1989. The quotation is from the attachment "Detail of Potential F.Y. 1991 Overtarget Items in Priority Order."

4. Galvin, "Trends in the Operations Budget," July 1989: 9–10.

5. Excluding the external grant-in-aid programs transferred to NPS from the Heritage Conservation and Recreation Service in 1981.

6. Poverty Point NM (La.); Salt River Bay NHP & Ecological Preserve (V.I.); and Marsh-Billings NHP (Vt.). In all three instances no lands had been acquired by NPS in time for the 1995 budget. *Budget Justifications, F.Y. 1995:* NPS-167, 169, 170.

7. Counting areas fails to account for an area's size, complexity, resource characteristics, and so forth. Over the mix of some 350-plus sites, however, some of those differences would tend to become less important.

8. The *r* value for the number of units and appropriation levels is 0.8, representing a very high positive correlation. Calculations were made using the data in Appendix 5, employing appropriations in constant 1990 dollars. The formula used was:

$$r = \frac{\Sigma xy - n\bar{y}}{n\sigma_x \sigma_y}$$

where x = the number of park system units
       y = appropriations for NPS operations in 1990 constant dollars.

9. For many years all accounting for people and jobs in the federal service was done on the basis of positions. Such accounting took no notice of part-time or seasonal workers, and gave managers almost no flexibility to use people in less than full-time permanent ways if they were to maximize their authorized positions. Beginning about fifteen years ago the Executive Branch began to use full-time equivalents (FTEs) as the preferred measure of people and jobs, giving managers enlarged flexibility to hire and use alternative work arrangements. For a long time, Congress insisted on the old counting system, but it now also uses FTEs to measure employment.

10. The Association of National Park Rangers links reduced seasonal staff to new park areas, noting that "the number of seasonal rangers . . . has decreased by about 1,000 positions (20%) since 1980, yet the National Park System during the same period grew by 37 areas (10% increase) and visitation increased by almost 40 million (15% increase). It's not uncommon . . . to spend an entire day in a park without seeing a ranger" (*Ranger* vol. 7, no. 4 [Fall 1991]: 10).

11. Not all uses of less than full-time and permanent staff have humanitarian motives. American business has adopted that strategy on many recent occasions in order to reduce wages, avoid paying all or most nonsalary benefits, and otherwise improve their competitive position.

12. *Reduction In Force*—laid off.

13. Appendix 7 was derived from the data in Appendix 6-1. For reasons of economy, these tables have been sampled, selecting the first and last ten units and every tenth unit in between. Interested readers may obtain the full text of the tables from the publisher (see details on p. 269).

14. I remember commenting on a draft General Management Plan in the late 1970s that proposed a staffing level that would have permitted visitors to be individually met as they entered the park. At some historic sites, such as Hamilton Grange (N.Y.) or Eugene O'Neill (Calif.), it might be possible for someone to meet and greet everyone coming through the door because of their physical layout and moderate visitation levels.

15. Some people define MISSION 66, a ten-year developmental program designed to catch up on both maintenance and new facility development following World War II, as a long-range program. While MISSION 66 was indeed ten years in the making and doing, the program did not exist up front except as a concept—a slogan—around which annual appropriations requests were developed. The program's scale, a giant by prior NPS experience, did force the development of multiyear projects and multiyear planning for them. The program did not, however, contain resource management components or companion financing of interpretation and visitor services. It was developmental in character, and even though it was undertaken as a means to catch up on many years of visitor growth without comparable investments in facilities, many people today believe MISSION 66 was too development directed. In many instances the Service has regretted the existence or placement of MISSION 66 buildings and other facilities. Those years were not, however, a time of great sensitivity to environmental values and impacts. For the story of MISSION 66, see Wirth, *Parks, Politics, and the People,* chap. 9; Everhart, *National Park Service,* 25–27; and Garrison, *The Making of a Ranger,* 255–65. These accounts regard MISSION 66 as a huge success, especially as it lifted the morale of NPS staff and gave them a sense of purpose and motion.

16. From the Foreword by Russell E. Dickenson to Everhart, *National Park Service,* x.

17. Almost all federal budgeting is done by accepting as a given the sums appropriated in prior years. Major focus each year during budget reviews is on the additions above the base. In zero-based budgeting (ZBB), the review is supposed to include the first dollar and everything above it, thereby subjecting older programs and operations to the same level of scrutiny as new ones. Attempts to implement ZBB in the federal government have foundered on the shoals of tradition and inertia, both in the Executive Branch and in Congress.

18. The total was drawn by telephone estimates from the regional offices and sample data from selected parks. No actual costs were kept in any formal way. NPS has no way of keeping track of the costs of projects like this undertaking. Some NPS officials argued that the project really didn't cost anything because the salaries of the Park Service employees involved "would have been paid anyway." The perception that activities undertaken by government employees "who are paid anyway" are without cost is a widely held view. In another setting, I overheard an explanation of such thinking as akin to a passenger arguing he should not have to pay for an airline ticket inasmuch as "the plane is going anyway." All activities of federal employees cost money. All programs cost money. However, surprisingly few government agen-

cies or parts of agencies have any idea what those costs might be. Many would prefer not to know or even guess. The only cost-accountable programs in the Park Service are fire fighting and construction projects. The Denver and Harpers Ferry Centers are the only large-scale activity operated on a cost accountable (project) basis.

19. About $210 million in 1991 dollars. All Basic Operations data are from: "Basic Operations: preliminary assessment," Washington, D.C., National Park Service, Mar. 30, 1982.

20. The parks were War in the Pacific NHP (Guam)—$4,700,000; Denali NP & NPres (Alaska)—$6,295,500; Petrified Forest NP (Ariz.)—$9,294,900; Yellowstone NP (Wyo., Idaho, Mont.)—$10,017,800; Big Bend NP (Tex.)—$11,385,500; Death Valley NM (Calif., Nev.)—$13,129,400; Yosemite NP (Calif.)—$22,254,000; Grand Canyon NP (Ariz.)—$47,939,300.

21. Director Dickenson was out of town on the day of the meeting with Secretary Watt and NPS was represented by Deputy Director Ira Hutchison. Hutchison had day-to-day oversight of the project during its compilation. It seems unlikely that Dickenson's personal participation in the meeting would have changed its outcome.

22. The STEWARDSHIP agenda (it is referred to all in capital letters) was attributed to President Bush who "has made stewardship a top priority of his administration. The president and I [Secretary Lujan] are dedicated to the preservation, conservation, and development of America's natural resources in an environmentally sound manner. The president and I have agreed that the idea of stewardship will guide us in this endeavor" . . . [From a "Dear Interior Employee" letter signed by Secretary Lujan and printed with a 10-point agenda for its implementation.]

The Legacy 99 initiative "consists of programs for hazardous waste, housing, operational maintenance and projects for the repair, rehabilitation and replacement of facilities. [From the Draft Guidelines for Development of Multi-Year Construction Schedules for Legacy 99, undated.]

23. The appropriation request for F.Y. 1995 was $103.7 million. *Budget Justifications, F.Y. 1995:* NPS-259.

24. If the president has the authority to veto individual projects in an appropriations act, OMB would become the focus of intense political pressures on every potentially affected project. It is likely the director of OMB and the staff would discover the unexperienced intensity of project lobbying. Though it is politically correct to support the line-item veto in some quarters, OMB can only shudder at the prospect of being the focus of so much political attention, if the power existed. The threat of it may be regarded by some people as a damper on Congressional excesses. A president would find exercise of such authority a very unpleasant new demand on his time and that of his OMB staff, and a political mine field of the first order. It is certain the net effect would not materially lower the annual budget deficit; the real budget and deficit problems have much larger dimensions.

TEN

Other People's Money and Support

From the beginning, private philanthropy has played an important—sometimes pivotal—role in the life and administration of the national park system. The Service's first director, Stephen T. Mather, spent his personal money to buy buildings, equipment, tools, and land. He also subsidized the salaries of Horace Albright, then his assistant director, and one or two others on the Washington, D.C., office staff. To supplement what he regarded as the miserly appropriations of Congress, Mather sought and accepted financial support from the business community, from the railroads, from hoteliers, and from others.

Director Mather plied members of Congress and others with no-cost travel, meals, vacations, and other amenities ranging from horses to sleeping bags. He understood such lobbying and special services to be the way to members' hearts. He aimed to provide influential people with personal experiences in and with the National Parks. In that way they would identify with his objectives for the system and support legislation and other actions he sought. By many measures Mather was superbly successful. His personal spending patterns have not been matched by any subsequent director, but parts of the activity have survived.[1] Philanthropy, gifts of money and land to the National Park Service, has been important over the years. Providing VIPs with special services was treated in chapter 5; that tradition similarly remains.

Two parks had their beginnings based on donations of land that could serve as the basis for a presidential proclamation as a National Monument: Muir Woods NM (Calif.) and Acadia NP (Maine).[2] Many other parks have benefited in substantial form from private philanthropic gifts: Shenandoah NP, Great Smoky Mountains NP, Grand Teton NP, the John D. Rockefeller, Jr., Memorial Parkway, Virgin Islands NP, and Pecos NHP, for examples. Cash or endowments have also been important though not to the extent of gifts of land. Several parks are supported by small endowments and occasional substantial gifts, some of which are managed by the National Park Foundation. A few parks have locally managed funds.

After the days of Mather and until the 1980s National Park Service policies regarding gifts and philanthropy of other sorts were to be an enthusiastic, but passive, recipient. Gifts were infrequently solicited of anyone and rarely by anyone except the then director. In the 1980s that changed under Reagan-Watt administration policies that encouraged donations of various sorts and facilitated, especially, corporate philanthropy. In the mid-1980s NPS promulgated its first formal policy document on the subject of fund-raising. For the first time the Service included the solicitation of gifts (fund-raising) as an element in the position descriptions and performance standards of regional directors and park superintendents. Corporate sponsorships of various types were authorized in exchange for promised donations or in the expectation of some share of sales or profits. Among those that have participated in some form of corporate fund-raising on behalf of the national park system are: Murphy's Oil Soap; Raisin Bran; Honda/Readers Digest; Kodak/Readers Digest; OFF (insect repellent); Target/Kodak; WD-40 (lubricant).

A 1991 campaign involving WD-40 illustrates how such participation works. Picture a full page add in a national newsmagazine. The headline reads: STOP SQUEAKS, PREVENT RUST AND PRESERVE NATIONAL PARKS. The ad pictured an outboard motor, a pocket knife, a fishing reel, a motor home, and a sign sporting a butterfly and labeled "National Park." The sign is captioned, "With our $50,000 donation, America's National Parks will be a little greener this Fall." The ad explains what a fine product WD-40 is and that "this Fall, WD-40 is donating $50,000 to the National Park Service to help protect the National Parks. If you'd like to add your contribution to WD-40's send your donation . . ."

While $50,000 is a sum of considerable significance to park employees and certain authors, it is, unfortunately, a trivial measure of support for the national park system. It was also, probably, a trivial part of the cost of the full page advertisement. Other donations to the National Park Service from such corporate promotions have generated as much as $100,000.

Another form of corporate linkage took the form of a "Special Advertising Section" by the Ford Motor Company in the May 25, 1992, issue of *Newsweek Magazine*. The insert was sixteen pages in full color, with eight pages of conventional advertising and eight pages devoted to "America the Beautiful: The National Park System." The article about the national park system was straight forward, containing photographs and descriptions of seven parks, some of them among those less familiar to many people. The article also provided, in a boxed column, the names of twelve "National Parks Allowing Off-Road Driving."

The advertising supplement showed the Ford logo on every page, including those devoted to materials relating to the national park system. It also suggested that contributions could be sent to the National Park Foundation and that additional information about the parks could be obtained from National Park Service headquarters in Washington, D.C. The descriptive materials on each park mentioned in the supplement were, in fact, written by National Park Service staff. The advertisement was reported to have cost $1.3 million. No money was paid or donated to NPS.

The obvious benefits to the Ford Motor Company from the association of its name and product with the national park system are not matched with an equally evident set of benefits for the national park system. For many years NPS has attempted to promote a list of less-visited parks, on the theory that by promoting visitation to them, crowding at other well-known sites might be reduced. To that end, the National Park Service has employed on its headquarters staff a full-time senior travel and tourism specialist to work with the travel industry and encourage visitation to the lesser-known parks. While some evidence suggests that the promotional aspects of the activity have been moderately successful (visitation at the newly-promoted parks has grown), no direct evidence demonstrates that growth there has reduced visitation or growth elsewhere.

Given perceived needs and available resources, the real question is whether NPS ought to promote and encourage park visitation at all—or encourage others to do so. A host of self-serving commercial forces at work—including the Ford Motor Company, park concessions, and so on—promote park visitation. For NPS to use its staff and money to pump up visitation even further seems a misplaced priority.

It is important to note, however, that the Ford Motor Company could have conceived and printed the materials described above entirely on its own, without any permission or cooperation from the National Park Service. Informational materials, photographs, and other publications of the National Park Service are not copyrighted and may be borrowed or copied freely. Only the NPS logo (the arrowhead shield) is protected from commercial uses. Whether using NPS staff to compose copy for such advertising is a proper use of government funds is more a question of ethics and taste than an issue of law. It is one way of assuring or improving the accuracy of what is said and printed about the parks.

Whether such cooperative arrangements with the business community are a form of undue commercialization of the national park system is a matter on which there are widely divergent views. In the early days of the Park Service, Directors Mather and Albright eagerly and openly sought involvement of the business community in the life of the national parks, notably the railroads, hotels, and other recreation and vacation services. The national park system has used private concessions to build and operate inpark visitor accommodations and services from the first days of the system.

Beginning in the 1960s and 1970s, largely in response to outside pressures against overdevelopment and perceived environmental impacts, the Park Service became more sensitive to commercial presence in the parks. Advertising, signs, building designs and locations became the objects of attitudes and policies that sought to reduce and sometimes eliminate the visible forms of commercialism in the parks. For all of thirty years there have, for example, been pressures to remove many of the commercial facilities in Yosemite Valley, sometimes including much or all of the overnight accommodations.

Back in the 1970s a well-known house paint supplier sought to capitalize on the fact that its product was used to repaint the White House (a National Park Service responsibility). The linkage was accurate since the paint was used for that purpose. Yet, NPS stopped the advertising, considering such to be unacceptable commercialization involving a park system unit. It seemed indeed poor taste.

Beginning in the Reagan-Bush years, the tide turned in the other direction, with new forms of commercial involvement in the parks gaining favor with the political leadership in the Department of the Interior and with the director. Evidences of business involvement in the parks are no longer automatically rejected or shunned. The business logo of a firm that donated money for refurbishment of a Yosemite NP trail appears on a sign at the trailhead. A booklet on Ellis Island containing general advertising was produced by the park concessioner. Advertising is to be allowed at a park site in Washington, D.C. Fund-raising has become a highly visible program at many park locations. New training programs teach professional staffs the ins and outs of raising money from philanthropic sources. Much fund-raising and commercialization have been allowed under the rubric of "partnerships," a politically correct concept that favors sharing costs and sometimes other responsibilities with non-NPS entities. Several fund-raising programs have recently been shifted to the National Park Foundation, the nongovernmental nature of which softens some objections to their commercialism and any alleged advertising excesses.

In 1993 NPS inaugurated a new "Challenge Cost-Share" program based on the partnership concept. Park-level projects cost-shared with private sources conduct trail maintenance, build or refurbish exhibits, and do other smallish, short-term projects to benefit the parks. In 1993 an appropriation of $1.87 million generated 152 projects with a reported dollar value of $5.8 million.

Other forms of fund-raising, largely for capital developments, are conducted by various "friends" organizations. Many parks have attached to them an association of people who raise money, sponsor volunteers, print publications, and conduct a wide variety of activities that support the park and its staff. Some friends organizations are very active in the day-to-day life of the park. Some friends leadership are important community figures, sometimes also members of a park Advisory Commission. Along with the support of friends organizations, the national park system also benefits significantly from donations of things and materials such as computers, radios, tools, and similar objects. Many of these donations have no commercial link.

During the early 1980s, efforts were made to develop written Servicewide policies to guide fund-raising activities in ways that would support the Service but avoid appearances of commercialization and exploitation of the Park Service name or its resources. It was a difficult and often frustrating undertaking because representatives of the Reagan administration were always willing to push (with enthusiasm) the limits of taste and decorum. Many of those officials never saw a problem in commercial use of everything from the NPS logo to the proposed donation of vehicles to a park that would have a company's logo painted on the door: "On Loan from the Whatever Corporation." One feature of such uses is that they were (and are) never competitive. All were the result of a corporation's initiative based on a self-interest in the association with the parks. There were endless debates about whether use of a national park system symbol is advertising. The arguments were never settled, in part because one person's advertising is another person's benefaction. There can, however, be no mistaking that the company believes it is in *their* best interest, however it may be defined.

The debate continues though. New proposals emerge and each is handled on its own terms. It would be ideal if all commercial ventures of such a nature could be summarily banned, on the grounds that the national park system is a public trust that may not be exploited for private gain. There is, however, no way to frame such a policy and make it stick. Exceptions abound, beginning with all the concessions in the parks, travel agencies, book writers, and a thousand mutations on the theme. The trick is to be consistent yet flexible, but acutely sensitive to elements of good taste and constructive association. Liquor ads or cigarette commercials should not be associated with the national park system. Any number of associations are more difficult to call, and often the context is as important as the subject.

Whether these and other forms of link up with the world of commerce and industry are offensive or whether they are just a reasonable way of stimulating alternatives to tax-supported appropriations is a subject very much in the eye of the beholder. The popular view sees nothing wrong with taking donations from anyone in support of the national park system. Every little bit can help. Actually, donations as small as $25,000 or $50,000 may represent a net loss to the National Park Service if the costs of staff time and other overhead spent supporting the activity were included in the accounting. Perhaps fortunately, few government agencies count the costs of any such activity, and never weigh overhead and support costs against the revenues or benefits derived.

Most gifts are unrestricted—that is, they can be used by the Park Service for any purpose it deems appropriate. Some gifts are, however, for specific things, such as for construction of a visitor center or for purchase of a specific tract of land. The hazard inherent in restricted gifts is that they can encourage the recipient (NPS) to do something that would otherwise not be undertaken at all. Gifts can also affect timetables by forcing something to happen ahead of schedule to satisfy a donor. It can distort local priorities by focusing attention on something that would otherwise not be important to park management. Its largest potential hazard is that only on the rarest of occasions are donors or recipients of gifts likely to consider thoroughly the imputed long-term costs to the park and the government of the donation about to be made. For example, though a donor may pay the costs of a new building, the park and the government must operate and maintain it over the long run. Many donations will ultimately require added staff or other new resources to operate and maintain them. Few superintendents and other officials document

the long-term consequences of today's philanthropy. On many occasions the long-term costs will far exceed the original costs for whatever is involved.

The apparent problems regarding long-term costs notwithstanding, many people feel that spillover benefits of having a wider constituency outweigh any added expenditures. The more people personally participating directly in the park system support structure the
better. Most people are connected with the parks only through their
general taxes. Even small donations are welcomed because they represent a personal level of interest and commitment that is not typical of the population as a whole.

In addition to corporate sponsorships and link ups, NPS has installed donation boxes in nearly all visitor centers and similar facilities systemwide. Boxes and their accompanying signs encourage visitors to make cash donations on the spot. Results have been mixed.
Donated sums are rarely of any great significance. Given the political significance attached to the concept, no serious weighing of its
costs is probable.

One recent national park system project has broken all the rules and
expectations for philanthropy: The Statue of Liberty–Ellis Island Project.
The project was structured around the rehabilitation of the Statue of
Liberty, but included both that National Monument and Ellis Island,
located a stone's throw from the statue in New York Harbor. Ellis Island was the site through which more than 12 million immigrants
entered the United States in the last century and in the early years of
this one. An impressive fraction of the contemporary U.S. population
has someone in their lineage with an Ellis Island connection.

In the 1950s Ellis Island was abandoned (by another federal agency) and ultimately transferred to the National Park Service. For most
of two decades it was the object of vandalism and decay, as nothing
was done by NPS to save or salvage it. In the early 1980s Park Service planners took a long hard look at the site and proposed a modest rehabilitation of the main immigration building. Planners knew
that costs would be high and were much concerned about whether
Ellis Island really had a long-term viable place in the national park
system. Americans are not inherently ancestor oriented. Many of us
do not even know our grandparents' names or where they came from,
and only a handful can recite much about their great grandparents.
NPS was, then, for several reasons very conservative in its approach
to adding Ellis Island to active sites in the system. Interestingly, Ellis
Island was not classified as an affiliated area. It was fully part of the
national park system.

The plan, though, was put on the table and a host of interested people, including many celebrities such as Bob Hope and Irving Berlin, came to its rescue and defense. They urged much larger investments in historic rehabilitation and the development of elaborate interpretive programs and technology on the island. A detailed history of the Statue of Liberty–Ellis Island Project is beyond the scope of this book. However, it is important to know that a secretarial level commission was chartered and formed to guide the project and to serve as the principal vehicle for raising tens of millions of dollars for the effort. Chrysler Motors President Lee Iacocca chaired the commission for much of its life and in the end over $350 million was raised and devoted to the project. The fund-raising effort ranged from proverbial pennies from school children to multimillion dollar gifts from many wealthy people and corporations. In addition the commission sponsored fund-raising activities across a wide front—many of which raised NPS eyebrows for their audacity. In the end the Statue of Liberty got a new torch and general face-lifting, along with both new and rehabilitated features on Liberty Island.

On Ellis Island the project financed restoration of the Great Hall, a spectacular example of historic preservation, complete with computerized interpretation. It is one of the most visited places in America today.[3] It is also a site with a large annual operating cost: estimated to be about $4.7 million and a staff of seventy-five in 1994.[4] By agreement between the Park Service and the private fund-raising foundation, an endowment of some $20 million was set aside toward annual operating costs. The endowment was created in 1993 and in 1994 contributed $1.1 million toward Ellis Island. The funding was to be used for exhibit maintenance and other facilities associated with interpretation of the site. Obviously, at current interest rates a $20 million endowment cannot cover present operating costs. The foundation is also continuing support for additional capital investments on the north end of the island.[5]

NPS will do well to study the lessons learned from the Statue of Liberty–Ellis Island project before repeating its mistakes and overlooking its successes in new ventures toward similar ends. Proposals advanced for the joint public-private conversion of the Presidio of San Francisco are a case in point.

Ellis Island also contained the seeds of a further funding innovation. When the plan was drawn for the Great Hall, a companion plan was drafted for the south half of the island that contains a hospital and other buildings. Those buildings have had no major effort made to keep or repair them. They are, however, the object of a Request

For Proposals (RFP), that has been on the table since the early 1980s.[6] The idea was to bid out the site to private developers and interests, attaching to the Request For Proposals strict historic preservation goals and standards. No ticky-tacky here!

The RFP was published and some thirteen concepts came in, of which nine were judged to be solid proposals. An evaluation panel of outside experts helped evaluate the proposals and after much vacillating two finalists, Tex McCrary and the Center for Housing Partnerships, joined forces and were selected for the project. The center proposed developing a hotel on the island, along with a conference facility and a marina.

The proposal turned out to be very controversial and when Lee Iacocca became chairman of the Statue of Liberty/Ellis Island Centennial Commission in May 1982, he quickly and vigorously objected to it. The proposal languished and became emersed in personal and institutional politics, reaching bitter dimension at times. Additional competing ideas and plans were put on the table and sides taken. The controversy dragged on for years. The project remains alive in 1994. Though it is now reduced to a conference center, entirely financed with private sector monies, it retains the historic preservation requirements on the buildings and other features.

Whether the idea of private development or redevelopment (restoration) of a national park system property can be accomplished under terms that do not compromise the integrity of the site or of the National Park Service is a question only time will answer. I believe the idea has great merit for the future, though the last decade of controversy makes it abundantly clear that private financing is no easy road out. It is filled with hazards and pitfalls and opportunities for compromises and self-serving manipulation of horrendous proportions. It is, in short, a risky business. It is, perhaps, doubly risky in the case of the National Park Service, given that bureau's very spotty record of disciplined management of concession operations, a subject suitable for an entire book.

The RFP concept has been tried elsewhere, also in New York, at Gateway NRA. Included are giant hangers at Floyd Bennett Field, New York City's first commercial airport (and the one from which Wrong Way Corrigan took off). Involved are large structures with enormous potential for enclosing things and activities compatible with the NRA. A Request For Proposals (RFP) has solicited offers for their redevelopment through private sponsorship and financing. Again, because Floyd Bennett Field is a historic district, the plan contains strict historic preservation standards and criteria. This application also awaits proving up.

Another important component of philanthropic contributions to the national park system are the Volunteers-in-Parks (VIPs). The Volunteers-in-Parks program is now nearly twenty years old, though its roots are much older. Volunteer interpreters, many of them school teachers who work during the summer months at a park, have made major contributions to the visitor experiences of literally millions of people. Many VIPs are talented people with unique knowledge of a specific site or event. Some have served the equivalent of a second career at "their" park. The program now receives a modest appropriation for its support, under which the Service can reimburse the volunteers for certain costs, lunch and bus fare, for example. VIPs have a distinctive uniform and can be seen in many parks, especially during the busiest parts of the season.

In 1993 some seventy-nine thousand volunteers contributed 1,635 work-years at 325 parks, with an estimated value of $39 million. The 1995 budget request in support of the Volunteers-in-Parks program was $1,599,000, the same level as in recent years.[7] Each volunteer costs about $20 a year in direct costs, for which the national park system receives back services estimated to return $30 for each dollar invested.

Another element in the philanthropic program is the National Park Foundation, a private congressionally chartered organization located in Washington, D.C. The NPF is privately funded, with an operating budget of about $9 million, including capital funds and various restricted fund activities. The foundation has a governing board chaired by the secretary of the Interior. Serving on the board are about twenty men and women with affiliations in business and industry.

An examination of the foundation's role and programs is not my purpose here, but in the years that I was familiar with its activities, its contributions to the national park system were significant chiefly because the foundation's independent legal status allowed it to do things a government agency could not—accept and spend money for certain things the Park Service cannot finance, or buy land without the legal requirements attached to federal land acquisitions. The foundation makes grants to individual parks for specific projects. On one occasion in 1994, it granted a total of $273,444 to twenty-two park projects. The present foundation leadership asserts there is to be "a new mission and focus" in the years ahead, including "orderly expansion, growth of funds, additions to staff and active board involvement in the foundation."[8]

One particular fund administered by the foundation has special relevance here: the Horace M. Albright Employee Development Fund.

This fund was established in 1986 by Laurance S. Rockefeller and Jackson Hole Preserve, Incorporated to make grants to individual Park Service employees in order "to pursue endeavors that increase their personal growth and enhance professional skills." The fund is characterized by the foundation as the only privately funded employee-development fund among government agencies. The Albright Fund supplements normal ongoing employee training and education programs by the National Park Service. In 1993 twenty-five grants were made totaling $72,000.

A further source of new and additional monies for the support of the national park system is user fees. In the earliest days of the National Park Service fees charged for automobile use of the parks were a very important source of funds for park operations. Motor fees at the National Parks in 1917 ranged from $0.50 at Mesa Verde NP and General Grant NP, to $7.50 at Yellowstone NP. Interestingly, motor fees at Yellowstone were reduced that year from $10 per car. The Yellowstone fee in 1917 was equal to approximately $76 in 1990 dollars! The 1994 entrance fee to Yellowstone was $10.

Entrance and user fees at units of the national park system have been a matter of debate and contention since the beginning. In Acting Director Albright's first annual report he noted that many people complained about the fees as "discriminatory and unjust."[9] The dominant school of thought asserts that the national park system is taxpayer owned and paid for, that it is available for everyone on an equal access basis (which is arguably untrue), and that it should be free to all. Alternative rationales have really never gained more than token support. Present entrance and user fees are intended to represent a symbolic contribution for the value received in the park experience. They have no defined or implied relationship to park operating costs, either in aggregate systemwide or on a park-by-park basis.

Evidence suggests, though, that user and entrance fees do have an impact on visitor attitudes. Fees help visitors understand that the parks are not really free. They cost money to create and more money to operate and care for. Also, fees may heighten people's awareness that the resource is public property and that littering, vandalism, and other destructive acts hurt their parks. Park managers believe intuitively (and perhaps based on at least generalized experience) that people take better care of something they have paid for than something provided entirely free. Many parks have charged entrance fees for much or all of their history, although many more never did.

Then, in the 1980s the Reagan-Watt administration saw park entrance and user fees as a means for "revenue enhancement." Fees were raised, although not dramatically, at parks where they were already collected, and new fees were begun at many sites previously free of charge. All receipts from such fees and user charges went into the General Fund of the Treasury—not to the park where they were collected and not to the National Park Service.

Continuing a long NPS tradition and practice, fee collections were a low priority activity. Many collection booths at entrance gates were operated only a few hours a day. Knowledgeable repeat visitors could plan their arrival easily to avoid fees. Superintendents did not feel happy about allocating staff time to collecting fees that would be funneled off to the Treasury in Washington, D.C. It costs money to collect the fees, and sometimes those costs were clearly more than the sums collected. New collection facilities and booths were built, gates installed, and staff trained, all at costs never reimbursed by way of the fees collected. Visitors also complained that their money was not used to benefit the park they paid to see.

In 1988 Congress changed the law, and NPS was allowed to use such fees. The system has solved many of the problems previously characteristic of fee collection. Now superintendents have an incentive to collect the fees. Collection facilities are not only open longer hours but also open on days formerly closed. NPS recreation fee revenues in 1993 were about $88.6 million, about 50 percent more than they were in the years before the change in the law.

Visitor fees remain very modest by all measures: equal to less than the cost of a dinner out or a movie in a theater, particularly for families. Alongside private recreational opportunities, such as those operated by Disney or other theme parks, fees for entrance and use of national park system resources are very low, by a factor of ten or more for a family of four.

The fee issue remains unresolved and a matter of dispute because neither Congress nor any administration has ever worked out a fee policy that could garner a consensus. In recent administrations, including that of Bill Clinton during his first year, fees have been used primarily as revenue enhancements and are not based on any principle or policy relationship between people who use the parks and the costs of providing park opportunities.

The Canadian park system has attempted to articulate such a relationship by saying that the general taxpayer (all citizens through general taxation) will pay to create the parks and the users will pay to operate them. The relationship does not succeed in any literal way, but the principle is now established and appears to be generally accepted. If such a principle were in effect for our national park system, the universal user fee for all park visitors would be less than $2.50 per visit. The sum is actually lower than many single-visit costs today, but, of course, it would not allow for any freebies (such as afforded senior citizens) and even repeat visitors would have to pay again. Nevertheless, the sum is not outrageous.

On a park-by-park basis a universal fee may not make sense under a policy that attempts to relate costs and users. As evident in Appendix 7-1, the actual imputed costs-per-visit vary widely from park to park—from a low of under twenty cents to values well over $100 per visitor. The range of costs displayed in Appendix 7-1 is itself interesting, and could perhaps serve as an ingredient in comparing the relative efficiency of park financial investments. While some resources can clearly justify larger than normal investments, the cost differences do not appear to be all related to obvious resource-related factors. The data merit a closer look and development of policy rationales or other explanations for the exceptional differences. Some costs may be quite hard to justify.

It seems very probable that a uniform fee of $2.50 or so would spark complaints from both ends of the spectrum: from those visiting parks where costs are much lower than that, and others who would assert that they should not be subsidizing visitors to high-cost parks. Very high cost parks might receive virtually no visitors. The policy dilemma is an important unresolved matter, awaiting someone with just the right statement of a policy rationale and a formula that can survive the political wars. In the meantime, recreation fee revenues are an important part of the Park Service budget. People who follow such things need to be ever watchful that fees supplement, and do not supplant, regular appropriated funds.

From time to time, the Service receives other proposals to increase funding for the national park system through excise taxes on something associated with recreation, through dedicated taxes on gas or other fossil (nonrenewable) fuels, through the sale of federally owned assets (land, oil and gas, surplus property, etc.), or through some sort of national lottery or subscription.

In addition, an array of financial and managerial alternatives to the present national park system are not treated in this book, including partial or total privatization (sell the parks, with or without clear and enforceable requirements that they be managed in a particular way); transfer of park system sites and assets to another level of government (perhaps with partial but not total federal funds to manage the sites); or management of the national park system by some sort of new public or private instrumentality.[10] None of these proposals has been treated here, in part because they seem totally unworkable in any form, but in larger part because they all seem far removed from the commitment this nation has so far made to its natural and historic heritage.

For the present and foreseeable future the most probable source of funding for national park system sites and programs is the regular annual appropriations of Congress, supplemented in an important, but minor, way by philanthropy. Given an extended history of congressional appropriations that usually exceed the formal budget request of the president, it is hard to argue that the Service has done poorly or is suffering from financial malnutrition, $2 billion backlogs notwithstanding.

If NPS had a long-range program and perspective, if there did exist a well thought out strategy for ensuring adequate basic operations of the national park system, and if NPS had a credible exposition of its mission for the year 2000 and beyond, it would be in far better position to substitute real programs for public relations initiatives and to defend its near-term and long-term requirements. Accordingly, the new strategic planning office in the Park Service has a large task ahead.

Some park system supporters have pushed well-intentioned panic buttons because they have seen examples of resources harmed by inadequate funds or staff. A historic building literally fell down a few years ago because the needed maintenance actions were not taken in time. Things were bad enough at Independence NHP for the National Trust for Historic Preservation to place the site on a recent "most endangered list." Other examples could be cited.

I am not an enthusiastic supporter of such cries of panic. The national park system is supported by a budget of over $1 billion. If a historic structure is genuinely endangered, if Independence Hall is in serious trouble, NPS already has the resources and the means to rescue it on an emergency basis. Difficult decisions would be required, to be sure, and something would necessarily have to give way.

The Park Service has in the past and will probably in the future be accused of carrying out what is called the Washington Monument Syndrome: if you are in money trouble, close the Washington Monument so the affected tourists will complain to Congress and get the money restored. The strategy works—even when it is only threatened—often enough to keep the concept very much alive. Are the panic buttons about Independence NHP and other sites a similar exercise? Squeaky wheels always get the oil.

In something of a mutation on the Washington Monument Syndrome, some NPS officials have recently suggested private fund-raising on behalf of rescue and emergency vehicles, law enforcement equipment (including guns), and other high-profile necessities, so that regular appropriations could be devoted to things with less public appeal. Such a strategy seems to me to reflect a very cynical view of philanthropic motivations and badly distorted budget priorities. What if the private fund-raising falls short of its goals?

I am a strong supporter of philanthropy as a matter of policy. I directed an organization for several years that depended on philanthropy to an important degree. I am aware, however, that fund-raising and gift solicitation can easily cross over from the tasteful and proper to tasteless and counter-productive. Philanthropy is not free money. It must also be cost-effective, either by honest accounting of costs and returns or by the clear-eyed evaluation of costs versus non-cash benefits that serve the needs and goals of the institution. In a public program the requirements for good taste and discipline are magnified by current public skepticism about efficiency in government. The public has demonstrated for many years its willingness to support the parks voluntarily with money, time, and talent. The tasks of marshalling those resources ought to remain tasteful and conservative, respectful of the common values the system seeks to preserve.

NOTES

1. Much of the personal financing done by Mather (such as augmenting part of his staff's salaries) is not legal today, some of it having been declared illegal even as Mather was doing it.

2. For a history of the beginnings of Muir Woods NM and Acadia NP (then Sieur de Monts NM) see Rothman, *Preserving Different Pasts*, 61–64, 105–6.

3. According to Weissmann Travel Reports, which compiles information about the most popular attractions in the U.S., Ellis Island was recently no. 2 of the top ten. It is the only national park system site on the list. As reported by Michael Iachetta for the *New York Daily News* and published in the Ft. Lauderdale (Fla.) *Sun-Sentinel*, Dec. 29, 1991, the top ten sites in 1991 were (1) Disney/MGM Studios and Universal Studios, Fla.; (2) the Museum of Immigration, Ellis Island, N.Y.; (3) the Futures Center and the Franklin Institute, Philadelphia, Pa.; (4) Washington National Cathedral, D.C.; (5) the Marine Mammal Pavilion of the National Aquarium, Baltimore, Md.; the Aquarium of the Americas, New Orleans, La.; and the Texas State Aquarium in Corpus Christi; (6) Technology Center of Silicon Valley, San Jose, Calif.; (7) Trump Taj Mahal Hotel/Casino, Atlantic City, N.J.; and Excalibur Hotel/Casino in Las Vegas; (8) Vermillion, an Acadian theme village in La.;

(9) the Richard Nixon Library, Yorba Linda, Calif.; and (10) Evergreen House, a newly restored art museum, in Baltimore, Md.

4. Costs and staffing have been estimated by Acting Superintendent Tom Bradley because the budgets and staffing for Ellis Island are merged with those for Statue of Liberty NM. Many of the staff serve both sites and no separate accounting is kept.

5. For a candid insider's account of the Statue of Liberty–Ellis Island project see Holland, *Idealists, Scoundrels, and the Lady.* F. Ross Holland is a former NPS associate director and historic preservation expert who worked for the commission as its director of restoration and preservation.

6. I wrote the first Ellis Island project Request For Proposals (RFP), a then major departure for the National Park Service from conventional project financing. The concept was experimental, trying to test whether private funds could be induced to restore and make an adaptive use of a historic structure and site. NPS at that time had no conceivable need for the massive concrete buildings on the south side of the island. Even demolition would have cost an estimated $40 million, a sum far beyond Park Service budget expectations. The RFP did not circumscribe potential uses to which the lands and buildings might be put, but the uses could not be incompatible with the monumental nature of the Great Hall. Although new structures were not encouraged, neither were they strictly prevented. Demolition was similarly not encouraged but not ruled out completely.

7. *Budget Justifications, F.Y. 1995:* NPS-94.

8. From the president's message, published in the *National Park Foundation Annual Report 1990:* 2.

9. Annual Report of the Director, National Park Service, published in *Annual Report of the Secretary of the Interior, 1917:* 803–4. Albright's rationale for the fees, which must have been regarded as significant in their day, was that they reflected "benefit received, rather than the ability to pay." He cited the following principles, which he attributed to Congress: "1. The parks are far from the center of population and are not visited by the majority of people, hence the burden of maintaining them should be shared in larger measure by the traveler. 2. There is a relatively large volume of local travel which should bear a heavy share of maintenance costs. People who live near a park necessarily are able to make a larger use of it than those who come from afar. 3. The tourist must pay for the use of roads and streets at home; also he must pay for service by public utilities, such as the gas company, the electric power company, the telephone company, the traction corporation, etc. There is no reason why he should not expect to help defray cost of similar service in the national parks where public utilities are very costly and expensive to maintain."

10. According to Rothman, in the years preceding creation of the National Park Service, Frank Bond, chief clerk of the General Land Office (a bureau in the Interior Department responsible for several national monuments), proposed privatizing the national monuments in hopes of thereby affording them care they were then not receiving from any source. (*Preserving Different Pasts*, 83).

ELEVEN

Toward a New National Park System

As the national park system moves toward the second millennium, its greatest shortcoming is that—for all its majesty, for all the irreplaceable wonders and artifacts it contains, for all the love bestowed upon it by millions of people, and for all the dedicated care and affection given to it by the men and women who care for it—it is not yet a real *system*.

Too little binds the 367 and more units together into a cohesive national stratagem that would make each unit a gem in a single crown of jewels, secured together forever. There are no agreed-upon criteria having the force of law to shape the future of the system. There is no certain agreement as to just what is even now in the national park system. There is no certainty as to its permanence. The parks and other sites under the jurisdiction of the National Park Service are not yet managed as a disciplined, integrated system that assures an equality of concern and professional care for every unit.

The congressional language of 1970 described in chapter 1 is not adequate. That enactment only defined the national park system to include everything managed by the National Park Service. As I showed in chapter 3, with the invention of affiliated areas that definition proved slippery. Mar-A-Lago NHS, Georgia O'Keeffe NHS, and other divestitures have proved that the system may not be secure from those who would shrink its extent or deny a new area of established merit.

Therefore, we need not only a new definition of the national park system but also one that conveys a concept and standard against which proposed new areas may be weighed and judged. The purpose of the standard is not to foreclose possibilities as much as it is to assure everyone that the merits of new areas have been carefully examined and that the process has thoughtfully considered the nature of the long-term commitment that membership in the national park system requires.

First, a new definition of the national park system needs to address the essential permanence of the system, which should not be fair game for second guessing and economic or political manipulation later. Obviously, one Congress cannot bind another to its will, but like the concept of legal precedent in the Supreme Court, Congress can set a stage for permanence by its own consistency, by the language in its laws, and by how it shapes public perceptions of its intent.

Areas long ago authorized but never established should be looked at again by Congress and the Executive with fresh intention to resolve their indeterminate status.[1] The Park Service and Congress should finish and settle the policy issues raised by the study of affiliated areas discussed in chapter 3, including a clear understanding about what is and what is not part of the national park system. In addition, Congress and the Executive Branch should settle with clarity the issue as to what legal protections affiliated areas have and what responsibilities the National Park Service has to enforce such protections. Equally important, a new definition of the national park system must contain no ambiguities about what is in the system and what is not. There must be no half-baked parks.

Accordingly, the National Park Service should reprise its experiences with Mar-A-Lago NHS for the lessons that might be learned and the processes that might benefit. NPS could also learn from reexamining the events surrounding the deauthorization-before-establishment of Georgia O'Keeffe NHS (N.Mex.). Deauthorization of the site came after preparation and release of a proposed General Management Plan that stirred up local opposition. Neighbors convinced Miss O'Keeffe to withdraw her donation of the property, a proposition to which NPS and Congress assented. Only the National Parks and Conservation Association tried to retain the site in the system in hope of eventually overcoming local objections. In this instance, NPS has evidenced a measure of professional inconsistency by ignoring earlier findings of national significance that have not led to actions that would protect the site over the long run.

Second, a new definition of the system can attempt to clarify and bring improved consistency to the nomenclature by which parks are known and managed. However, name changes should be done only with the most serious of intents and with utmost regard for historical usages. And finally a new definition of the system can help frame the grand design and its accompanying criteria by which the shape and content of the system's future can be projected. Perhaps the present National Park System Plan (described in chap. 1) can serve as a useful beginning. If so, it needs to be tested in the halls of Congress and among the public whose aspirations will also shape the content of the growing system. The role of Congress is critical to the success of that undertaking.

Beginning in 1994 the Park Service reinstituted a form of new area studies, this time acknowledging the role of studies conducted at the request of outside entities (including Congress), but also undertaking several studies on its own initiative. The Service set up an interdisciplinary panel of professionals to review and rank new area study proposals based on ten criteria. For 1994–95 it proposed to begin work on two new studies on the Service's own list of high-priority sites, study five sites mandated by Congress, and continue work on eleven studies begun in prior years.[2]

The Park Service should keep the pressure on to have a positive role in the identification and evaluation of new areas and in the analysis of proposals pending in Congress and elsewhere—a role largely denied the bureau in the Reagan-Bush years. The assertion of that role, however, is not to argue that only NPS is capable of correctly judging the merits of a proposed addition to the national park system. The Service's opinion is but one ingredient in that mixture. The Service's explicit statement that planning can "help defend the integrity of the park system against expansions into areas that fail to meet established standards" conveys a level of defensiveness against the views of others that is troublesome.[3]

The National Park Service must understand in a much deeper and more explicit way that it is the guardian and steward of resources whose ultimate membership in the system is defined by others—the Congress—not by it. The political processes by which units are added to the national park system are the people's best guarantee of the system's integrity. Those same political processes and the timing of each new area's entry into the system are important parts of each site's history. The Park Service must find satisfaction and motivation in that reality, not grounds for withholding support or playing the dog in the manger. Further, the Park Service needs to talk out and work out its discomforts with new departures and find compatible rationales for undertaking an enlarged mission whose boundaries do not remain fixed. There is no reasonable prospect that the boundaries and extent of the national park system will remain fixed and unchanging in the decades ahead, the state of the economy and partisan politics aside.

Characterizations of the national park system today as "10 park systems" or "367 park systems" come far too close to truth. The system has grown without strong linkages between and among the parks and without a clear and directed sense of a unified mission

However, far more than a new definition in law and popular culture a new national park system is also a new process, a new formulation for actions and attitudes. Every unit of the national park system needs to be electronically linked with every other unit through compatible systemwide networks of communication that foster the exchange of information, ideas, problems, and solutions. Such linkage can also support wider standardization of administrative systems, resource and historical data, and other record-keeping and management reporting systems. The "cc:mail" system in place in 1994 is not yet systemwide. Used only for "the Director's Bulletin Board" and vacancy announcements, it falls far short of the potential benefits that modern electronic communications systems can provide.

A new management discipline needs to reflect a more mature National Park Service. The powers of the modern computer and electronic communications can help. A higher level of toleration by NPS managers and staff for modern reporting and compliance requirements would similarly help. While it is popular culture to disparage all paperwork and reports as a waste of time, it is unrealistic to believe that there will be less of it in the future. The parks and their managers need more information, not less. If any level of serious interpark analyses are undertaken, needed data and information requirements will inevitably generate additional paperwork. Regularized reporting, as opposed to sporadic data collection, can make even large tasks easier in the long run. The strategy is to keep reports lean and do them well.

The Park Service and its supporters need to understand the consequences of the crown jewels syndrome and of the effects of branding some parks lesser or inferior. While it is probably impossible to avoid having favorites or ascribing special virtues to those parks dubbed the crown jewels, great care needs to be taken by NPS management and staff to ensure that having a favorite does not mean practicing favoritism. Bad jokes that denigrate individual parks should go the way of ethnic slurs—they have many of the same possible effects.

The role and status of approved park plans need to be strengthened. *All* developments should require a formal finding of consistency with the plan, including its scale and timing. A bridge between park budgets and park plans should be fashioned and enforced. Superintendents should be held accountable for park plans and for their accomplishment. If a superintendent cannot support the park plan, steps should be taken either to revise the plan or change the opinion of the person objecting. Park plans are rarely circulated for their educational and precedent values. Wheels are constantly reinvented. Plans should be widely distributed and innovative features or solutions to particularly knotty problems given generous internal publicity.

While the absence of detailed administrative and management policies and procedures may, indeed, promote individual initiative and suppress the dead hand of conformity, consistency is often a virtue in the conduct of public business. The public has a right to expect that its communal assets will be treated in a common and dependable manner. It is also important that those resources be managed according to publicly validated goals and standards, not the idiosyncratic agendas of individual managers.

Every new park area should begin its role in the national park system with the full measure of legal and staff support necessary to protect its values and assure its success. Beginning in Congress, the authority to create new park areas should be joined at the outset by the responsibility to provide for their care and custody. Also, park units should be counted one by one—numbered 367, 368, and so forth. Numbering highlights the depth of the present and future obligation inherent in every new unit. Numbering could also strengthen the hand and role of the substantive committees in Congress. Legislative end-runs would be perhaps less likely.

In addition, start-up activities and capabilities at new park units should have a high measure of standardization, making the best use of the institution's memory for prior beginnings. A consistent written plan should guide all new park activations. New parks also offer special challenges and opportunities for creativity and innovation. Park organizations should exhibit increased standardization and parallel staffing to foster improved opportunities for career mobility and the development of so-called career ladders. Such standardization should cut across all regions and should include job titles, extent of supervisory oversight, and output or performance measures.

Perhaps most important the Park Service needs to resolve its internal ambivalence on the role of science and research in the parks. The lack of an adequate scientific basis for management decisions has too long excused inaction or promoted finger pointing.

There is little doubt that the National Park Service, the system and its employees are going through a crisis in these years. The results of the 1991 Vail, Colorado, symposium present the picture of an agency seriously struggling with a wide variety of issues. A number of the problems identified at Vail have been treated here. Many of the topics on which concern was voiced are matters within the director's province to remedy. Money is only a part of any answer. Some problems involve the need for improved administrative discipline and "tougher" management.

Although extensive in some fields, the Vail report failed in one important area: the participants and speakers lacked an explicit understanding of the National Park Service as a part of the United States government and in turn a part of the larger economy and political body of all the United States. While the participants may know those relationships as individuals, in their papers and presentations they lacked clarity on the point.

Issues regarding low entrance salaries, the inability of younger and lower graded employees to buy homes on today's market, the professional stagnation that comes with an economy that is barely growing (if at all), and the lack of psychic income in working for a federal government whose general image and value are the object of derision and humorless jokes—all these and more are part of a set of national circumstances of which the National Park Service is only a part.

In many ways the Park Service is just now feeling the effects of forces in the American economy that have troubled other elements of society for a decade and more. These include the stagnation of real incomes, the impacts of technology, the explosion of information needs and accessibility, skills obsolescence, and so forth. Geography and mission have sheltered NPS for many years. Realization of the larger trends and contexts can help enormously by making it possible for the Park Service to focus on its strengths and build on its past successes with a much clearer understanding of where and why change is essential. Understanding the national context could suggest looking to other areas of the economy for possible approaches, solutions, and sources of aid. Improved understanding of larger national trends that will effect the Service ought to be a central concern of the new NPS strategic planning effort.

The final report of the Vail conference contains a statement that must have deeply impressed many of the people who attended. It was repeated in press accounts based on the final written report. The official conference report gloomily asserted that "the core operational budget of the Park Service has remained flat in real terms since 1983."[4] The statement, however, is untrue.

Figure 3 shows a ten-year trend of the Park Service budget since 1983 in relation to the growth of park units and visitation, using

Figure 3. Recent Trends, 1983–92 (in constant 1990 dollars).

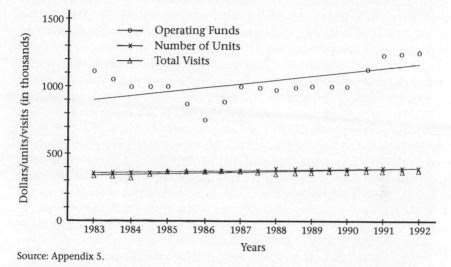

Source: Appendix 5.

financial information in constant dollars. Appropriations have shown ups and downs, with 1986 being a particularly low year, but the trend has been well above "flat," after taking into account the effects of inflation. It is, however, true that not every park managed to do so well. But what of an agency that *thinks* it is doing so poorly? What does this error do to employees' understandings of their own reality? How would it effect the tone of the conference and the morale of its participants—in conference and when they return to their parks? I made every effort to discover the basis for the error and uncover the reasoning behind it. I found nothing. It was apparently one of those things said out loud at a meeting or passed along in a draft paper and never questioned. Perhaps it found its way into the report because it fit the mood of the times and the expectations of the people involved. It is a serious error, made worse by its inclusion in the final report—where many readers will uncritically accept its veracity.

This reality only underscores the need for National Park Service leadership and employees to look into the larger national economy and see themselves in perspective. It will potentially help in understanding the forces and realities of which the Service and the system are a part. It may also convince some people that the national park system grass is actually greener than other pastures, because, indeed, it is. NPS has done much better than average financially in the administrations of Presidents Reagan and Bush. There are blessings that ought to be counted.

The status of the modern American economy also contains other messages. Government budgets will not likely soon again be in an expansionist mode and the requirement will therefore be to make more efficient use of present resources. OMB and the Congress may well force the Park Service to shift toward more disciplined administrative practices, including the development of productivity indicators and movement toward standardization in organizational arrangements, staffing patterns and so forth.

NPS must place itself in a position to compete for scarce Federal dollars from a position of strength. It must know its own needs better. Informed professional guesstimates of the extent of its financial requirements are not good enough. Something the equivalent of the Basic Operations Survey, described in Chapter 9, that inventories and scales out the needs of each park should exist in the background of every annual budget.

Allocations of both old and new money should be based on measured needs. Explicit systems for funding allocations can go a long way against the grain of funding decisions based on informal networks and the perpetuation of any form of the crown jewels syndrome. The Service should be acutely mindful of the effects of monetary inflation and not permit parks to slide behind the curve except by a conscious decision to cut the budget, assuming such choices are possible.

Perhaps the Service and the system need a modern equivalent of MISSION 66—without the undue focus on new development and with a more acute sensitivity to environmental impacts. Any such effort should also include resource management, visitor services, and other software components. By a variety of measures MISSION 66 was a clear-cut success. However, I am not certain such an effort can succeed again in the same way. Today's federal government is rarely able to mount sustained program efforts at anything. Wars on poverty and drugs seem to lose steam quickly. After the momentum is lost, skepticism and then cynicism soon set in. One possibility might be a reinvestment-in-infrastructure program tied to some new source of dedicated revenues. However, governmentwide strategies for deficit reduction and other economic development may militate against the success of such an approach.

It seems unlikely that large-scale progress will be made in dealing with the infrastructure needs of the national park system except as the nation as a whole begins to address those same needs in other aspects of national life. If that is true, the National Park Service, then, must work harder than ever to identify and justify the needs it knows so well.

NPS must be able to demonstrate more clearly to the Department, to OMB, and to the Congress that it is making the most intelligent use of its present human and financial resources. Staff, supervisors, and members in those bodies are mindful of present realities. The plain fact is that the National Park Service is not managed very efficiently. Even if all or part of it were, there is no meaningful way to prove it. Explicit change can help convince everyone of the reality of the needs and of the probabilities that new money will be wisely spent.[5]

The National Park Service pays a heavy price today for the institutional and administrative isolation of the parks. Career opportunities are stunted. Problems identified in one location remain hidden from view in others. Solutions found in one location may never reach another place. Inefficiencies are likely to go unrecognized because no one ever attempts to measure outputs or productivity. Park-to-park comparisons are viewed as an impertinent threat, even by the managers whose responsibilities include the capacity to see the larger picture. The proposition that all parks are independently unique and that all forms of comparative and structural analysis are unfair or inappropriate must be replaced by the certainty that the units of the national park system have far more in common than differences that separate them. Cost and productivity comparisons between and among parks are not inherently unfair as long as the comparisons are explicit and subject to analysis.

The hardest part of all will be convincing present National Park Service management of the necessity for and opportunity to change. The data displayed in Appendixes 6, 7, and 8 alone contain strong hints of the need for critical appraisals of organizations, budgets, staffing, and costs. Along with conveying the need to change, management must have proof that change will have its rewards. Such is no small undertaking in a federal government that for a long time has placed little to no importance on improved efficiency and effectiveness in public programs. The burden on NPS leadership is, therefore, even heavier.

Competition for entry level professional jobs in the American economy will become even more acute in the years ahead. While the number of people looking for jobs remains high it will remain an employer's market. NPS needs to decide what sort of professional skills it will need in the next generation of workers and then must move on its own to recruit and retain the best and the brightest available. The Service can no longer afford to hire only from among those who apply on their own. The Park Service should also seek new talent in the form of experienced persons who could bring to the bureau the ability to move up on the learning curve at an accelerated pace. Outside recruiting can also help make significant improvements in career placement and opportunities for minorities and women. New blood, both at the bottom of the career ladder and on higher rungs, holds the potential for serious adverse effects on the morale and effectiveness of the present labor force. Large new training and retraining efforts must go hand in hand with outside recruiting to help overcome those effects.

The so-called professionalization of the ranger force is a particularly thorny issue. The Service faces some very serious dilemmas: to the degree it defines the new ranger in professional terms analogous to those of a forest ranger, who must have a four-year degree in forestry, for example, it isolates a large part of the existing labor force who would not qualify. As full-fledged professionalization occurs within the ranks of the park ranger force, the existing complement of rangers must be brought up to speed through training, advanced education, back-to-college programs, and, perhaps as a last resort, early retirements and new hires. Other occupational groups require similar attention and help. Such needs are not unlike those in many occupations and industries in the American economy. If NPS has lagged in its awareness of the problem, it ought not further lag in moving toward constructive ways to deal with the issues. The ultimate pain only deepens.

Because the National Park Service is such a small, closely knit organization, many institutional changes are especially difficult. The people who make and carry out the decisions know personally many of the people who will be affected. They may be long-standing friends. Through career rotations they may someday have reversed roles; today's regional director may be tomorrow's superintendent or vice versa. It is hard to imagine any solution that will avoid hurting some people. In this dimension, too, NPS is close to larger trends in the national economy over which it has very limited control.

However, in the final analysis, and taking nothing whatever away from the wonders and significance of the cultural and natural resources administered by the National Park Service, the agency's greatest single asset is its people. By all measures the Park Service is extraordinarily fortunate to employ a staff of highly motivated, dedicated people. The talent and skills of many NPS staff are outstanding. Very much about them and about their line of work if changed would be a great loss to the Service. People fortunate enough to have linked their life's work to the parks may do so because they understand more deeply than others the parks true meaning to the quality of modern life. Or they may have chosen that work because they wished to find that meaning in their own lives, or to share it with others.

One of the National Park Service's most respected career rangers, the late Lemuel A. ("Lon") Garrison, articulated in writing his feelings for the parks. In his autobiographical accounting of *The Making of a Ranger* Garrison wrote of his special feelings about the parks:[6]

> I ride on horseback to the very top of the trail through Donahue Pass on the eastern boundary of Yosemite National Park and stop abruptly. Suddenly, I see to the far edge of the world in the eastern distance, across an endless jumble of wild mountain tops. Standing as tall as I can before the Lord, I am humbled and bareheaded and silent. I have met Creation.
>
> An old lady at the Grand Canyon murmurs to her companion, "I feel that I must whisper."[7]
>
> A visitor to the Liberty Bell drops to her knees and quite obviously offers a silent prayer, rises, kisses the bell, and walks out. Why does this seem a natural place for her to offer her devotions?

Garrison was neither the first nor the last to raise the things that belong to the national park system to a level of profound spirituality and sublime, even religious, significance.[8] Many people will always see the parks through a sentimental window, and for the visitors who experience them and others who wish they could, that window is the essential reality. Others view the parks as "Islands of Hope" that have the capability to preserve and sustain an irreplaceable diversity of biotic forms and invaluable artifacts of human intelligence and creativity, all sentiment aside.[9]

The parks are also the object of disagreements and on occasion they are battlegrounds between opposing forces who would wish their will on the future of the parks. The antagonists almost never attack the essence of the park—only its management or the way things happen or fail to happen. The policies and practices by which the parks live out their days are often controversial, and strong feelings and powerful, self-serving interests wage earnest pressures to prevail.

The National Park Service and its staff are not always right, of course. Sometimes they forget. Sometimes they resist even the best of changes. Sometimes they simply do not know. Sometimes a policy or practice, believed right at the time, turns out to have been a mistake. Sometimes the hardest thing of all is to admit being wrong, even when a better course of action becomes clear.

For many decisions at the interface of Mankind and Nature hindsight is the only way of knowing. The modern environmental movement is largely constructed on the knowledge that hindsight affords. We know now that many earlier decisions on growth, the destruction of wetlands, nonrenewable resource extraction, and the disposal of wastes were wrong. Writer James Hamilton-Paterson has observed, "Conservation is only ever a rear guard action, fought from a position of loss."[10]

Every day we gain some new evidence of the degree to which all people are inexorably linked to other species, resources, and systems on this planet, our home. If only our learning and reaction could catch up with the speed of growth and resource consumption. A sustainable earth must be the policy of every nation. As the world's largest consumer of almost everything, the United States has a special obligation for leadership.

Much hindsight is critical and costly to remedy and the National Park Service tends to defend its past with resolute conviction and righteous protectionism. All institutions find it much harder to admit error than people do, even when the mistakes were made by well-intentioned people long gone from the scene.

The policy and management decisions facing the National Park Service in the future exist in a particularly difficult framework. The essential nature of managing the parks is to prevent change, because most change is seen as bad. Rust, decay, fires, scale, mold, even the inevitable processes of aging, are all to be prevented. Such an orientation is not often the wellspring of change. The conservation framework is made even less receptive to change when added to it is the fact that many National Park Service employees, perhaps most, enjoy their work and the environments within which they labor, to a measure in no way typical of the average worker in America. Park Service employees can with some seriousness observe, "It is hard to call this work. And I get paid for doing it!" No small number of outside observers may jokingly agree, but the joke is only in part a funny.

Work in the parks, especially that of the ranger force, often involves activities many people label recreation. Working in the parks is rarely boring and often it is fun—from horseback trips into the back country to wildlife counts, from escorted trips with a member of Congress or tourists from Japan, to an underground tour of the Lincoln Memorial. Again, such work conditions do not make change easy.

These conservative elements place a special burden on the leadership of the National Park Service to bring about constructive change in an ever-changing world. Change needs an institutional mentor and at least as many surrogates as there are units in the national park system. It must, of course, begin with the director, and even if it can begin there, it needs the like-minded support of the secretary of the Interior and the president. For much too long change in the federal government has meant doing less, even doing nothing. Rewards did not often attend those who tried to do their job better or more efficiently—an incredible irony in recent administrations dominated by conservative businessmen. Only time will tell whether the administration of President Bill Clinton will successfully reinvent the National Park Service.[11]

However, the stakes are high and the resources at risk are as irreplaceable as anything on this planet. Though I am not someone who sees Armageddon in any one year's presidential budget or in the failure of Congress to throw defense-sized dollars at the National Park Service, the system has real unmet needs that can be defined and described in plain English. Park professionals must see that the parks' needs are met. It is, however, not enough to ask for money simply "because." There are too many competitors whose stake in national priorities has at least an equal claim.

A National Park Service for the future will require types and levels of expertise whose nature and extent are only vaguely felt today. I suspect that a significant part of the current dissatisfactions expressed by NPS employees reflects a deep discomfort with self-capacities to comprehend the future. This is an important precursor to change, although no guarantee that change will actually occur or that it will move the institution in the right direction.

The national park system holds sites and artifacts whose value cannot be measured in dollars. Their real value is best measured by what we humans know for certain is more valuable than money, that is, time. The parks have captured time and hold it for us—for all of us—to experience and to strive to understand.

Some critics of the system, or at least of some things in it, assert that the national park system cannot be all things to all people. Why not? By its own diversity, it can illuminate the diversity of the American people and of their values, circumstances, and aspirations. By representing diversity we give it honor and identity, and, ultimately, make it easier to understand each of our places as individuals in the mosaic of our world and culture. We will better understand, then, that we cannot live as if we were alone.

Controversies will assuredly continue, in part because for many of the policy questions, including most of the ones asked in this volume, there are no single, and seldom easy, answers. The issues and problems that face the national park system in these closing years of the twentieth century appear formidable, even daunting. However, a well-motivated work force with caring leadership can move mountains. If they have the help of informed citizens willing to do the necessary political homework and legwork, almost nothing is impossible.

Now is the time for new beginnings. The future of the national park system depends on all of us who care.

NOTES

1. The following list of authorized-but-never-established sites was compiled by Hogenauer and published in "Gone But Not Forgotten." His list also included the Columbus Battlefield Marker (Ga.), approved April. 10, 1936 (49 STAT. 1195), for which there does not appear to be any evidence that Congress intended the site to be part of the national park system. Along with all of the sites now listed as affiliated areas, some of which have also been authorized-but-never-established, the following authorizations merit a new, definitive examination in light of current circumstances and future expectations: (1) Grandfather Mountain NM (N.C.), June 12, 1917 (40 STAT. 152); (2) Palm Canyon NM (Calif.), August 26, 1922 (42 STAT. 832); (3) Pioneer NM (Ky.), June 18, 1934 (48 STAT. 982); (4) Spanish War Memorial Park (Fla.), August 20, 1935 (49 STAT. 661); (5) Belvoir Mansion Site, Lord Fairfax Estate (Va.), Aug. 29, 1935 (49 STAT. 967); (6) Eutaw Springs Battlefield Site (S.C.), June 26, 1936 (49 STAT. 1975); (7) Fort Saint Marks NHS (Fla.), Oct. 10, 1962 (76 STAT. 807); (8) Wolf NSR (Wis.), Oct. 2, 1968 (16 STAT. 1274).

2. *Budget Justifications, F.Y. 1995:* NPS-299-300.

3. Ibid. NPS-299.

4. *National Parks for the 21st Century,* 12.

5. Not everyone agrees that change is really needed, at least when it comes to parks and recreation. Authors Osborne and Gaebler, whose *Reinventing Government* offers a multitude of examples of ways to improve government services, assert that "Bureaucratic institutions still work in some instances. If the environment is stable, the task relatively simple, every customer wants the same service, and the quality of performance is not critical, a traditional public bureaucracy can do the job. Social security still works. . . . [A]gencies that provide libraries and parks and recreational facilities still work" (pp. 15–16). The characterization of both library and park and recreation services is downright wrongheaded. Neither is simple; the quality of performance is critical; neither ought to suffer poor performance.

6. The quotation is on pages 300–301. See also Sholly, *Guardians of Yellowstone,* for another ranger's feelings about one park in particular.

7. On the other hand, historian-economist John Ise wrote in *Our Nation-*

al Park Policy (p. 8) that he heard a woman at Grand Canyon say: "Hell of a ditch! Let's go get something to eat."

While such a statement may reflect only a superficial appreciation of what she was seeing, it is also possible that she took away from that experience, however brief, an image on which she will have cause to reflect and wonder at her leisure. In any event, people will react to the parks with the myriad of differences that define the human condition.

8. For an interesting collection of papers linking nature and the environment to the great religions of the modern world see Rockefeller and Elder, *Spirit and Nature*, a collection of papers delivered at a 1990 conference covering presentations involving Christian, Jewish, Islamic, Native American, and Buddhist viewpoints.

9. See Brown, *Islands of Hope*.

10. Hamilton-Paterson, *The Great Deep*, 282.

11. In the May 21, 1993, press release announcing Roger G. Kennedy as the new Park Service director, Secretary of the Interior Bruce Babbitt charged him to "redirect and reinvent the National Park Service during this time of great challenges and opportunities."

Epilogue

The national park system was not a topic of any significant visibility in the presidential campaign of 1992. However, the presence of Senator Al Gore on the ticket stood as substantial evidence of Bill Clinton's compatibility with at least the broad sweep of conservation ideology. Senator Gore's attachment to a global conservation ethic is manifest in his book *Earth in the Balance,* though parks per se are not mentioned in his treatise. To be sure, most of the ecological issues he addresses in a worldwide context have impacts on all present and future parks and other conservation reserves.

President Clinton's first executive action affecting the National Park Service was the selection of former Arizona Governor Bruce Babbitt to serve as secretary of the Interior. Much of the community of conservation interests applauded Clinton's choice. Later they urged him to stick with it when Secretary Babbitt was on two occasions mentioned as a potential appointee to the Supreme Court. Shortly after taking office, Secretary Babbitt named former President of the Wilderness Society George Frampton as assistant secretary for fish and wildlife and parks, again to the plaudits of many people on the conservation scene.

A protracted search for a new National Park Service director ended with the swearing in of Roger G. Kennedy on June 1, 1993. Kennedy came to the Park Service from the position as director of the Museum of American History, part of the Smithsonian Institution in Washington, D.C.

Secretary Babbitt's most important early action affecting the National Park Service was creation of the National Biological Survey (NBS), a new bureau modeled on the U.S. Geological Survey (USGS). NBS will conduct research, gather data, and inventory information about the animate landscape. Secretary Babbitt created the new bureau without generic legislation by pulling staff and money from four bureaus in the department: the Fish and Wildlife Service, National Park Service, Bureau of Land Management, and the Bureau of Reclamation. Subsequently, NBS received congressional sanction and funding. For starters NBS received an appropriation of $163 million and a staff of 1,840 employees.[1] A missing ingredient in the NBS makeup is the very substantial research and scientific capability of the U.S. Forest Service in the Department of Agriculture. Including part of that agency's scientific resources in NBS would be intellectually justifiable but probably impossible politically.

The immediate effect of creating the new organization was to remove much of the scientific staff and funding from the National Park Service and place it in the new institution. NBS staff located in parks and regional offices were to remain there. They will, however, report to the new bureau chief. The transfer of scientific expertise out of the National Park Service to the National Biological Survey in 1993–94 was not, however, a first. The same was done in 1939–40 by Secretary of the Interior Harold L. Ickes, who transferred the then NPS staff of about twenty-seven biologists, the bureau's only acknowledged "scientists," to an earlier Bureau of Biological Survey.[2]

The National Biological Survey is a timely reinvention, reflecting many years of frustration felt in the scientific community about the absence of a biological counterpart to the Geological Survey. USGS surveys and topographic maps are largely taken for granted today, but for over a century they have helped large portions of the Nation's oil, gas, mining, and realty economy.[3] NBS is probably a splendid idea whose time has come.

It may, however, be much less certain that its existence will greatly benefit the national park system in the short term. The Park Service has been struggling to build a scientific capability to serve park management needs. Success has been sharply limited by inadequate staffing and funding. Success has also been hampered by deep levels of ambivalence within the ranks of the Service. Among many old-line rangers science has restricted utility in a management system largely defined by the limits of intuition and pragmatic problem solving. While there has not often been overt institutional hostility to science in the parks, each scientific advance has had to meet special tests of relevancy and utility to gain wide park management support. How science will fare under the new arrangement remains to be discovered. It will take management skills of noteworthy proportion to avoid the stranger-in-a-strange-land syndrome among NBS employees continuing to reside and work in the parks.

If the list of NPS professional staff has in the past appeared to lack in-depth capability to deal with complex resources management issues and decisions, that list is shortened further by the existence of NBS. It is all the more important under such circumstances for the National Park Service to examine its professional resource management needs and accelerate a transition from resource custodian to resource manager. The need for more advanced college level training and qualifications for tomorrow's labor force—whether labeled "rangers" or by another title—will be magnified in a major way by the new organization. NBS will face many dilemmas: whether to support basic research and data collection or focus its scientific resources on solving specific management problems identified by park managers. Uncharacteristic of many similar bureaucratic situations, both the official and unofficial attitudes within the National Park Service appear to say: "The National Biological Survey is going to happen. We need the help. Let's make it succeed."

Almost immediately after taking office NPS Director Roger Kennedy adopted as his own the Seventy-fifth anniversary (1991) "Vail Agenda." He will emphasize recommendations aimed at bettering the morale and working conditions of National Park Service professionals. One set of initiatives, "Ranger Futures," is pointed toward improving the salaries of the ranger corps, upgrading their role in the management and leadership of the Park Service, improving in-park housing, providing twenty-year retirement for law enforcement rangers, and gaining senior executive service status for several superintendents at the larger parks.[4]

Another area of significant projected change relates to agency boundaries and responsibilities. Director Kennedy outlined the idea at the 1993 George B. Hartzog, Jr., Lecture at Clemson University on September 15. Though specifics are missing at this writing, Kennedy predicted that

> There is going to be radical transformation in the way in which those agencies dealing with public—meaning common—land go about their business . . . We will not have the current structures as between the agencies of the Department of the Interior or those in the Department of Agriculture. . . . Old boundaries are coming down. We are going to have co-management of areas. We are going to have a focus upon regions as defined by their genuine biological and historical and social imperatives, not the political happenstance of where boundaries were drawn before. . . . It's going to look a lot different three years from now, maybe even six months from now, than it looks right now.

The clear scientific merit in treating lands and resources according to biological and ecological units rather than along boundaries determined by politics and budgets supports high hopes for the success of the proposal Director Kennedy has articulated. Accomplishment of the idea will be very controversial. It will require a large measure of administrative skill and bureaucratic savvy. Congress may want a say in the details of how any co-management is carried out.

The bad news is that all this change most likely must be accomplished within financial constraints that may allow budget levels no better than staying even with the annual effects of inflation. Director Kennedy, who sees only level or declining budgets ahead, attributed future financial realities to a new national bipartisan consensus that maintains that "the first duty of [the federal] government is paying down the mortgage, and not to fixing the bridges, not to educating the children, not to taking care of the national parks. . . . we are going to put our first emphasis, we as a nation, on debt service. . . . we're going to pay down the mortgage."[5]

Actually, there is not widespread agreement to do anything with the national debt (the mortgage), only a tenuous political compact to slow the growth of the annual deficit. Working on the debt would change the scope of the problem by orders of great magnitude. Also, American budgetary priorities are not arrayed to do anything at all "instead of" anything else. The U.S. political process ultimately forms a negotiated mix of programs and activities that fall far short of satisfying any one objective in order to make at least some progress toward other social needs and economic goals. The reality is that NPS is in a stiff competition for budget dollars, vying against a large universe of also-worthy needs and objectives. That competition makes it even more important that the Service know its needs and express them forcefully to the president, to Congress and to the public. It must also prove to the best of its ability that it is making efficient use of present resources.[6]

As a consequence of the National Performance Review accomplished under the leadership of Vice President Gore, new initiatives will be undertaken in the Park Service to bring park decision making closer to the consumer, the park visitor.[7] This change appears to be occurring through steps taken by Director Kennedy to downplay the role of the regional offices and to upgrade the role of the park superintendents. It is said the regional offices will be more helpers than overseers. The idea is consistent with higher grades at the park superintendent level, and with extended program responsibilities beyond individual park boundaries. Many park level people will warmly welcome any diminution of the role played by regional offices or the Washington, D.C., headquarters. The hazard is that the characterization of the National Park Service as "10 Park Services" may come closer to "367 Park Services." NPS does not have a tradition or history of administrative cohesion and discipline. Park unit management could become highly balkanized and idiosyncratic with the character and goals of individual park superintendents—something even now felt by many people to be a serious problem requiring action.[8] Weak regions and a weak national headquarters could make all forms of interpark standardization and cost-effective analysis exceedingly difficult. More connected consumer services at the local level really have very little to do with levels of supervision and organizational discipline. The distinction should be in the forefront of any steps to shift functions between parks, regions, and the Washington, D.C., headquarters.

In addition, the National Park Service has been targeted for its share of the 252,000-job reduction to which President Clinton has committed his administration as part of the deficit reduction actions. Director Kennedy has said it will involve up to 1,300 NPS jobs. Such cuts, however and wherever carried out, will be painful, although Kennedy says the cuts will not be made in park operations. That leaves only the Washington office, the ten regional offices, and the two Service centers to absorb up to a 25 percent reduction. Such reductions will make improvements in processes and programs absolutely mandatory, and will make it even more important to look deep into present operations for savings. However, the parks ought not be insulated from the search for new efficiencies. Collectively they account for the majority of the park system's operating appropriations.

Finally, the new administration is considering strategies to make the National Park Service more entrepreneurial. This may be done through the collection of new and higher user fees, larger returns from the profits made by concessioners in the parks, and through the expanded use of private funding sources, notably the National Park Foundation. One proposal likely on the Clinton administration's next legislative agenda would allow half of any new revenues generated at the park level to be retained by the Service for immediate use without appropriation by Congress. Proponents argue that such an off-budget funding mechanism would help guarantee that Congress does not simply offset new revenues with equal cuts in the annual appropriation. Both Congress and the Office of Management and Budget, however, have a long history of opposing off-budget funding, so the outlook for such a proposal is uncertain.

The Clinton administration's list of actions and proposals affecting the national park system is a useful beginning. Many of its proposals are completely compatible with conclusions and recommendations suggested here. A few, such as strengthening the existing role and attributes of the present ranger force may be potentially regressive. According to the spring 1994 "Newsletter of the Employees and Alumni Association," the "standards for [ranger positions] did not change but the methods and philosophies for evaluating and crediting [ranger] work did." While this welcomed step may go a long way toward solving the salary equity problems of the present ranger force, it does nothing to address the larger issues of work force educational and skills requirements for the longer haul. Companion efforts underway to hire or train additional resource specialists may make it possible to do both if the scale is sufficient to make a real difference. We must hope so, though enhancement of the ranger corps needs to take account of the often equal needs of maintenance, history, archaeology, and other staff who do not wear the ranger badge and hat.

However, nowhere in the Vail agenda or elsewhere is there at this time an effort by the new administration to look ahead to the definition of and requirements for what can be a genuine national park *system* for the long term, as outlined and characterized in this book. Most of the policy subjects discussed here, such as the status of affiliated areas and criteria for new parks, will become no easier to address by delay. To be sure, the oft-stated constraints of budgets that will not grow in any spectacular way can serve to dampen hopes for new departures. In a highly competitive budget environment, however, self-preservation can be powerful motivation for change.

In the Hartzog lecture Director Kennedy characterized the climate for change as "buoyant." When the nation's leadership is willing to push for change, there is room for genuine optimism that innovation will be seen as helping the goals of the organization and, by that, gain its willing, even eager, support. We sincerely hope it is true.

Now is, indeed, the time for new beginnings.

NOTES

1. According to a June 8, 1993, Department of the Interior release, NBS was to be staffed initially by 1,180 scientific personnel from the Fish and Wildlife Service, 156 from the National Park Service, 27 from the Bureau of Land Management, and 5 from the Bureau of Reclamation, a total of 1,366. The remainder were support staff.

2. The Bureau of Biological Survey had been transferred by President Roosevelt to the Interior Department from the Department of Agriculture earlier in 1939. The Biological Survey was in turn merged with the Bureau of Fisheries to become the Fish and Wildlife Service later that same year. See

Richard West Sellars, "The Rise and Decline of Ecological Attitudes in National Park Management, 1929–1940, Part 1," in *George Wright Forum* vol. 10, no. 1 (1993): 56.

3. The U.S. Geological Survey was founded in 1881 under the leadership of its first director, John Wesley Powell. A geologist and ethnologist, Powell's notable explorations of the West included a survey by boat of the Grand Canyon in 1869.

4. The *Budget Justifications, F.Y. 1995* sometimes uses the term "Employee Futures" and sometimes "Ranger Futures" (see NPS-99 and NPS-100). The focus does appear to be on the ranger corps. One NPS official characterized the effort as one "to give the Park Service back to the rangers." The statement reflects a long-standing belief among many older rangers that "bean counters" and technocrats in the Washington, D.C., and regional offices have taken away the authority and capacity of the rangers to run the parks. By many measures the statement contains truth, because in times past within memory each superintendent had substantial autonomy, inconsistent supervision, and virtually no systematic performance evaluation.

Early in 1994 four park superintendencies were reclassified in the senior executive service: Yellowstone, Yosemite, Everglades, and Grand Canyon NPs. Also elevated to SES was the job supervising planning for the Presidio, the large defunct army base in San Francisco that is in the process of becoming part of the national park system. In addition, the 1995 budget includes $12.7 million to upgrade 2,244 permanent park ranger positions "approximately two grades per position to make the grades more in line with comparable occupations at the federal and state level." (*Budget Justifications, F.Y. 1995:* NPS-100).

5. From the 1993 George B. Hartzog, Jr., Lecture at Clemson University, Sept. 15, 1993.

6. The 1995 budget for the National Park Service reflected an *increase* of $45.3 million for operating programs, but reductions of $66.0 million in other activities. The total for all national park system activities was $1.127 billion.

7. See especially chap. 2, "Putting Customers First," in Gore, *From Red Tape to Results.*

8. John Reynolds, named deputy director by Roger Kennedy, has said that "each of us must dedicate ourselves to the mission of the Service as it is defined from Congress, not as we might like it to be. We need to realize and embrace the responsibilities we have been given, not just the ones we personally like. It is not just the grand natural parks, nor is it just the historic or recreation areas that comprise the system" (*Courier* vol. 36, no. 3 [Fall 1991]: 7).

Appendix 1

Units of the National Park System

Class and Unit[a]	Year[b]	How?[c]	Acreage[d]
National Parks (51)			
Acadia (Maine)	1916	P	41,409
Arches (Utah)	1929	P	73,379
Badlands (S.Dak.)	1929	L	243,244
Big Bend (Tex.)	1935	L	802,541
Biscayne (Fla.)	1968	L	173,039
Bryce Canyon (Utah)	1923	P	35,835
Canyonlands (Utah)	1964	L	337,570
Capitol Reef (Utah)	1937	P	241,904
Carlsbad Caverns (N.Mex.)	1923	P	46,755
Channel Islands (Calif.)	1938	P	249,354
Crater Lake (Oreg.)	1902	L	183,224
Denali (Alaska)	1917	L	4,716,726
Dry Tortugas (Fla.)	1935	P	64,700
Everglades (Fla.)	1934	L	1,398,938
Gates of the Arctic (Alaska)	1978	P	7,523,888
Glacier Bay (Alaska)	1925	P	3,225,284
Glacier (Mont.)	1910	L	1,013,572
Grand Canyon (Ariz.)	1893	P	1,218,375
Grand Teton (Wyo.)	1929	L	309,994
Great Basin (Nev.)	1922	P	77,109
Great Smoky Mountains (Tenn., N.C.)	1926	L	520,269
Guadalupe Mountains (Tex.)	1966	L	86,416
Haleakala (Hawaii)	1916	L	28,655
Hawaii Volcanoes (Hawaii)	1916	L	229,177
Hot Springs (Ark.)	1832	P	5,839

Appendix 1, continued

Class and Unit[a]	Year[b]	How?[c]	Acreage[d]
Isle Royale (Mich.)	1931	L	571,790
Katmai (Alaska)	1918	P	3,716,000
Kenai Fjords (Alaska)	1978	P	669,541
Kings Canyon (Calif.)	1890	L	461,901
Kobuk Valley (Alaska)	1978	P	1,750,421
Lake Clark (Alaska)	1978	P	2,636,839
Lassen Volcanic (Calif.)	1907	P	106,372
Mammoth Cave (Ky.)	1926	L	52,419
Mesa Verde (Colo.)	1906	L	52,085
Mount Rainier (Wash.)	1899	L	235,404
NP of American Samoa	1988	L	undetermined
North Cascades (Wash.)	1968	L	504,781
Olympic (Wash.)	1909	P	921,924
Petrified Forest (Ariz.)	1906	P	93,533
Redwood (Calif.)	1968	L	110,132
Rocky Mountain (Colo.)	1915	L	265,200
Sequoia (Calif.)	1890	L	402,503
Shenandoah (Va.)	1926	L	195,382
Theodore Roosevelt (N.Dak.)	1947	L	70,416
Virgin Islands (V.I.)	1956	L	14,689
Voyageurs (Minn.)	1971	L	218,036
Wind Cave (S.Dak.)	1903	L	28,292
Wrangell–St. Elias (Alaska)	1978	P	8,331,604
Yellowstone (Wyo., Idaho, Mont.)	1872	L	2,219,791
Yosemite (Calif.)	1890	L	761,170
Zion (Utah)	1909	P	146,598
			47,384,021

National Preserves (13)

Aniakchak (Alaska)	1978	P	465,603
Bering Land Bridge (Alaska)	1978	P	2,784,960
Big Cypress (Fla.)	1974	L	716,000
Denali (Alaska)	1978	P	1,311,365
Gates of the Arctic (Alaska)	1978	P	948,629
Glacier Bay (Alaska)	1925	P	57,884
Katmai (Alaska)	1918	P	374,000
Lake Clark (Alaska)	1978	P	1,407,293
Noatak (Alaska)	1978	P	6,574,481
Wrangell–St. Elias (Alaska)	1978	P	4,856,721
Yukon–Charley Rivers (Alaska)	1978	P	2,523,509

Timucuan Ecological & Historic Preserve (Fla.)	1988	L	35,000
Big Thicket (Tex.)	1974	L	802,541
			22,155,498

National Reserves (2)

Ebey's Landing NHRes (Wash.)[e]	1978	L	19,000
City of Rocks (Idaho)	1988	L	14,407
			33,407

National Monuments (76)

Agate Fossil Beds (Nebr.)	1965	L	3,055
Alibates Flint Quarries (Tex.)	1965	L	1,371
Aniakchak (Alaska)	1978	P	137,176
Aztec Ruins (N.Mex.)	1923	P	319
Bandelier (N.Mex.)	1916	P	32,737
Black Canyon of the Gunnison (Colo.)	1933	P	20,766
Booker T. Washington (Va.)	1956	L	224
Buck Island Reef (V.I.)	1961	P	880
Cabrillo (Calif.)	1913	P	144
Canyon de Chelly (Ariz.)	1931	L	83,840
Cape Krusenstern (Alaska)	1978	P	659,807
Capulin Volcano (N.Mex.)	1916	P	793
Casa Grande (Ariz.)	1889	L	473
Castillo de San Marcos (Fla.)	1924	P	20
Castle Clinton (N.Y.)	1946	L	1
Cedar Breaks (Utah)	1933	P	6,154
Chiricahua (Ariz.)	1924	P	11,985
Colorado (Colo.)	1911	P	20,454
Congaree Swamp (S.C.)	1976	L	22,200
Craters of the Moon (Idaho)	1924	P	53,545
Death Valley (Calif.)	1933	P	2,067,628
Devils Postpile (Calif.)	1911	P	798
Devils Tower (Wyo.)	1906	P	1,347
Dinosaur (Colo., Utah)	1915	P	211,142
Effigy Mounds (Iowa)	1949	P	1,481
El Malpais (N.Mex.)	1987	L	114,716
El Morro (N.Mex.)	1906	P	1,279
Florissant Fossil Beds (Colo.)	1969	L	5,998
Fort Frederica (Ga.)	1936	L	216
Fort Matanzas (Fla.)	1924	P	228
Ft. McHenry NM & Historic Shrine (Md.)	1925	L	43
Fort Pulaski (Ga.)	1924	P	5,623
Fort Stanwix (N.Y.)	1935	L	16

Appendix 1, continued

Class and Unit[a]	Year[b]	How?[c]	Acreage[d]
Fort Sumter (S.C.)	1948	L	197
Fort Union (N.Mex.)	1954	L	721
Fossil Butte (Wyo.)	1972	L	8,198
George Washington Birthplace (Va.)	1930	L	538
George Washington Carver (Mo.)	1943	L	210
Gila Cliff Dwellings (N.Mex.)	1907	P	533
Grand Portage (Minn.)	1951	P	710
Great Sand Dunes (Colo.)	1932	P	38,662
Hagerman Fossil Beds (Idaho)	1988	L	4,394
Hohokam Pima (Ariz.)	1972	L	1,690
Homestead NM of America (Nebr.)	1936	L	194
Hovenweep (Colo., Utah)	1923	P	785
Jewel Cave (S.Dak.)	1908	P	1,274
John Day Fossil Beds (Oreg.)	1974	L	14,014
Joshua Tree (Calif.)	1936	P	559,953
Lava Beds (Calif.)	1925	P	46,560
Little Bighorn Battlefield (Mont.)	1879	P	765
Montezuma Castle (Ariz.)	1906	P	858
Muir Woods (Calif.)	1908	P	554
Natural Bridges (Utah)	1908	P	7,636
Navajo (Ariz.)	1909	P	360
Ocmulgee (Ga.)	1934	L	683
Oregon Caves (Oreg.)	1909	P	488
Organ Pipe Cactus (Ariz.)	1937	P	330,689
Petroglyph (N.Mex.)	1990	L	5,262
Pinnacles (Calif.)	1908	P	16,265
Pipe Spring (Ariz.)	1923	P	40
Pipestone (Minn.)	1937	L	282
Poverty Point (La.)	1988	L	911
Rainbow Bridge (Utah)	1910	P	160
Russell Cave (Ala.)	1961	P	310
Saguaro (Ariz.)	1933	P	83,574
Salinas Pueblo Missions (N.Mex.)	1909	P	1,077
Scotts Bluff (Nebr.)	1919	P	2,997
Statue of Liberty (N.Y.)	1924	P	58
Sunset Crater Volcano (Ariz.)	1930	P	3,040
Timpanogos Cave (Utah)	1922	P	250
Tonto (Ariz.)	1907	P	1,120
Tuzigoot (Ariz.)	1939	P	801
Walnut Canyon (Ariz.)	1915	P	2,249
White Sands (N.Mex.)	1933	P	143,733

Wupatki (Ariz.)	1924	P	35,253
Yucca House (Colo.)	1919	P	10
			4,844,340

National Historic Sites (71)

Abraham Lincoln Birthplace (Ky.)	1916	L	117
Adams (Mass.)	1946	L	10
Allegheny Portage Railroad (Pa.)	1964	L	1,247
Andersonville (Ga.)	1970	L	476
Andrew Johnson (Tenn.)	1935	L	17
Bent's Old Fort (Colo.)	1960	L	800
Boston African American (Mass.)	1980	L	f
Carl Sandburg Home (N.C.)	1968	L	264
Charles Pinckney (S.C.)	1988	L	25
Chimney Rock (Nebr.)	1956	L	83
Clara Barton (Md.)	1974	L	9
Dorchester Heights (Mass.)	1974	L	g
Edgar Allen Poe (Pa.)	1978	L	1
Edison (N.J.)	1955	P	21
Eisenhower (Pa.)	1967	P	690
Eleanor Roosevelt (N.Y.)	1977	L	181
Eugene O'Neill (Calif.)	1976	L	13
Ford's Theatre (D.C.)	1866	L	< 1
Fort Bowie (Ariz.)	1964	L	1,000
Fort Davis (Tex.)	1961	L	460
Fort Laramie (Wyo.)	1938	P	833
Fort Larned (Kans.)	1964	L	718
Fort Point (Calif.)	1970	L	29
Fort Raleigh (N.C.)	1941	P	157
Fort Scott (Kans.)	1965	P	17
Fort Smith (Ark., Okla.)	1961	L	75
Fort Union Trading Post (N.Dak., Mont.)	1966	L	442
Fort Vancouver (Wash.)	1948	L	209
Frederick Douglass (D.C.)	1962	L	9
Frederick Law Olmsted (Mass.)	1979	L	2
Friendship Hill (Pa.)	1978	L	675
Golden Spike (Utah)	1957	P	2,735
Grant-Kohrs Ranch (Mont.)	1972	L	1,499
Hampton (Md.)	1948	L	62
Harry S Truman (Mo.)	1983	L	< 1
Herbert Hoover (Iowa)	1965	L	187
Home of Franklin D. Roosevelt (N.Y.)	1944	P	290
Hopewell Furnace (Pa.)	1938	P	848
Hubbell Trading Post (Ariz.)	1965	L	160
James A. Garfield (Ohio)	1980	L	8

Appendix 1, continued

Class and Unit[a]	Year[b]	How?[c]	Acreage[d]
Jimmy Carter (Ga.)	1987	L	[h]
John Fitzgerald Kennedy (Mass.)	1967	L	< 1
John Muir (Calif.)	1964	L	339
Knife River Indian Villages (N.Dak.)	1974	L	1,293
Lincoln Home (Ill.)	1971	L	12
Longfellow (Mass.)	1972	L	2
Maggie L. Walker (Va.)	1978	L	1
Martin Luther King, Jr. (Ga.)	1980	L	23
Martin Van Buren (N.Y.)	1974	L	40
Mary McLeod Bethune Council House (D.C.)[i]	1992	L	undetermined
Ninety-Six (S.C.)	1976	L	989
Palo Alto Battlefield (Tex.)	1978	L	50
Pennsylvania Avenue (D.C.)	1965	P	[1]
Puukohola Heiau (Hawaii)	1972	L	80
Sagamore Hill (N.Y.)	1962	L	83
Saint-Gaudens (N.H.)	1964	L	148
Saint Paul's Church (N.Y.)	1978	L	6
Salem Maritime (Mass.)	1938	P	9
San Juan (P.R.)	1949	P	75
Saugus Iron Works (Mass.)	1968	L	9
Springfield Armory (Mass.)	1974	L	55
Steamtown (Pa.)	1986	L	62
Theodore Roosevelt Birthplace (N.Y.)	1962	L	< 1
Theodore Roosevelt Inaugural (N.Y.)	1966	L	1
Thomas Stone (Md.)	1978	L	328
Tuskegee Institute (Ala.)	1974	L	74
Ulysses S. Grant (Mo.)[k]	1989	L	??
Vanderbilt Mansion (N.Y.)	1940	P	212
Weir Farm (Conn.)	1990	L	177
Whitman Mission (Wash.)	1936	L	98
William Howard Taft (Ohio)	1969	L	3
			18,468

National Historical Parks (32)

Appomattox Court House (Va.)	1930	L	1,325
Boston (Mass.)	1974	L	41
Chaco Culture (N.Mex.)	1907	P	33,974
Chesapeake and Ohio Canal (Md., D.C., Va.)	1938	P	20,781
Colonial (Va.)	1930	L	9,327

Cumberland Gap (Ky., Va., Tenn.)	1940	L	20,274
George Rogers Clark (Ind.)	1966	L	26
Harpers Ferry (W.Va., Md., Va.)	1944	L	2,238
Hopewell Culture NHP (Ohio)	1923	P	270
Independence (Pa.)	1948	L	45
Jean Lafitte NHP and Pres (La.)	1907	P	20,020
Kalaupapa (Hawaii)	1980	L	10,779
Kaloko-Honokohau (Hawaii)	1978	L	1,161
Kino Mission (Ariz.)	1908	P	17
Klondike Gold Rush (Alaska, Wash.)	1976	L	13,191
Lowell (Mass.)	1978	L	136
Lyndon B. Johnson (Tex.)	1969	L	1,571
Minute Man (Mass.)	1959	P	750
Morristown (N.J.)	1933	L	1,671
Natchez (Miss.)	1988	L	1
Nez Perce (Idaho)	1965	L	2,108
Pecos (N.Mex.)	1965	L	365
Pu'uhonua o Honaunau (Hawaii)	1955	L	182
San Antonio Missions (Tex.)	1978	L	493
San Francisco Maritime (Calif.)	1988	L	50
San Juan Island (Wash.)	1966	L	1,752
Saratoga (N.Y.)	1938	L	3,393
Sitka (Alaska)	1910	P	107
Valley Forge (Pa.)	1976	L	3,468
War in the Pacific (Guam)	1978	L	1,960
Women's Rights (N.Y.)	1980	L	6
Zuni-Cibola (N.Mex.)	1988	L	800
			151,633

National Memorials (26)

Arkansas Post (Ark.)	1960	L	389
Arlington House, The Robert E. Lee Memorial (Va.)	1925	L	28
Chamizal (Tex.)	1966	L	55
Coronado (Ariz.)	1941	L	4,750
De Soto (Fla.)	1948	L	27
Federal Hall (N.Y.)	1939	P	< 1
Fort Caroline (Fla.)	1950	L	138
Fort Clatsop (Oreg.)	1958	L	125
General Grant (N.Y.)	1958	L	< 1
Hamilton Grange (N.Y.)	1962	L	< 1
Jefferson National Expansion Memorial (Mo.)	1854	L	191
John F. Kennedy Center for the Performing Arts (D.C.)	1958	L	18
Johnstown Flood (Pa.)	1964	L	164

Appendix 1, continued

Class and Unit[a]	Year[b]	How?[c]	Acreage[d]
Lincoln Memorial (D.C.)	1911	L	110
Lincoln Boyhood (Ind.)	1962	L	200
Lyndon B. Johnson Memorial Grove on the Potomac (Va.)	1973	L	17
Mount Rushmore (S.Dak.)	1925	L	1,278
Perry's Victory and International Peace Memorial (Ohio)	1936	P	25
Roger Williams (R.I.)	1965	L	5
Thaddeus Kosciuszko (Pa.)	1972	L	< 1
Theodore Roosevelt Island (D.C.)	1932	L	89
Thomas Jefferson Memorial (D.C.)	1934	L	18
USS Arizona Memorial (Hawaii)	1980	L	m
Vietnam Veterans Memorial (D.C.)	1980	L	2
Washington Monument (D.C.)	1848	L	106
Wright Brothers (N.C.)	1927	L	431
			7,949

National Recreation Areas (18)			
Amistad Recreation Area (Tex.)	1965	L	57,292
Bighorn Canyon (Mont., Wyo.)	1966	L	120,296
Chattahoochee River (Ga.)	1978	L	9,265
Chickasaw (Okla.)	1902	L	9,522
Coulee Dam (Wash.)	1946	L	100,390
Curecanti (Colo.)	1965	L	42,114
Cuyahoga Valley (Ohio)	1974	L	32,460
Delaware Water Gap (Pa., N.J.)	1965	L	66,652
Gateway (N.Y., N.J.)	1972	L	26,311
Gauley River (W.Va.)	1988	L	undetermined
Glen Canyon (Utah, Ariz.)	1958	L	1,236,880
Golden Gate (Calif.)	1972	L	73,080
Lake Chelan (Wash.)	1968	L	61,889
Lake Mead (Nev., Ariz.)	1936	L	1,495,666
Lake Meredith (Tex.)	1965	L	44,978
Ross Lake (Wash.)	1968	L	117,574
Santa Monica Mountains (Calif.)	1978	L	150,050
Whiskeytown-Shasta-Trinity (Calif.)	1965	L	42,503
			3,686,923

National Battlefields (11)

Antietam (Md.)	1890	L	3,244
Big Hole (Mont.)	1910	P	656
Cowpens (S.C.)	1929	L	842
Fort Donelson (Tenn.)	1928	L	537
Fort Necessity (Pa.)	1931	L	903
Monocacy (Md.)	1934	L	1,647
Petersburg (Va.)	1926	L	2,735
Stones River (Tenn.)	1927	L	331
Tupelo (Miss.)	1929	L	1
Wilson's Creek (Mo.)	1960	L	1,750
Yorktown (Va.)	1930	L	n

12,772

National Seashores (10)

Assateague Island (Md., Va.)	1965	L	39,631
Canaveral (Fla.)	1975	L	57,662
Cape Cod (Mass.)	1961	L	43,557
Cape Hatteras (N.C.)	1937	L	30,319
Cape Lookout (N.C.)	1966	L	28,415
Cumberland Island (Ga.)	1972	L	36,415
Fire Island (N.Y.)	1964	L	19,579
Gulf Islands (Fla., Miss.)	1971	L	65,817
Padre Island (Tex.)	1962	L	130,697
Point Reyes (Calif.)	1962	L	71,047

597,096

National Lakeshores (4)

Apostle Islands (Wis.)	1970	L	69,372
Indiana Dunes (Ind.)	1966	L	12,857
Pictured Rocks (Mich.)	1966	L	72,899
Sleeping Bear Dunes (Mich.)	1970	L	71,132

227,244

National Military Parks (9)

Chickamauga and Chattanooga (Ga., Tenn.)	1890	P	8,106
Fredericksburg and Spottsylvania County Battlefields Memorial (Va.)	1927	P	9,327
Gettysburg (Pa.)	1895	P	3,896
Guilford Courthouse (N.C.)	1917	P	220
Horseshoe Bend (Ala.)	1956	L	2,040

Appendix 1, continued

Class and Unit[a]	Year[b]	How?[c]	Acreage[d]
Kings Mountain (S.C.)	1931	P	3,945
Pea Ridge (Ark.)	1956	L	4,300
Shiloh (Tenn.)	1894	P	3,838
Vicksburg (Miss.)	1899	P	1,620
			34,047
National Wild and Scenic Rivers and Riverways (9)			
Alagnak (Alaska)	1980	L	24,038
Bluestone (W.Va.)	1988	L	undetermined
Delaware (Pa., N.J.)	1978	P	1,973
Kobuk (Alaska)	1980	L	o
Lower Saint Croix (Wis., Minn.)	1972	L	9,475
Obed (Tenn.)	1976	L	5,077
Rio Grande (Tex.)	1978	L	9,600
Saint Croix (Wis., Minn.)	1968	L	67,434
Salmon (Alaska)	1980	L	p
			292,597
National Rivers (7)			
Big South Fork NR and RA (Tenn., Ky.)	1974	L	122,960
Buffalo (Ark.)	1972	L	94,219
Delaware National Scenic River (Pa., N.J.)	1978	L	1,973
Mississippi National River and Recreation Area (Minn.)	1988	L	undetermined
Missouri National Recreational River (S.Dak., Nebr.)	1978	L	undetermined
New River Gorge (W.Va.)	1978	L	62,663
Niobrara National Scenic Riverway (Nebr.)	1991	L	undetermined
			360,630
Parkways (4)			
Blue Ridge (N.C., Va.)	1933	L	85,955
George Washington Memorial (Va., Md.)	1930	L	7,131
John D. Rockefeller, Jr., Memorial (Wyo.)	1972	L	23,777
Natchez Trace (Miss., Ala., Tenn.)	1934	L	51,756
			168,618

National Battlefield Parks (3)

Kennesaw Mountain (Ga.)	1917	L	2,884
Manassas (Va.)	1940	P	5,114
Richmond (Va.)	1936	L	769
			8,767

National Scenic Trails (3)

Appalachian (Maine to Ga.)	1968	P	161,208
Natchez Trace (Ga., Ala., Tenn.)	1983	L	10,995
Potomac Heritage (Md., D.C., Va., Pa.)	1983	L	undetermined
			172,203

International Historic Sites (1)

Saint Croix Island (Maine)	1949	L	35

National Battlefield Sites (1)

Brices Cross Roads (Miss.)	1929	L	1

Other (11)

Catoctin Mountain Park (Md.)	1936	P	5,770
Constitution Gardens (D.C.)	1978	L	52
Fort Washington Park (D.C.)	1930	P	341
Greenbelt Park (Md.)	1950	P	1,176
National Capital Parks (D.C.)q	1790	L	6,468
National Mall (D.C.)	1790	L	146
Piscataway Park (Md.)	1961	L	4,263
Prince William Forest Park (Va.)	1936	P	18,572
Rock Creek Park (D.C.)	1890	L	1,754
White House (D.C.)	1790	L	18
Wolf Trap Farm Park for the Performing Arts (Va.)	1966	L	130
			40,121

Total acreage	approx. 80,000,000

Sources: *The National Parks: Index 1989;* computer update from the NPS Office of Public Affairs as of September 1991; "Compilation of National Park Service Laws of 102d Congress" compiled by Dorothy J. Whitehead, National Park Service, Office of Legislation, May 11, 1993.

a. Classification and unit name as of September 1991, unless otherwise indicated.
b. The year shown is the earliest year major action was taken to protect an area and may have involved only a part of what later became a unit of the system.

c. Units created by an act of Congress are labeled "L"; those created by a presidential proclamation, with a "P."

d. Acreages are as of December 31, 1988, unless otherwise indicated, and generally include all land within the exterior boundaries of a park unit. Totals may, therefore, include other federal, state, local, or private lands, some of which may ultimately become part of the park, some not, depending on the terms of the specific park legislation, the availability of land acquisition funds, near-term priorities, and other factors.

e. Reclassified a unit of the system from status as an affiliated area after publication of the *Index 1989*.

f. Acreage undetermined. Contains 15 pre–Civil War black history structures, linked by the 1.6-mile Black Heritage Trail.

g. Part of Boston NHP that includes Bunker Hill, Old North Church, Paul Revere House, Faneuil Hall, Old State House, Old South Meeting House, and part of the Charlestown Navy Yard, including the *USS Cassin Young*, the *USS Constitution*, and the *USS Constitution* Museum. Total acreage: 41.

h. Acreage undetermined. Site includes President Carter's residence, boyhood home, high school, and the railroad depot.

i. Added to the system by an act of Congress (105 STAT. 1652) subsequent to publication of the *Index 1989*.

j. Acreage undetermined. The historic district runs from the Capitol to the White House.

k. Added to the system after publication of *Index 1989* by Act of Congress, approved October 2, 1989 (103 STAT. 677.)

l. Acreage undetermined; includes Melrose, a historic planter's home.

m. Owned by the U.S. Navy.

n. Acreage included in Colonial NHP.

o. Acreage included in Gates of the Arctic NP & NPres, length 110 miles.

p. Acreage included in Kobuk Valley NP, length 70 miles.

q. The National Capital Parks were part of the original action in 1790 to establish a permanent National Capital, beginning with 17 public reservations purchased in the early years, and now made up of some 300 sites in Washington, D.C.

Appendix 2

Areas Affiliated with the National Park System

1. American Memorial Park, Saipan; recreational park and memorial honoring those who died in the Marianas campaign during World War II; authorized 1978; 133 acres, all nonfederal.

2. Benjamin Franklin NMem, statue in the Rotunda of the Franklin Institute, Philadelphia, Pa.; designated 1972; less than 1 acre, all nonfederal.

3. Blackstone River Valley National Historic Corridor; forty miles of river and canals and their associated mills, villages, and transportation networks from Worcester, Mass. to Providence, R.I.; established 1986; 263,901 acres, all nonfederal.

4. Chicago Portage NHS, Ill.; part of the portage between Lake Michigan and the Mississippi River; designated 1952; 91 acres, all nonfederal.

5. Chimney Rock NHS, Nebr.; 500-foot feature above the Platte River on the Oregon Trail; designated 1956; 83 acres, all nonfederal.

6. David Berger NMem, Cleveland, Ohio; honoring 11 Israeli athletes assassinated at the 1972 Olympics; authorized 1980; less than 1 acre, all nonfederal.

7. Delaware and Lehigh Navigation Canal National Heritage Corridor, Pa.; two nineteenth-century canals and their associated railroads; designated 1988; acreage undetermined but includes a state park and other state, county, local and private owners.

8. Ebey's Landing NHRes, on Whidbey Island, Wash.; authorized 1978; acreage undetermined. (Reclassified a unit of the system subsequent to publication of the *Index 1989*. See chap. 3).

9. Father Marquette NMem, in Straits State Park, Mich.; authorized 1975; 52 acres, all nonfederal.

10. Gloria Dei (Old Swedes') Church NHS, in Philadelphia, Pa.; designated 1942; 3.71 acres, 2.08 federal, 1.63 nonfederal.

11. Green Springs Historic District, in Louisa County, Va.; an "unmarred landscape" of fine rural manor houses and related buildings; declared a National Historic Landmark in 1974; 14,000 acres, for which NPS holds preservation easements on about half.

12. Historic Camden, S.C.; site of two Revolutionary War battles; authorized 1982; 105 acres, all nonfederal.

13. Ice Age NST, Wis.; a 1,000-mile trail linking six of the nine units of Ice Age National Scientific Reserve; authorized 1980; approximately 450 miles open to public hiking, all nonfederal.

14. Ice Age National Scientific Reserve, Wis.; features nationally significant features of continental glaciation; authorized 1964; 32,500 acres, all nonfederal.

15. Iditarod NHT, Alaska; a 2,037-mile trail from Seward to Nome, developed during the gold rush at the turn of the century; authorized 1978; on and off federal lands, acreage undetermined.

16. Illinois and Michigan Canal National Heritage Corridor, Ill. and Mich.; canal and railroad corridor; designated 1984; 322,000 acres, all nonfederal.

17. International Peace Garden, N.Dak. (and Manitoba, Canada); commemorates peaceful relations between the U.S. and Canada; originated by North Dakota 1931; 2,330 acres, all nonfederal.

18. Jamestown NHS, Va.; part of the first permanent English settlement in North America, adjoins Colonial NHP; designated 1940; 21 acres, all nonfederal.

19. Lewis and Clark NHT, commemorates the 1804–6 Lewis and Clark Expedition; authorized 1978; some 4,500 miles of water routes, planned trails, and marked highways; acreage undetermined.

20. McLoughlin House NHS, Oreg.; home of Dr. John McLoughlin, chief factor of Fort Vancouver and referred to as the "Father of Oregon"; designated 1941; less than 1 acre, all nonfederal.

21. Mary McLeod Bethune Council House NHS, Washington, D.C.; headquarters of the National Council of Negro Women; designated 1982; nonfederal. (Made part of the national park system by an act of Congress subsequent to publication of *Index 1989*.)

22. Mormon Pioneer NHT, follows the 1,300-mile route of Brigham Young from Nauvoo, Ill., to Salt Lake City, Utah; authorized 1978; an auto tour has been marked approximating the route; all nonfederal.

23. North Country NST, some 3,200 miles from Crown Point, N.Y., to the Missouri River and Lake Sakakawea in N.Dak.; authorized 1980; about 1,400 miles open to public; mixed ownerships.

24. Oregon NHT, 2,000-mile route from Independence, Mo., to Portland, Oreg.; authorized 1978; not developed for public use.

25. Overmountain Victory NHT, 272-mile route of revolutionary patriots through parts of Va., Tenn., and N.C. to Kings Mountain, S.C.; authorized 1980; acreage undetermined.

26. Pinelands NRes, N.J.; the largest undeveloped tract on the eastern seaboard created to test intergovernmental and private preservation; authorized 1978; over 1 million acres, mixed ownerships.

27. Red Hill Patrick Henry NMem, Va.; the law office and grave of Patrick Henry at the site of his last home; authorized 1986; 117 acres, all nonfederal.

28. Roosevelt Campobello International Park, located in New Brunswick,

Canada, the summer home of President Franklin D. Roosevelt; the first jointly administered international park; established 1964; 2,722 acres, all nonfederal.

29. Santa Fe NHT, Mo. to N.Mex., established 1987, all nonfederal.

30. Sewall-Belmont House NHS, Washinton, D.C.; headquarters of the National Women's Party; authorized 1974; less than 1 acre, all nonfederal.

31. Touro Synagogue NHS, in Newport, R.I.; example of colonial religious architecture and an active congregation; designated 1946; less than 1 acre, all nonfederal.

32. Trail of Tears NHT, N.C. to Okla., established 1987, all nonfederal.

Sources: *The National Parks: Shaping the System,* 112–13; *The National Parks: Index 1989.*

Appendix 3

Thematic Representation in the National Park System

Natural History (Extract)

Cascade Range
Landforms of the Present
  Mountain Systems
    Crater Lake National Park
    Lassen Volcanic National Park
    Mount Rainier National Park
    North Cascades National Park
    *Mount Shasta, Calif.
  Works of Volcanism
    Crater Lake National Park
    Lassen Volcanic National Park
    Mount Rainier National Park
    *Burney Falls, Calif.
    *Mount Shasta, Calif.
  Hot Water Phenomena
    Crater Lake NP
    Lassen Volcanic NP
  Mount Rainier NP
  **

Sculpture of the Land
  Crater Lake National Park
  Lassen Volcanic National Park
  Mount Rainier National Park
  North Cascade NPS Service Complex
  *Burney Falls, Calif.
  *Crown Point, Oreg.
Eolian Landforms[a]
  *Burney Falls, Calif.
  *Crown Point, Oreg.
  ***

River Systems and Lakes
  Crater Lake National Park
  Lassen Volcanic National Park
  Mount Rainier National Park
  North Cascades National Park
Works of Glaciers
  Crater Lake National Park
  Mount Rainier National Park
  North Cascades National Park
  **

[etc.]

History and Prehistory (Extract)

XV. Communications
  A. Written Word (Newspapers and Periodicals)
    *Hearst San Simeon Estate, Calif.
    *H. L. Mencken House, Md.
    *New York Amsterdam News Building, N.Y.
    *Tampa Bay Hotel, Fla.
    ***
  B. Mail Service (Overland, Water, and Air Routes)
    Fort Bowie National Historic Site, Ariz.
    Fort Laramie National Historic Site, Wyo.
    *William Aiken House and associated railroad structures, S.C.
    *Fort Churchill, Nev.
    *Fort Ruby, Nev.
    *Hollenburg Pony Express Station, Kans.
    *Patee House, Mo.
    *Pony Express Terminal (B. F. Hastings Building), Calif.
  C. Telegraph and Telephone
    *Bell Telephone Laboratories, N.Y.
    *The Factory, Speedwell Village, N.J.
    *Fort Churchill, Nev.
    *Fort Ruby, Nev.
    *Joseph Henry House, N.J.
    *Pony Express Terminal (B. F. Hastings Building), Calif.
    *Volta Bureau, D.C.
    ***
  D. Radio
    Cape Cod National Seashore (Marconi's Wireless Station), Mass.
    *Reginald A. Fessenden House, Pa.
  E. Television
    **
    ***
  F. Post-World War II Electronic

 **
 ***
 G. Spoken Word (Oratory and Public Speaking)
 Gettysburg National Military Park, Pa.
 Red Hill, Patrick Henry National Memorial, Pa. (an affiliated area)
 *St. John's Episcopal Church, Va.
 *Westminster College Gymnasium, Mo.

 [etc.]

Key: *   = registered Natural or Historic Landmark[b] (not in federal ownership)
   ** = not represented by a Registered Natural or Historic Landmark
   *** = not represented in the national park system

Sources: *Natural History in the National Park System and on the National Registry of Natural Landmarks,* Natural Resource Report NPS/NR/NRTR-90/03, (National Park Service, 9/1990): 35, 74; *History and Prehistory in the National Park System and the National Historic Landmarks Program* (National Park Service, Washington, D.C., 1987), II-10, II-11, III-24, and II-25.

a. Sand or rock formations formed by wind.
b. Registered Natural Landmarks are designated by the secretary of the Interior from nominations by the director of the National Park Service. They recognize and encourage the long-term protection of "the best remaining examples of ecological and geological components of the nation's natural heritage." The National Registry of Natural Landmarks contained 587 sites at the end of 1993, though the program was temporarily suspended in 1989 pending a formal review. It was anticipated new regulations would be completed in 1994. The National Historic Landmarks program garners about 50 properties annually for designation by the secretary. As of 1994, there were about 2,100 properties listed.

Appendix 4

Areas No Longer Part of the National Park System

1. Atlanta Campaign NHS (Ga.); 1944–50; five sites, fifteen acres. All five sites are managed to commemorate General Sherman's Atlanta Campaign: one part of a larger state historic site, one by the Ga. State Patrol, and three by the Ga. Department of Transportation.

2. Camp Blount Tablets NM (Tenn.); 1930–44; acreage unknown. Site of an encampment by Andrew Jackson's troops in 1813 and a second encampment by troops enroute to the Second Seminole War in 1836. Originally under War Department; moved to NPS in 1933, but nothing was ever done with the site. Site abolished in 1944.

3. Castle Pinckney NM (S.C.); 1924–56; 3.5 acres. Under War Department until transferred to NPS in 1933. Closed to public in 1935; sold in 1958 to South Carolina Ports Authority for $12,000. Now owned by the Sons of Confederate Veterans.

4. Chattanooga NCem (Ga.); 1867–1944. Transferred to NPS, 1933; to War Department, 1944; now under the Veterans Administration. Cemetery is still active.

5. Father Millet Cross NM (N.Y.); 1925–40; 1 acre. Part of Old Fort Niagara State Historic Site.

6. Flaming Gorge NRA (Colo.); 1962–68. Began as a NRA administered jointly by the Forest Service and NPS. Divested to reduce areas jointly administered by the two agencies. See Hartzog, *Battling for the National Parks,* chap. 10.

7. Fossil Cycad NM (S.Dak.); 1922–56; 320 acres. Set aside in 1922 to protect a deposit of fossil cycads, a palm-like evergreen bearing large cones and said to be the most primitive form of seed-bearing plants from the Permian Period. The site was never afforded any on-site protection and between 1922 and the 1950s amateur and professional fossil hunters cleaned the site of fossils. Lacking an obvious reason for existence, the site was returned to the public domain in 1956. Today the lands remain under the Bureau of Land Management. According to BLM, "due to the high resource values on that tract, disposal is unlikely." The land "is leased for grazing and has been di-

vided (north and south) by a highway." The former NM status is not marked, nor are the lands available for public use. No visible fossils remain.

8. Georgia O'Keeffe NHS (N.Mex.); 1980–83; three acres. Authorized but then deauthorized before it was formally established due to local opposition generated by a draft plan for the site. Now owned by O'Keeffe Foundation.

9. Holy Cross NM (Colo.); 1929–50; 1,392 acres. Created to protect a "seasonal cross formation resulting from snow deposits in a 1,500-foot vertical crevasse and 750-foot horizontal ledges," above 13,000-feet elevation. The feature remains, now part of Holy Cross Wilderness in the White River National Forest.

10. Lake Texoma NRA (Tex.); 1946–49; acreage unknown. Now two state parks, Lake Texoma and Eisenhower. Public access around the lake is a small fraction of the original NRA.

11. Lewis & Clark Cavern NM (Mont.); 1908–37. A State park.

12. Mackinac NP (Mich.); 1875–95; about 1,000 acres. Mackinac was the second National Park in the U.S., under the War Department—the same as Yellowstone NP. The debate in Congress on the proposal advanced by Senator Thomas W. Ferry, who was born on the island, paralleled the earlier history of Yellowstone. The enabling legislation is almost identical. The park was transferred to the State of Michigan in 1895 because the Army proposed to abandon the island's fort, thereby leaving no one to care for the park. Though often characterized today as a site obviously unsuited to be a National Park because of developments that had already taken place on the island, it is interesting to note that there were only thirty-five homes on the island in 1895.[a] The then-existing hotels were not unlike those later developed in Yellowstone, Yosemite, and Grand Canyon NPs. Today the state park is about the same size as in 1895.

13. Mar-A-Lago NHS (Fla.); 1972–80; 17 acres. See chap. 5.

14. Millerton Lake NRA (Calif.); 1945–57; 11,605 acres. Now Millerton Lake [State] Recreation Area.

15. National Visitor Center (D.C.); 1968–81. Washington, D.C.'s, Union Station. Originally planned to become a place to meet and greet visitors to the Nation's Capital, the conversion of the old railroad station was plagued by insufficient funding, unrealistic planning, and bureaucratic squabbles. The concept was abandoned and the station redeveloped privately—and successfully. Again used as a railroad station the site now contains a large mall, theaters, and shops on the D.C. subway system. Major architectural and historic features of the original building were restored.

16. New Echota Marker NM (Ga.); 1933–50; 1 acre. The marker, a granite pillar some twenty-five feet high, was moved about one-quarter mile to the site of the Cherokee National Capitol (1819–38). The original one-acre site adjoins a golf course; it is still owned by the State of Georgia.

17. Old Kasaan NM, (Alaska); 1916–55; 39.7 acres. The monument was originally set aside to protect a collection of totem poles of the Haida Indians. Transferred to NPS in 1933, no development took place at the site between that year and 1955, when it was returned to the forest service, Ton-

gass National Forest. In about 1970 several of the totem poles in condition to be moved were taken to a "Totem Heritage Center" in Ketchikan. In 1974 the lands were selected by the Kavilco Corporation, an Alaska native village, under terms of the Alaska Native Claims Settlement Act of 1971. In 1979 title passed to Kavilco.

18. Papago-Saguaro NM, (Ariz.); 1914–30; 2,050 acres. A city and state park and Arizona National Guard installation.

19. Santa Rosa Island NM (Fla.); 1939–46; 9,500 acres. Transferred to Escambia County (Fla.). The area was subsequently included in Gulf Islands NS in 1971.

20. Shadow Mountain NRA (Colo.); 1952–78; 19,004 acres. Now Arapaho NRA, managed by U.S. Forest Service.

21. Shoshone Caverns NM (Wyo.); 1909–54; 210 acres. Transferred to the City of Cody, the site was returned to the federal government in 1978 because of failure of the city to develop or use the site. The land reverted to the public domain, under the jurisdiction of the Bureau of Land Management. BLM removed all traces of the "Show Cave," put a gate on the entrance, and now limits public use to people having a special caving permit. The site was renamed Spirit Mountain Caverns.

22. Sully's Hill NP (N.Dak.); 1909–31; 960 acres. Long maligned as a National Park[b] for its lack of spectacular scenery, Sully's Hill was transferred in 1931 to the Department of Agriculture and renamed a National Game Preserve. Today it is administered by the U.S. Fish and Wildlife Service.

23. Verendrye NM (N.Dak.); 1917–56; 253 acres. Much of the original NM was flooded by a reservoir. A state marker exists today. Set aside originally to mark the spot French explorer Sieur de la Verendrye "first saw beyond the Missouri River" in 1738, later opinion suggested the site was inaccurately located.

24. Wheeler NM (Colo.); 1908–50; 300 acres. Set aside to preserve uniquely sculptured volcanic dust formations, the area never received on-site protection, even after transfer to the National Park Service in 1933. Totally surrounded by the Rio Grande National Forest the NM was abolished in 1950 and the lands transferred to the Forest Service. The lands were withdrawn from entry under the mining laws, enlarged to 640 acres, and renamed Wheeler Geologic Area.

25. Oak Mountain NRDA (Ala.); 1936–42; 8,000 acres. A state park, now 9,940 acres.

26. Mendocino Woodlands NRDA (Calif.); 1936–42; 6,000 acres. Now Jackson State Forest.

27. Hard Labor Creek NRDA (Ga.); 1936–42; 4,500 acres. A state park.

28. Alexander Stephens Memorial NRDA (Ga.); 1936–42; 900 acres. A state park.

29. Pine Mountain NRDA (Ga.); 1936–42; 3,500 acres. Now Franklin D. Roosevelt State Park.

30. Pere Marquette NRDA (Ill.); 1936–42; 3,000 acres. Now part of 8,000-acre Pere Marquette State Park.

31. Versailles NRDA (Ind.); 1936–42; 6,000 acres. A state park.

32. Winemac NRDA (Ind.); 1936–42; 6,500 acres. A state park.

33. Otter Creek NRDA (Ken.); 1936–42; 8,000 acres. Actual acquisition was about 2,500 acres. Transferred to state then to the City of Louisville in 1947. Now about 3,000 acres.

34. Camden Hills, NRDA (Maine); 1936–42; 7,000 acres. A state park. Actual acreage conveyed to the State was 4,965 in 1948. Now 5,535 acres.

35. Waterloo NRDA (Mich.); 1936–42; 13,000 acres. Renamed Waterloo Recreation Area; part of state park system.

36. Yankee Springs NRDA (Mich.); 1936–42; 4,000 acres. Yankee Springs Recreation Area; part of state park system.

37. St. Croix NRDA (Minn.); 1936–42; 20,500 acres. Part of St. Croix State Park of some 34,070 acres.

38. Lake of the Ozarks NRDA (Mo.); 1936–42; 14,500 acres. A state park, now 17,213 acres.

39. Cuivre River NRDA (Mo.); 1936–42; 5,500 acres. A state park, now 6,271 acres.

40. Montserrat NRDA (Mo.); 1936–42; 5,000 acres. Actual acreage conveyed was 3,341; now 3,549 acres. Renamed Knob Noster State Park.

41. Bear Brook NRDA (N.H.); 1936–42; 5,500 acres. A state park, about 10,000 acres.

42. Crabtree Creek NRDA (N.C.); 1936–42; 6,000 acres. Crabtree Creek State Park was combined with Reedy Creek State Park in 1966. The then-combined park was renamed William B. Umstead State Park, now 5,337 acres.

43. Lake Murray NRDA (Okla.); 1936–42; 3,000 acres. A state park, now 12,496 acres.

44. Silver Creek NRDA (Oreg.); 1936–42; 10,800 acres. Acreage conveyed was 5,990. A state park now 8,706 acres.

45. Raccoon Creek NRDA (Pa.); 1936–42; 5,000 acres. A state park, now 7,572 acres.

46. French Creek NRDA (Pa.); 1936–42; 7,000 acres. A state park, now 7,344 acres.

47. Laurel Hill NRDA (Pa.); 1936–42; 3,000 acres. A state park, now 3,935 acres.

48. Blue Knob NRDA (Pa.); 1936–42; 8,000 acres. A state park, now 5,614 acres.

49. Hickory Run NRDA (Pa.); 1936–42; 13,500 acres. A state park, now 15,500 acres.

50. Beach Pond NRDA (R.I.); 1936–42; 2,200 acres. Now part of Arcadia Management Area, some 75 square miles including parts of five towns. Within the Arcadia area the state owns about 15,000 acres, including the Beach Pond NRDA lands.

51. Cheraw NRDA (S.C.); 1936–42; 4,500 acres. A state park.

52. Waysides (S.C.); 1936–42; 300 acres in seven counties. Wayside in Greenville County renamed Wildcat Wayside, now 300 acres. Other sites remain under the jurisdiction of the state.

53. Kings Mountain NRDA (S.C.); 1936–42; 10,500 acres. A state park.

54. Custer Park NRDA (S.Dak.); 1936–42; 20,500 acres. A state park, now 73,000 acres.

55. Montgomery Bell NRDA (Tenn.); 1936–42; 4,000 acres. A state park, now 3,782 acres.

56. Shelby Forest Park NRDA; (Tenn.); 1936–42; 10,000 acres. Renamed Meeman-Shelby State Park.

57. Falls Creek Falls NRDA (Tenn.); 1936–42; 7,500 acres. A state park, renamed Falls Creek Falls State Resort Park.

58. Swift Creek NRDA (Va.); 1936–42; 7,500 acres. A state park.

59. Waysides (Va.); 1936–42; 384 acres in six counties. All transferred to Virginia Department of Transportation. Four parcels have been further transferred to local jurisdictions for receational uses. DOT still owns two of the tracts, one described as "closed," the other under negotiation for transfer to Pulaski County.

60. Lake Guernsey NRDA (Wyo.); 1936–42; 1,900 acres. Guernsey State Park, 6,538 acres.

61. St. Thomas NHS (Virgin Islands); 1960–75; acreage unknown. Fort Christian, built in 1671–80, is the oldest remaining building in the Virgin Islands. Located in downtown Charlotte Amalie, the building was used to house the fire department and civil defense activities of the Virgin Islands government. Though created in 1960 no development took place and the site was transferred to the Virgin Islands government in 1975.

62. White Plains National Battlefield Site (N.Y.); 1926–56; four sites, acreage unknown. Commemorates the Battle of White Plains, involving the forces of George Washington and British General Howe, between October 28 and November 1, 1776. No development ever took place and the site was abolished in 1956. A private group was formed to identify and preserve as many sites associated with the battle as possible. A nine-mile Heritage Trail remains, voluntarily maintained.

Total: approximately 290,000 acres in 28 states

Much of the original research on the sites listed in this Appendix was done by park enthusiast Alan K. Hogenauer, the results of which were published in Hogenauer, "Gone But Not Forgotten." Quotations are from that source, unless otherwise indicated. Hogenauer's data have been updated and supplemented. The years shown are the one in which the unit was created and the one in which the unit was divested or otherwise dropped from the list of national park system areas.

a. Widder, Keith R., *Mackinac National Park, 1875–1895*, Reports in Mackinac History and Archeology, No. 4 (Lansing: Mackinac Island State Park Commission, 1975): 42.

b. There is doubt whether Sullys Hill Park was ever intended to be a National Park. Both an enabling Congressional resolution and the Presidential Proclamation in 1909 omitted the word "National." In later usage, however, the site came to be known as a National Park and was referred to as such in subsequent legislation and at the time it was transferred to the Park Service in 1916.

Appendix 5

Financial History of the National Park Service, 1916–95

Year	Appropriations (in dollars)					Units[a] in the System	Revenues (in dollars)		Total Recorded Visits
	Operating Programs	Grants and Assistance Programs[b]	Acquisitions, Planning, and Development	Total[c]	Total in 1990 Constant Dollars[d]		General Fund	Special Fund	
1916e				253,647	3,041,000	36	177,471		358,006
1917f				537,367	5,487,000	38	180,652		487,368
1918g				530,680	4,593,000	40	217,331		451,661
1919h				966,364	7,301,000	43	196,678		755,325
1920				907,071	5,928,000	43	316,878		919,504
1921				1,058,969	7,732,000	44	396,928		1,007,335
1922				1,533,230	11,928,000	44	432,965		1,049,502
1923				1,579,520	12,073,000	48	513,706		1,280,996
1924				1,759,601	13,449,000	49	663,886		1,422,353
1925				3,027,657	22,612,000	50	670,921		1,760,872
1926				3,258,409	24,061,000	53	826,454		1,930,955
1927				3,933,920	29,550,000	53	703,850		2,354,643
1928				4,874,685	37,259,000	55	808,256		2,522,188
1929				4,771,515	36,470,000	58	849,273		2,680,597
1930				7,890,321	61,752,000	60	1,015,741		2,774,561
1931				15,289,435	131,469,000	61	940,365		3,152,845

1932			9,595,250	91,540,000	65	820,654	2,948,507
1933	2,816,620	8,004,000	10,820,620	108,789,000	129	628,182	3,481,590
1934	2,518,190	2,567,000	5,085,790	49,605,000	134	729,153	6,337,206
1935	6,799,540	5,000,000	11,799,540	112,569,000	139	905,935	7,676,490
1936	9,110,780	7,585,500	16,696,280	156,993,000	192[1]	1,136,026	11,989,793
1937	11,198,395	6,635,000	17,833,395	161,863,000	198	1,398,692	15,133,432
1938	11,052,834	10,618,546	21,671,380	200,883,000	204	1,508,127	16,331,467
1939	12,202,047	13,832,650	26,034,697	244,801,000	209	1,567,334	15,530,636
1940	12,954,267	8,144,015	21,098,282	196,968,000	214	1,928,078	16,755,251
1941	4,622,649	4,747,381	9,370,030	83,310,000	215	2,179,119	21,236,957
1942	5,715,005	8,894,770	14,609,775	117,147,000	172	2,080,702	9,370,969
1943	5,079,342	408,023	5,487,365	41,457,000	174	1,061,992	6,828,420
1944	4,563,560	0	4,563,560	33,890,000	174	807,601	8,339,775
1945	4,736,810	4,000	4,740,810	34,424,000	176	824,078	11,713,852
1946	5,457,125	30,250	5,487,375	36,779,000	179	1,592,947	21,752,315
1947	11,032,334	14,995,621	26,027,955	152,549,000	180	2,923,587	25,534,188
1948	9,660,055	968,000	10,628,055	57,638,000	184	3,303,328	29,858,828
1949	11,542,299	2,505,350	14,047,649	77,144,000	187	3,467,606	31,726,402
1950	15,150,982	14,953,868	30,104,850	163,266,000	187	3,527,607	33,252,589
1951	16,288,200	17,687,500	33,975,700	170,793,000	188	3,534,372	37,106,440
1952	16,878,564	11,370,000	28,248,564	139,324,000	191	3,568,094	42,299,836
1953	18,131,920	15,030,410	33,162,330	162,334,000	192	4,190,643	46,224,794
1954	18,437,550	15,416,300	33,853,850	164,487,000	194	4,037,551	47,833,913
1955	18,494,095	14,199,895	32,693,990	159,444,000	194	4,914,239	50,007,838
1956	20,787,000	28,079,300	48,866,300	234,810,000	195	5,065,784	54,923,443
1957	22,970,000	45,050,000	68,020,000	316,378,000	194	5,658,040	59,284,869
1958	27,581,530	48,000,000	75,981,530	343,626,000	197	5,744,920	58,676,953
1959	29,962,600	50,000,000	79,962,600	359,145,000	198	5,688,138	62,812,000
1960	32,682,000	46,735,000	79,417,000	350,669,000	203	5,685,176	72,287,800
1961	37,890,000	51,528,000	89,418,000	390,867,000	209	5,660,349	79,039,800[i]

Appendix 5, continued

| Year | Appropriations (in dollars) | | | | | Units[a] in the System | Revenues (in dollars) | | Total Recorded Visits |
	Operating Programs	Grants and Assistance Programs[b]	Acquisitions, Planning, and Development	Total[c]	Total in 1990 Constant Dollars[d]		General Fund	Special Fund	
1962	42,223,851		67,976,000	110,199,851	476,925,000	217	5,841,761		88,457,100
1963	48,017,054		72,775,500	120,792,554	515,934,000	218	6,450,559		94,092,900
1964	48,553,529	1,056,400	63,466,900	112,020,429	472,293,000	228	7,085,877		107,446,700
1965	53,087,000	1,238,000	73,860,600	126,947,600	526,732,000	244	5,581,436	1,768,524	113,703,200
1966	58,179,200	1,119,500	68,469,500	126,648,700	510,895,000	254	1,707,748	6,371,967	127,440,300
1967	64,320,600	1,257,600	57,488,400	121,809,000	476,660,000	256	1,747,071	6,544,330	135,325,600
1968	73,201,200	1,745,500	53,238,100	126,439,300	474,874,000	265	1,858,361	6,996,063	145,342,200
1969	76,905,700	1,501,500	26,328,600	103,234,300	367,649,000	270	1,929,915	7,135,505	157,356,500
1970	93,417,770	2,607,900	33,232,986	126,650,756	426,630,000	274	2,187,246	6,581,443	166,900,000
1971	114,363,900	8,321,600	41,643,300	156,007,200	503,460,000	278	2,182,501	12,093,209	186,188,000
1972	127,655,400	10,043,600	103,742,800	231,398,200	723,535,000	292	2,114,753	12,989,286	206,441,900
1973	162,666,000	17,759,000	55,362,000	218,028,000	641,808,000	293	2,425,692	12,780,975	215,051,300
1974	201,833,000	22,642,000	72,590,000	274,423,000	727,527,000	304	2,773,839	11,101,946	209,251,200
1975	230,746,000	31,422,000	83,123,000	313,869,000	762,702,000	304	3,410,551	13,796,382	228,985,800
1976	260,385,000	31,379,000	72,322,000	332,707,000	765,226,000	312	4,295,046	15,268,967	255,821,700
1977[k]	387,631,000	43,122,000	170,048,000	558,111,000	1,203,715,000	313	5,887,109	23,405,952	365,120,000
1978	345,709,000	6,254,000	198,851,000	544,560,000	1,089,120,000	346	5,608,000	17,281,000	267,137,555
1979	398,187,000	4,814,000	122,746,000	520,933,000	937,679,000	347	5,942,000	15,121,000	279,210,110
1980	404,096,000	3,494,000	127,400,000	531,496,000	845,079,000	366	6,131,750	14,956,369	294,582,280
1981[l]	471,801,000	210,217,000	186,504,000[m]	658,305,000	947,959,000	364	6,731,000	16,161,000	327,348,000
1982	533,185,000	41,456,000	226,140,000	759,325,000	1,025,089,000	365	7,717,000	17,814,000	331,445,176
1983	601,167,000	208,478,000	253,775,000	854,942,000	1,119,974,000	368	3,370,000	29,764,000	337,947,177

Year									
1984	625,997,000	112,770,000	204,062,000	830,059,000	1,045,874,000	368	103,000	36,067,000	328,392,400[n]
1985	645,732,000	103,146,000	205,467,000	851,199,000	1,029,951,000	368	961,000	49,598,000	347,221,086
1986[o]	627,288,000	74,926,000	141,803,000	627,429,803	746,641,000	370	1,549,000	49,150,000	352,155,500
1987	705,683,000	71,666,000	166,131,000	871,814,000	1,002,586,000	373	42,153,000[p]	28,649,000	370,982,172
1988	741,021,000	54,441,000	162,942,000	903,963,000	994,359,000	385	1,123,000	76,073,000[q]	371,489,100
1989	799,531,000	59,479,000	218,916,000	1,018,447,000	1,069,369,000	386	906,000	85,344,000	354,937,100[r]
1990	783,776,000	60,748,000	267,927,000	1,051,699,000	1,051,699,000	390	1,004,000[s]	77,569,000	359,875,800
1991	896,681,000	97,712,000	380,983,000	1,277,064,000	1,226,070,000	394	1,065,000	77,039,000	364,520,600
1992	1,010,657,000	75,279,000	384,790,000	1,395,447,000	1,299,964,000	397	1,034,000	87,226,000	371,847,000[t]
1993	1,019,141,000	79,215,000	314,817,000	1,333,960,000	1,206,565,000	399	837,000	88,619,000	361,174,000[t]
1994[u]	1,112,762,000	85,578,000	268,921,000	1,379,683,000	1,210,236,000	398	837,000	115,934,000	371,527,000[t]
1995[u]	1,158,061,000	84,735,000	203,790,000	1,361,851,000	1,159,570,000	398	837,000	160,965,000[v]	382,673,000[t]

Sources: The first appropriations to the Park Service came in 1920. From 1916 to 1919 appropriations for the parks and monuments were split between the Departments of the Interior, War, and Agriculture. For 1916–21, *Annual Report of the Director of the National Park Service*, in the *Annual Report of the Secretary of the Interior* (Washington, D.C., GPO, 1920): 359; for 1922–41, *Annual Report of the Director*, in the *Annual Report of the Secretary of the Interior*, 1941: 319. Sources 1941–65: *Budget Justifications for the U.S. Department of the Interior, National Park Service, F.Y. 1966*: 1-2 and 1-3; 1966–73, from the *Budget Justifications, F.Y. 1975*: 1; 1974–80, from the *Budget Justifications, F.Y. 1989: NPS-6*; 1981–88, from the *Budget Justifications, F.Y. 1989: NPS-11*; 1989–91, from the *Budget Justifications, F.Y. 1991: NPS-12*. The source of visitation data for the years 1918–32 is the *Annual Report of the Director, 1933*: 194. Visitation records for the National Parks under the jurisdiction of the Department of the Interior were kept from 1909, and published in the *Annual Report of the Superintendent of National Parks, 1917*. See also note t below. Technical footnotes in the sources have not been reproduced here unless they were deemed essential to understanding the numbers. The reader will notice that certain appropriations titles have changed over the years. The arrangement here has been adapted for literary purposes and may not conform to official government classifications. The column showing appropriation equivalents in constant dollars was computed from the published Consumer Price Index (CPI-U), All Urban Consumers, U.S. city average, all items, on the base period 1982–84 = 100, published by the Bureau of Labor Statistics, U.S. Department of Labor, Washington, DC 20212, dated February 17, 1994 (3 pages). For purposes of this table the base was shifted to 1990.

a. Includes affiliated areas; net of divestitures in the year they happened; also includes certain National Cemeteries originally treated as separate national park system units.

b. These external programs of the National Park Service are not included in the "Total Appropriations" column to the right inasmuch as they do not contribute directly to the care and custody of the units of the national park system. Of course, indirectly these programs, administered by the staff of the National Park Service, make substantial contributions to the national milieu within which the Park Service operates. Programs in historic preservation, in particular, often benefit sites directly related to units of the national park system—occasionally sites later made a part of the system.

c. All sums have been rounded to the nearest whole dollar.

d. Sums calculated have been rounded to the nearest thousand.

e. Interior Department only. War Department appropriations were $245,000.

f. Interior Department only. War Department appropriations in 1917 were $247,200.

g. Interior Department only. War Department appropriations were $70,000.

h. Interior Department only. War Department appropriations were $50,000.

i. Includes 46 National Recreation Demonstration Areas in 24 States. In 1942 forty-four of the NRDAs were divested.

j. A new basis for counting visitors was implemented in 1960. The comparable figure on the old basis of counting was 65,827,000.

k. Includes a transition year when the federal fiscal year was changed from July 1–June 30 to October 1–September 30 of each year.

l. Heritage Conservation and Recreation Service (formerly the Bureau of Outdoor Recreation) appropriations merged with the National Park Service in May 1981.

m. Land and Water Conservation Fund transferred to the National Park Service from the Heritage Conservation and Recreation Service beginning in 1981. Amounts do not include the yearly $30,000,000 of contract authority for land acquisition.

n. The 1984 visitation figure reflects a change in counting methodology at Golden Gate NRA (Calif.) and at Rock Creek Park (D.C.) that resulted in a decrease of approximately 14 million in the total of recorded visits.

o. Reductions attributable to Graham-Rudman-Hollings are included.

p. Changes in appropriation language by Congress authorized the National Park Service to establish increased entrance fees in 1987 and directed that all revenues from these fees be deposited in the General Fund of the Treasury.

q. Legislation in F.Y. 1988 provided for the deposit of all recreation fee revenues into a special fund for use by NPS.

r. "The change from 1988 to 1989 results primarily from changes in statistical counting procedures at Assateague NS, Blue Ridge Parkway, George Washington Memorial Parkway, Gulf Islands NS, the Lincoln Memorial, Natchez Trace Parkway, and the Vietnam Veterans Memorial. Corrections procedures in those areas resulted in an artificial drop of 17.3 million visits. Hurricane Hugo and the San Francisco earthquake resulted in decreases of another 0.3 million visits. Had these changes and events not occurred, visits in 1989 would have shown a +0.3 percent increase over 1988." *Budget Justifications, F.Y. 1991: NPS-12.*

s. Beginning in F.Y. 1990 concessioner fees were deposited to the General Fund.

t. NPS is again changing its counting methods at many parks. Most changes are downward. The actual visitation reported for 1991 through 1995 in the F.Y. 1995 budget document are 267, 273, 265, 273, and 281 million, respectively. Earlier years are being similarly reduced as the study progresses in order to preserve trend information. Data for 1991–95 have here been "inflated" by the same factors used in NPS's newly revised series in order to extend the trend data displayed here over prior years and in figure 1.

u. Based on the president's F.Y. 1995 budget. Assumes an annual inflation rate of 4.5 percent in each of 1994 and 1995.

v. Includes revenues retained by the National Park Service for fee collection support, as authorized by P.L. 103–66.

Appendix 6-1

Comparative Resources of Units of the
National Park System

Park Unit	Budget	FTE[a]	1,000 Visits[b]	Acreage[c]
Abraham Lincoln Birthplace NHS	$384,000	10	297	117
Acadia NP	2,839,000	94	2,615	41,973
Adams NHS	911,000	22	41	14
Agate Fossil Beds NM	362,000	6	19	3,055
Allegheny Portage Railroad NHS	1,046,000	30	189	1,247
Amistad RA	1,439,000	40	1,486	58,500
Andersonville NHS	608,000	16	129	495
Andrew Johnson NHS	316,000	8	45	17
Aniakchak NM & Preserve	149,000	4	2	602,779
Antietam NB	1,269,000	36	189	3,256
Apostle Islands NL	1,444,000	39	130	69,372
Appalachian NST	648,000	6	0	166,400
Appomattox Court House NHP	668,000	18	233	1,594
Arches NP	696,000	24	770	73,379
Arkansas Post NMem	279,000	8	52	389
Assateague Island NS	2,161,000	68	1,962	39,733
Aztec Ruins NM	352,000	9	84	319
Badlands NP	1,374,000	42	845	242,756
Baltimore-Washington Parkway	666,000	14	0	0
Bandelier NM	1,412,000	46	364	32,737
Bent's Old Fort NHS	583,000	21	47	800
Bering Land Bridge NPres	567,000	6	0	2,784,960
Big Bend NP, Rio Grande WSR	3,241,000	90	320	810,763
Big Cypress NPres	1,765,000	62	235	716,000

Appendix 6-1, continued

Park Unit	Budget	FTE[a]	1,000 Visits[b]	Acreage[c]
Big Hole NB	206,000	5	64	656
Big South Fork NR&RA	2,317,000	59	726	125,000
Big Thicket NPres	1,422,000	45	83	96,563
Bighorn Canyon NRA	1,865,000	41	414	120,296
Biscayne NP	1,438,000	32	16	172,924
Black Canyon of the Gunnison NM	529,000	15	312	20,766
Blue Ridge Parkway	8,653,000	242	17,910	88,159
Booker T. Washington NM	421,000	12	26	224
Boston African American NHS	424,000	7	329	0
Boston NHP	4,937,000	120	1,900	41
Bryce Canyon NP	1,724,000	50	1,109	35,835
Buffalo NR	2,795,000	72	1,034	94,219
Cabrillo NM	831,000	22	1,153	137
Canaveral NS	1,146,000	31	1,172	57,662
Canyon de Chelly NM	863,000	22	767	83,840
Canyonlands NP	2,779,000	78	437	337,570
Cape Cod NS	2,986,000	99	5,153	43,570
Cape Hatteras NS, Fort Raleigh NHS, Wright Brothers NMem	4,577,000	124	3,043	31,263
Cape Krusenstern NM, Kobuk Valley NP, Noatak NPres	1,191,000	15	13	8,985,025
Cape Lookout NS	992,000	25	295	28,243
Capitol Reef NP	1,007,000	31	633	241,904
Capulin Volcano NM	357,000	12	54	793
Carl Sandburg Home NHS	506,000	15	64	264
Carlsbad Caverns NP	3,251,000	96	670	46,766
Casa Grande Ruins NM, Hohokam Pima NM	338,000	10	164	2,163
Castillo de San Marcos NM, Fort Matanzas NM	1,040,000	28	1,114	248
Castle Clinton NM	472,000	9	1,297	1
Catoctin Mountain Park	1,356,000	38	622	5,770
Cedar Breaks NM	259,000	6	508	6,155
Chaco Culture NHP	1,178,000	31	67	33,974
Chamizal NMem	1,287,000	27	254	55
Channel Islands NP	2,997,000	66	182	249,354
Charles Pinckney NHS	319,000	5	0	28
Chattahoochee River NRA	1,519,000	39	2,841	9,260
Chesapeake and Ohio Canal NHP	4,761,000	136	4,013	19,237

Chickamauga and Chattanooga NMP	1,228,000	33	1,012	8,106
Chickasaw NRA	1,791,000	39	1,369	9,930
Chiricahua NM, Fort Bowie NHS	803,000	24	132	12,985
Christiansted NHS, Buck Island Reef NM	513,000	13	176	907
City of Rocks NRes	201,000	1	84	14,407
Colonial NHP	3,725,000	96	2,369	9,330
Colorado NM	740,000	21	449	20,454
Congaree Swamp NM	301,000	8	52	22,200
Coronado NMem	220,000	7	78	4,750
Coulee Dam NRA	2,482,000	75	1,168	100,390
Cowpens NB	247,000	8	157	842
Crater Lake NP	2,459,000	72	381	183,224
Craters of the Moon NM	504,000	14	236	53,545
Cumberland Gap NHP	1,240,000	36	1,012	20,446
Cumberland Island NS	1,081,000	26	38	36,415
Curecanti NRA	1,858,000	48	1,091	42,114
Cuyahoga Valley NRA	4,539,000	134	2,065	32,525
De Soto NMem	271,000	8	218	27
Death Valley NM	3,616,000	94	1,001	2,067,628
Delaware Water Gap NRA	5,085,000	134	3,970	69,178
Denali NP & NPres	6,696,000	63	505	6,076,528
Devils Postpile NM	88,000	2	131	798
Devils Tower NM	525,000	16	429	1,347
Dinosaur NM	1,626,000	47	534	210,844
Dry Tortugas NP	439,000	8	24	64,700
Ebey's Landing NHRes	128,000	0	0	19,000
Edgar Allen Poe NHS	251,000	4	15	1
Edison NHS	1,491,000	39	62	21
Effigy Mounds NM	402,000	14	96	1,481
Eisenhower NHS	843,000	20	96	690
El Malpais NM	520,000	16	86	115,077
El Morro NM, Zuni Cibola NHP	316,000	9	79	1,279
Eleanor Roosevelt NHS	455,000	12	89	181
Eugene O'Neill NHS	226,000	7	3	13
Everglades NP	8,102,000	225	898	1,506,499
Federal Hall NMem	355,000	3	60	1
Fire Island NS	2,410,000	67	649	19,579
Florissant Fossil Beds NM	327,000	10	88	5,998
Ford's Theatre NHS	513,000	18	921	1
Fort Caroline NMem	304,000	11	136	138
Fort Clatsop NMem	481,000	16	212	125
Fort Davis NHS	527,000	16	73	460
Fort Donelson NB	591,000	17	207	552
Fort Frederica NM	436,000	12	308	241

Appendix 6-1, continued

Park Unit	Budget	FTE[a]	1,000 Visits[b]	Acreage[c]
Fort Laramie NHS	681,000	20	94	833
Fort Larned NHS	499,000	13	47	718
Fort McHenry NM	1,056,000	28	486	43
Fort Necessity NB	687,000	21	142	903
Fort Point NHS	296,000	10	1,501	29
Fort Pulaski NM	574,000	15	356	5,623
Fort Scott NHS	537,000	16	75	17
Fort Smith NHS	358,000	10	145	75
Fort Stanwix NM	483,000	15	55	16
Fort Sumter NM	847,000	26	338	195
Fort Union NM	424,000	11	21	721
Fort Union Trading Post NHS	311,000	9	27	442
Fort Vancouver NHS	665,000	20	256	209
Fossil Butte NM	328,000	10	27	8,198
Frederick Law Olmsted NHS	1,248,000	48	4	2
Fredericksburg and Spotsylvania County Battlefield Memorial NMP	1,921,000	50	455	7,793
Friendship Hill NHS	286,000	8	23	675
Gates of the Arctic NP & NPres	972,000	11	2	8,472,517
Gateway NRA	13,615,000	397	2,281	26,579
Gauley NRA, Bluestone NSR	240,000	2	182	14,568
General Grant NMem	121,000	1	16	1
George Rogers Clark NHP	507,000	13	145	26
George Washington Carver NM	452,000	13	41	210
George Washington Mem Pky	6,834,000	153	6,746	7,390
George Washington Birthplace NM	753,000	22	162	550
Gettysburg NMP	2,902,000	76	1,355	5,896
Gila Cliff Dwellings NM	171,000	0	60	533
Glacier Bay NP & NPres	1,722,000	28	242	3,283,168
Glacier NP	6,980,000	202	2,137	1,013,572
Glen Canyon NRA	5,901,000	134	1,800	1,236,880
Golden Gate NRA	9,481,000	198	16,723	73,180
Golden Spike NHS	530,000	14	51	2,735
Grand Canyon NP	11,214,000	294	4,530	1,217,158
Grand Portage NM	534,000	16	60	710
Grand Teton NP	5,675,000	159	2,590	309,993
Grant-Kohrs Ranch NHS	636,000	20	27	1,498
Great Basin NP	1,385,000	37	90	77,180

Great Sand Dunes NM	578,000	17	297	38,662
Great Smoky Mountains NP	9,296,000	284	9,277	520,269
Greenbelt Park	709,000	18	212	1,176
Guadalupe Mountains NP	1,306,000	33	164	86,416
Guilford Courthouse NMP	385,000	10	186	220
Gulf Islands NS	3,760,000	92	5,460	135,625
Hagerman Fossil Beds NM	230,000	7	0	4,280
Haleakala NP	2,243,000	51	1,343	28,099
Hamilton Grange NMem	131,000	3	0	1
Hampton NHS	367,000	9	26	62
Harpers Ferry NHP	3,490,000	98	380	2,287
Harry S Truman NHS	596,000	20	75	1
Hawaii Volcanoes NP	3,052,000	74	1,123	229,177
Herbert Hoover NHS	715,000	21	235	187
Home of Franklin D. Roosevelt NHS	1,017,000	25	175	290
Homestead NM of America	356,000	10	49	195
Hopewell Culture NHP	410,000	10	35	1,032
Hopewell Furnace NHS	636,000	18	112	848
Horseshoe Bend NMP	303,000	9	78	2,040
Hot Springs NP	2,329,000	61	1,523	5,543
Hovenweep NM, Yucca House NM	98,000	2	26	795
Hubbell Trading Post NHS	433,000	12	250	160
Independence NHP	9,015,000	202	3,141	45
Indiana Dunes NL	4,908,000	118	1,895	14,981
Isle Royale NP	2,063,000	54	22	571,790
Jean Lafitte NHP & Pres	3,338,000	67	919	20,020
Jefferson National Expansion Memorial	3,668,000	118	2,443	91
Jewel Cave NM	430,000	15	132	1,274
Jimmy Carter NHS	374,000	9	29	71
John D. Rockefeller, Jr., Memorial Parkway	318,000	7	1,330	23,777
John Day Fossil Beds NM	603,000	17	131	14,014
John F. Kennedy NHS	208,000	5	13	1
John Muir NHS	348,000	10	23	340
Johnstown Flood NMem	475,000	8	132	164
Joshua Tree NM	2,399,000	70	1,190	558,750
Kalaupapa NHP	964,000	11	0	10,779
Kaloko-Honokohau NHP	532,000	10	41	1,161
Katmai NP & NPres	1,243,000	14	53	4,114,038
Kenai Fjords NP	632,000	9	184	669,541
Kennesaw Mountain NBP	686,000	17	897	2,885
Kings Mountain NMP	424,000	12	231	3,945
Klondike Gold Rush NHP (Wash.)	263,000	8	109	0

Appendix 6-1, continued

Park Unit	Budget	FTE[a]	1,000 Visits[b]	Acreage[c]
Klondike Gold Rush NHP	1,131,000	21	403	13,191
Knife River Indian Village NHS	297,000	9	17	1,758
Lake Clark NP & NPres	871,000	12	12	4,044,132
Lake Mead NRA	9,184,000	194	9,022	1,495,666
Lake Meredith NRA, Alibates Flint Quarry NM	1,369,000	33	1,420	46,349
Lassen Volcanic NP	2,401,000	58	369	106,372
Lava Beds NM	733,000	22	160	46,560
Lincoln Boyhood NMem	569,000	16	177	200
Lincoln Home NHS	1,506,000	51	456	12
Little Bighorn Battlefield NM	571,000	15	342	765
Longfellow NHS	362,000	11	16	2
Lowell NHP	5,232,000	130	596	137
Lyndon B. Johnson NHP	2,049,000	54	188	1,572
Martin Luther King, Jr., NHS	1,119,000	28	848	23
Maggie L. Walker NHS	195,000	5	9	1
Mammoth Cave NP	3,795,000	114	2,404	52,824
Manassas NBP	984,000	29	710	5,072
Martin Van Buren NHS	593,000	14	14	40
Mary McLeod Bethune Council House NHS	291,000	3	0	0
Mesa Verde NP	3,035,000	90	665	52,122
Minute Man NHP	1,384,000	37	939	790
Mississippi NR and RA	464,000	8	0	53,775
Monocacy NB	228,000	3	7	1,647
Montezuma Castle NM, Tuzigoot NM	764,000	21	1,012	1,658
Moores Creek NB	221,000	5	60	87
Morristown NHP	1,263,000	31	716	1,684
Mount Rainier NP	6,660,000	154	1,396	235,613
Mount Rushmore NM	1,061,000	34	1,920	1,278
Muir Woods NM	260,000	7	1,521	554
Natchez NHP	846,000	16	103	108
Natchez Trace Parkway, Brices Crossroads NBS, Tupelo NB	5,906,000	129	5,764	62,745
National Capital Parks-East	6,979,000	162	280	350
National Capital Parks-Central	18,200,000	436	14,009	6,960
Natural Bridges NM	308,000	11	152	7,636
Navajo NM	430,000	12	102	360
New River Gorge NR	3,745,000	110	997	62,144

Nez Perce NHP	768,000	21	239	2,110
Ninety Six NHS	184,000	5	29	989
Niobrara NSR	370,000	5	0	0
North Cascades NP, Lake Chelan NRA, Ross Lake NRA	3,392,000	101	374	684,243
NP of American Samoa	135,000	1	0	9,000
Obed WSR	176,000	6	220	5,067
Ocmulgee NM	454,000	11	115	702
Olympic NP	6,521,000	183	2,667	922,651
Oregon Caves NM	333,000	10	91	488
Organ Pipe Cactus NM	946,000	26	253	330,689
Ozark National Scenic Riverways	3,352,000	99	1,385	80,790
Padre Island NS	1,909,000	52	770	130,434
Palo Alto Battlefield NHS	267,000	2	0	3,357
Pea Ridge NMP	462,000	12	82	4,300
Pecos NM	1,014,000	19	44	6,569
Perry's Victory and International Peace Mem	477,000	13	184	25
Petersburg NB	1,576,000	40	265	2,744
Petrified Forest NP	1,844,000	52	931	93,533
Petroglyph NM	695,000	12	68	5,262
Pictured Rocks NL	1,131,000	25	619	73,174
Pinnacles NM	1,157,000	33	198	16,265
Pipe Spring NM	256,000	8	56	40
Pipestone NM	418,000	13	108	282
Piscataway Park	367,000	9	115	4,263
Point Reyes NS	2,753,000	64	2,620	71,049
Poverty Point NM	212,000	0	0	911
President's Park	1,436,000	36	0	70
Presidio	1,537,000	34	0	0
Prince William Forest Park	1,753,000	44	271	18,572
Pu'uhonua O Honaunau NHP	652,000	19	445	182
Puukohola Heiau NHS	230,000	8	43	80
Rainbow Bridge NM	94,000	2	120	160
Redwood NP	5,194,000	120	415	110,232
Richmond NBP	815,000	24	167	772
Rock Creek Park	4,014,000	97	1,567	1,754
Rocky Mountain NP	6,435,000	195	2,760	265,727
Roger Williams NMem	270,000	8	51	5
Russell Cave NM	187,000	6	32	310
Sagamore Hill NHS	690,000	20	55	83
Saguaro NM	1,460,000	47	830	87,691
Saint Croix NSR, Lower Saint Croix NSR	1,776,000	47	389	92,736
Saint Croix Island NHS	50,000	0	0	35

Appendix 6-1, continued

Park Unit	Budget	FTE[a]	1,000 Visits[b]	Acreage[c]
Saint Paul's Church NHS	266,000	0	2	6
Saint-Gaudens NHS	495,000	14	27	148
Salem Maritime NHS	906,000	26	724	9
Salinas Pueblo Missions NM	594,000	18	49	1,101
San Antonio Missions NHP	1,419,000	41	1,052	819
San Francisco Maritime NHP	3,764,000	70	3,340	50
San Juan Island NHP	360,000	12	248	1,752
San Juan NHS	1,529,000	52	1,400	75
Santa Monica Mountains NRA	2,830,000	69	393	150,050
Saratoga NHP	846,000	24	167	3,393
Saugus Iron Works NHS	564,000	16	39	9
Scotts Bluff NM	521,000	22	157	3,003
Sequoia NP, Kings Canyon NP	8,514,000	252	1,685	864,384
Shenandoah NP	7,058,000	177	1,969	196,466
Shiloh NMP	757,000	19	355	3,973
Sitka NHP	782,000	9	120	107
Sleeping Bear Dunes NL	2,073,000	60	1,196	71,189
Springfield Armory NHS	552,000	13	13	55
Statue of Liberty NM, Ellis Island	8,322,000	127	4,110	58
Steamtown NHS	2,325,000	76	145	62
Stones River NB	352,000	9	277	740
Thaddeus Kosciuszko NMem	113,000	2	4	1
Theodore Roosevelt NP	1,297,000	35	472	70,447
Theodore Roosevelt Birthplace NHS	189,000	4	9	1
Theodore Roosevelt Inaugural NHS	147,000	0	29	1
Thomas Stone NHS	161,000	4	4	328
Timpanogos Cave NM	460,000	16	98	250
Timucuan Ecological and Historic Preserve	466,000	11	53	46,000
Tonto NM	301,000	12	67	1,120
Tumacacori NHP	333,000	9	50	47
Tuskegee Institute NHS	433,000	12	321	58
Ulysses S. Grant NHS	459,000	6	2	10
Upper Delaware Scenic and Recreational River	2,182,000	36	257	75,000
USS Arizona Memorial	1,363,000	35	1,493	0
Valley Forge NHP	3,596,000	93	1,776	3,468

Vanderbilt Mansion NHS	886,000	25	463	212
Vicksburg NMP	1,378,000	42	984	1,742
Virgin Islands NP	2,174,000	57	764	14,689
Voyageurs NP	1,920,000	49	230	218,035
War in the Pacific NHP	542,000	13	65	1,960
Weir Farm NHS	343,000	3	3	59
Whiskeytown NRA	1,746,000	47	429	42,503
White House	2,837,000	62	1,169	18
White Sands NM	646,000	19	354	143,733
Whitman Mission NHS	357,000	10	75	98
William Howard Taft NHS	263,000	7	7	3
Wilson's Creek NB	677,000	20	198	1,750
Wind Cave NP	1,134,000	39	457	28,295
Wolf Trap Farm Park	2,526,000	59	621	130
Women's Rights NHP	746,000	17	26	6
Wrangell-Saint Elias NP & NPres	1,519,000	22	32	13,176,391
Wupatki NM, Sunset Crater Volcano NM, Walnut Canyon NM	1,252,000	35	992	40,543
Yellowstone NP	17,404,000	469	2,934	2,219,791
Yosemite NP	15,430,000	489	3,809	761,236
Yukon-Charley Rivers NPres	609,000	12	2	2,523,509
Zion NP	3,016,000	104	2,361	146,598

Source: *United States Department of the Interior, Budget Justifications, F.Y. 1995, National Park Service:* 160-72.

a. Full-time equivalent (FTE). May include both permanent and temporary staff and full-time and part-time employees. A listing of "0" FTEs indicates the activity is served by staff from another site in an amount less than one FTE annually. Funding shown under such circumstances will include the salary and benefits for the partial FTE and all other objects of expenditure (supplies, travel, and so forth.)
b. Listings of "0" visits may mean that the data are not available or that the site was temporarily closed to the public (such as Hamilton Grange NMem, which was undergoing major restoration during the year), or that the site was too new to generate visitation information.
c. Acreage listed as "0" indicates it is a new area, the area of which has not yet been officially determined. Acreages listed as "1" may be only a fraction of an acre, such as Theodore Roosevelt Birthplace NHS, a brownstone house in New York City occupying approximately 0.11 acre.

Appendix 6-2

Sample Comparative Budgets of Units of the National Park System

Park Unit	Budget	FTE	1,000 Visits	Acreage
Saint Croix Island NHS	$50,000	0	0	35
Devils Postpile NM	88,000	2	131	798
Rainbow Bridge NM	94,000	2	120	160
Hovenweep NM, Yucca House NM	98,000	2	26	795
Thaddeus Kosciuszko NMem	113,000	2	4	1
General Grant NMem	121,000	1	16	1
Ebey's Landing NHRes	128,000	0	0	19,000
Hamilton Grange NMem	131,000	3	0	1
NP of American Samoa	135,000	1	0	9,000
Theodore Roosevelt Inaugural NHS	147,000	0	29	1
[etc.]				
Big Hole NB	206,000	5	64	656
Cowpens NB	247,000	8	157	842
De Soto NMem	271,000	8	218	27
Natural Bridges NM	308,000	11	152	7,636
Casa Grande NM, Hohokam Pima NM	338,000	10	164	2,163
San Juan Island NHP	360,000	12	248	1,752
Hopewell Culture NHP	410,000	10	35	1,032
Fort Frederica NM	436,000	12	308	241
Castle Clinton NM	472,000	9	1,297	1
Christiansted NHS, Buck Island Reef NM	513,000	13	176	907

Fort Scott NHS	537,000	16	75	17
Fort Donelson NB	591,000	17	207	552
White Sands NM	646,000	19	354	143,733
Sagamore Hill NHS	690,000	20	55	83
Montezuma Castle NM, Tuzigoot NM	764,000	21	1,012	1,658
Canyon de Chelly NM	863,000	22	767	83,840
Capitol Reef NP	1,007,000	31	633	241,904
Pictured Rocks NL	1,131,000	25	619	73,174
Wupatki NM, Sunset Crater Volcano NM, Walnut Canyon NM	1,252,000	35	992	40,543
Vicksburg NMP	1,378,000	42	984	1,742
Saguaro NM	1,460,000	47	830	87,691
Bryce Canyon NP	1,724,000	50	1,109	35,835
Voyageurs NP	1,920,000	49	230	218,035
Steamtown NHS	2,325,000	76	145	62
Buffalo NR	2,795,000	72	1,034	94,219
Big Bend NP, Rio Grande WSR	3,241,000	90	320	810,763
New River Gorge NR	3,745,000	110	997	62,144
Delaware Water Gap NRA	5,085,000	134	3,970	69,178
George Washington Mem Pky	6,834,000	153	6,746	7,390
[etc.]				
Blue Ridge Parkway	8,653,000	242	17,910	88,159
Independence NHP	9,015,000	202	3,141	45
Lake Mead NRA	9,184,000	194	9,022	1,495,666
Great Smoky Mountains NP	9,296,000	284	9,277	520,269
Golden Gate NRA	9,481,000	198	16,723	73,180
Grand Canyon NP	11,214,000	294	4,530	1,217,158
Gateway NRA	13,615,000	397	2,281	26,579
Yosemite NP	15,430,000	489	3,809	761,236
Yellowstone NP	17,404,000	469	2,934	2,219,791
National Capital Parks-Central	18,200,000	436	14,009	6,960

Source: Derived from Appendix 6-1. Includes the first ten parks, the last ten, and every tenth park in between. A complete listing for all parks for Appendixes 6-2, 6-3, 7-1, 7-2, and 7-3 is available for $5.00 from the publisher (University of Illinois Press, ATTN: Business Office, 1325 South Oak Street, Champaign, IL 61820).

Appendix 6-3

Sample Comparative Visitation to Units of the
National Park System

Park Unit	1,000 Visits	Budget	FTE	Acreage
Aniakchak NM & Preserve	2	$149,000	4	602,779
Gates of the Arctic NP & NPres	2	972,000	11	8,472,517
Saint Paul's Church NHS	2	266,000	0	6
Ulysses S. Grant NHS	2	459,000	6	10
Yukon-Charley Rivers NPres	2	609,000	12	2,523,509
Eugene O'Neill NHS	3	226,000	7	13
Weir Farm NHS	3	343,000	3	59
Frederick Law Olmsted NHS	4	1,248,000	48	2
Thaddeus Kosciuszko NMem	4	113,000	2	1
Thomas Stone NHS	4	161,000	4	328
[etc.]				
Edgar Allen Poe NHS	15	251,000	4	1
Dry Tortugas NP	24	439,000	8	64,700
Ninety Six NHS	29	184,000	5	989
Puukohola Heiau NHS	43	230,000	8	80
Arkansas Post NMem	52	279,000	8	389
Grand Portage NM	60	534,000	16	710
Fort Scott NHS	75	537,000	16	17
El Malpais NM	86	520,000	16	115,077
Natchez NHP	103	846,000	16	108
Devils Postpile NM	131	88,000	2	798
Natural Bridges NM	152	308,000	11	7,636
Christiansted NHS, Buck Island Reef NM	176	513,000	13	907
Pinnacles NM	198	1,157,000	33	16,265

Big Cypress NPres	235	1,765,000	62	716,000
Upper Delaware Scenic and Recreational River	257	2,182,000	36	75,000
Big Bend NP, and Rio Grande WSR	320	3,241,000	90	810,763
North Cascades NP, Lake Chelan NRA, Ross Lake NRA	374	3,392,000	101	684,243
Canyonlands NP	437	2,779,000	78	337,570
Cedar Breaks NM	508	259,000	6	6,155
Manassas NBP	710	984,000	29	5,072
Martin Luther King, Jr., NHS	848	1,119,000	28	23
Death Valley NM	1,001	3,616,000	94	2,067,628
Cabrillo NM	1,153	831,000	22	137
Chickasaw NRA	1,369	1,791,000	39	9,930
Rock Creek Park	1,567	4,014,000	97	1,754
Glacier NP	2,137	6,980,000	202	1,013,572
Rocky Mountain NP	2,760	6,435,000	195	265,727
[etc.]				
Grand Canyon NP	4,530	11,214,000	294	1,217,158
Cape Cod NS	5,153	2,986,000	99	43,570
Gulf Islands NS	5,460	3,760,000	92	135,625
Natchez Trace Parkway, Brices Crossroads, Tupelo NB	5,764	5,906,000	129	62,745
George Washington Memorial Parkway	6,746	6,834,000	153	7,390
Lake Mead NRA	9,022	9,184,000	194	1,495,666
Great Smoky Mountains NP	9,277	9,296,000	284	520,269
National Capital Parks-Central	14,009	18,200,000	436	6,960
Golden Gate NRA	16,723	9,481,000	198	73,180
Blue Ridge Parkway	17,910	8,653,000	242	88,159

Source: Derived from Appendix 6-1. Does not include seventeen parks reporting "0" visitation. Sample includes the first ten parks, the last ten, and every tenth park in between. A complete listing for all parks for Appendixes 6-2, 6-3, 7-1, 7-2, and 7-3 is available for $5.00 from the publisher (University of Illinois Press, ATTN: Business Office, 1325 South Oak Street, Champaign, IL 61820).

Appendix 7-1

Sample Comparative Costs per Visit to Units of the National Park System

Park Unit	Budget	1,000 Visits	Cost per Visit[a]
Muir Woods NM	$260,000	1,521	$0.17
Fort Point NHS	296,000	1,501	0.20
John D. Rockefeller, Jr., Memorial Pky	318,000	1,330	0.24
Castle Clinton NM	472,000	1,297	0.36
Blue Ridge Parkway	8,653,000	17,910	0.48
Cedar Breaks NM	259,000	508	0.51
Chattahoochee River NRA	1,519,000	2,841	0.53
Mount Rushmore NM	1,061,000	1,920	0.55
Ford's Theatre NHS	513,000	921	0.56
Golden Gate NRA	9,481,000	16,723	0.57
[etc.]			
USS Arizona Memorial	1,363,000	1,493	0.91
Acadia NP	2,839,000	2,615	1.09
Salem Maritime NHS	906,000	724	1.25
Martin Luther King, Jr., NHS	1,119,000	848	1.32
Jefferson National Expansion Memorial	3,668,000	2,443	1.50
Haleakala NP	2,243,000	1,343	1.67
Kings Mountain NMP	424,000	231	1.84
Coulee Dam NRA	2,482,000	1,168	2.13
Rocky Mountain NP	6,435,000	2,760	2.33
Fort Sumter NM	847,000	338	2.51
Coronado NMem	220,000	78	2.82
Piscataway Park	367,000	115	3.19
Cape Lookout NS	992,000	295	3.36
Fire Island NS	2,410,000	649	3.71

Yosemite NP	15,430,000	3,809	4.05
Pipe Spring NM	256,000	56	4.57
Carlsbad Caverns NP	3,251,000	670	4.85
Allegheny Portage Railroad NHS	1,046,000	189	5.53
Gateway NRA	13,615,000	2,281	5.97
Tumacacori NHP	333,000	50	6.66
General Grant NMem	121,000	16	7.56
Lowell NHP	5,232,000	596	8.78
Lyndon B. Johnson NHP	2,049,000	188	10.90
Sagamore Hill NHS	690,000	55	12.55
Booker T. Washington NM	421,000	26	16.19
Theodore Roosevelt Birthplace NHS	189,000	9	21.00
Cumberland Island NS	1,081,000	38	28.45
[etc.]			
Eugene O'Neill NHS	226,000	3	75.33
Biscayne NP	1,438,000	16	89.88
Cape Krusenstern NM, Kobuk Valley NP, Noatak NPres	1,191,000	13	91.62
Isle Royale NP	2,063,000	22	93.77
Weir Farm NHS	343,000	3	114.33
Saint Paul's Church NHS	266,000	2	133.00
Ulysses S. Grant NHS	459,000	2	229.50
Yukon-Charley Rivers NPres	609,000	2	304.50
Frederick Law Olmsted NHS	1,248,000	4	312.00
Gates of the Arctic NP & NPres	972,000	2	486.00

Source: Derived from Appendix 6-1. Does not include seventeen parks reporting "0" visitation. Sample includes the first ten parks, the last ten, and every tenth park in between. A complete listing for all parks for Appendixes 6-2, 6-3, 7-1, 7-2, and 7-3 is available for $5.00 from the publisher (University of Illinois Press, ATTN: Business Office, 1325 South Oak Street, Champaign, IL 61820).

a. Readers are cautioned to use these calculated values with care. Many park units are highly seasonal in character, and many park costs continue the year around regardless of visitation levels. Some parks are very remote (such as the Alaska parks), and visitation will never reach high levels. Isle Royale NP, for example, is a wilderness (roadless) park with a short visitor season and is only reachable by boat or float plane. Many parks, such as those associated with former presidents, have a limited potential clientele. Small differences between costs-per-visit are not significant. There are, however, anomalies that possibly merit further study. Such values may be useful for policy-making purposes in the setting of user fees. Such calculations are obviously sensitive to visitation counts; at this writing NPS is again revising its visitation counting methods, mostly downward. Some visitation counts are affected by forces beyond the Service's capacity to influence; Biscayne and Everglades NPs, for example, were severaly affected by Hurricane Andrew in 1992–93 visitor seasons. Hamilton Grange NMem was closed for 1992–93 for repairs.

Appendix 7-2

Sample Comparative Costs per Full-Time Equivalent at Units of the National Park System

Park Unit	Budget	FTE	Cost per FTE[a]
Scotts Bluff NM	$521,000	22	$23,682
Tonto NM	301,000	12	25,083
Frederick Law Olmsted NHS	1,248,000	48	26,000
Fort Caroline NMem	304,000	11	27,636
Bent's Old Fort NHS	583,000	21	27,762
Natural Bridges NM	308,000	11	28,000
Big Cypress NPres	1,765,000	62	28,468
Ford's Theatre NHS	513,000	18	28,500
Jewel Cave NM	430,000	15	28,667
Effigy Mounds NM	402,000	14	28,714
[etc.]			
Capulin Volcano NM	357,000	12	29,750
Jefferson National Expansion Memorial	3,668,000	118	31,085
Fort Stanwix NM	483,000	15	32,200
Vicksburg NMP	1,378,000	42	32,810
Fort Vancouver NHS	665,000	20	33,250
Carl Sandburg Home NHS	506,000	15	33,733
Richmond NBP	815,000	24	33,958
Pu'uhonua O Honaunau NHP	652,000	19	34,316
George Washington Carver NM	452,000	13	34,769
Antietam NB	1,269,000	36	35,250
Lincoln Boyhood NMem	569,000	16	35,563
Wupatki NM, Sunset Crater Volcano NM, Walnut Canyon NM	1,252,000	35	35,771
Fort Frederica NM	436,000	12	36,333

Apostle Islands NL	1,444,000	39	37,026
Great Basin NP	1,385,000	37	37,432
Andersonville NHS	608,000	16	38,000
Fort Larned NHS	499,000	13	38,385
Buffalo NR	2,795,000	72	38,819
Greenbelt Park	709,000	18	39,389
Martin Luther King, Jr., NHS	1,119,000	28	39,964
Santa Monica Mountains NRA	2,830,000	69	41,014
Cumberland Island NS	1,081,000	26	41,577
Point Reyes NS	2,753,000	64	43,016
Moores Creek NB	221,000	5	44,200
Natchez Trace Parkway, Brices Crossroads NBS, Tupelo NB	5,906,000	129	45,783
Yukon-Charley Rivers NPres	609,000	12	50,750
Mississippi NR and Recreation Area	464,000	8	58,000
Kenai Fjords NP	632,000	9	70,222
Bering Land Bridge NPres	567,000	6	94,500
[etc.]			
Mary McLeod Bethune Council House NHS	291,000	3	97,000
Denali NP & NPres	6,696,000	63	106,286
Appalachian NST	648,000	6	108,000
Weir Farm NHS	343,000	3	114,333
Federal Hall NMem	355,000	3	118,333
Gauley NRA, Bluestone NSR	240,000	2	120,000
General Grant NMem	121,000	1	121,000
Palo Alto Battlefield NHS	267,000	2	133,500
NP of American Samoa	135,000	1	135,000
City of Rocks NRes	201,000	1	201,000

Source: Derived from Appendix 6-1. Does not include six parks reporting "0" FTEs. Sample includes the first ten parks, the last ten, and every tenth park in between. A complete listing for all parks for Appendixes 6-2, 6-3, 7-1, 7-2, and 7-3 is available for $5.00 from the publisher (University of Illinois Press, ATTN: Business Office, 1325 South Oak Street, Champaign, IL 61820).

a. Readers are cautioned to use these calculated values with care because the budgets for all park units are not strictly comparable on their content and coverage. The very wide variations in costs-per-FTE evident here, however, are not explained by such things as higher salary costs in Alaska or other obvious structural differences. Over all 360-plus park units one would expect such things as within-grade salary differences to even out. Whether such things as merit pay, park-specific grade structures, or classification anomalies can explain the differences could be determined only by a much more detailed analysis of park-specific data. If the differences are caused chiefly by nonsalary/benefit costs, they may suggest needed standardization in the way other items of expenditure are treated at the park level.

Appendix 7-3

Sample Comparative Annual Visits per Full-Time
Equivalent at Units of the National Park System

Park Unit	1,000 Visits	FTE	Annual Visits per FTE[a]
Frederick Law Olmsted NHS	4	48	83
Yukon-Charley Rivers NPres	2	12	167
Gates of the Arctic NP & NPres	2	11	182
Ulysses S. Grant NHS	2	6	333
Isle Royale NP	22	54	407
Eugene O'Neill NHS	3	7	429
Aniakchak NM & Preserve	2	4	500
Biscayne NP	16	32	500
Cape Krusenstern NM, Kobuk Valley NP, Noatak NPres	13	15	867
Lake Clark NP & NPres	12	12	1,000
[etc.]			
Women's Rights NHP	26	17	1,529
Thaddeus Kosciuszko NMem	4	2	2,000
John F. Kennedy NHS	13	5	2,600
Agate Fossil Beds NM	19	6	3,167
North Cascades NP, Lake Chelan NRA, Ross Lake NRA	374	101	3,703
Capulin Volcano NM	54	12	4,500
War in the Pacific NHP	65	13	5,000
Andrew Johnson NHS	45	8	5,625
Allegheny Portage Railroad NHS	189	30	6,300
Effigy Mounds NM	96	14	6,857
Mesa Verde NP	665	90	7,389
Navajo NM	102	12	8,500

Oregon Caves NM	91	10	9,100
Glacier NP	2,137	202	10,579
Greenbelt Park	212	18	11,778
Fort Sumter NM	338	26	13,000
Natural Bridges NM	152	11	13,818
Cuyahoga Valley NRA	2,065	134	15,410
Johnstown Flood NMem	132	8	16,500
White Sands NM	354	19	18,632
Capitol Reef NP	633	31	20,419
Curecanti NRA	1,091	48	22,729
Hot Springs NP	1,523	61	24,967
Salem Maritime NHS	724	26	27,846
Arches NP	770	24	32,083
Point Reyes NS	2,620	64	40,938
Cape Cod NS	5,153	99	52,051
[etc.]			
Chattahoochee River NRA	2,841	39	72,846
Blue Ridge Parkway	17,910	242	74,008
City of Rocks NRes	84	1	84,000
Golden Gate NRA	16,723	198	84,460
Cedar Breaks NM	508	6	84,667
Gauley NRA, Bluestone NSR	182	2	91,000
Castle Clinton NM	1,297	9	144,111
Fort Point NHS	1,501	10	150,100
John D. Rockefeller, Jr., Memorial Parkway	1,330	7	190,000
Muir Woods NM	1,521	7	217,286

Source: Derived from Appendix 6-1. Does not include twenty parks reporting either "0" visits or "0" FTEs. Sample includes the first ten parks, the last ten, and every tenth park in between. A complete listing for all parks for Appendixes 6-2, 6-3, 7-1, 7-2, and 7-3 is available for $5.00 from the publisher (University of Illinois Press, ATTN: Business Office, 1325 South Oak Street, Champaign, IL 61820).

a. Readers are cautioned to use these calculations with care, remembering that perhaps half of a park staff has no regular duties involving visitor contacts. In many parks, however, the maintenance staff are the people most regularly seen by visitors (such as those handling campground maintenance.) In other parks (such as smallish historic sites) almost everyone has visitor contacts. This index of visitors-per-FTE is, however, valuable for the wide variations it reveals, particularly at the extremes. A more refined index may help explain the differences or suggest needed staffing adjustments.

Appendix 8

Systemwide Occupational Summary

Code[a]	Occupation	Full-time Permanent	All Other	Seasonal[b]
0025	Park Management/Ranger[c]	3,281	2,105	237
4749	Maintenance Mechanic	1,558	496	249
0318	Secretary	681	56	9
0083	Police[d]	619	0	0
0303	Miscellaneous Clerk & Assistant	511	154	10
0401	General Biological Science	345	30	4
5716	Engineering Equipment Operation	290	27	20
5703	Motor Vehicle Operating	272	134	71
0203	Personnel Clerical & Assistance	227	15	4
0322	Clerk-Typist	195	146	9
0503	Financial Clerical & Assistance	182	12	1
0807	Landscape Architecture	176	28	1
0341	Administrative Officer	172	2	0
1640	Facility Management	165	1	0
0808	Architecture	153	24	2
4607	Carpentry	145	79	26
0170	History	130	50	6
5003	Gardening	129	9	5
1102	Contracting	129	2	0
0334	Computer Specialist	128	19	3
0193	Archeology	120	64	4
0810	Civil Engineering	119	8	1
1105	Purchasing	119	3	1
5823	Automotive Mechanic	112	10	8
3502	Laboring	111	674	37
2805	Electrician	109	15	11
1016	Museum Specialist & Technician	100	137	10
5705	Tractor Operation	98	30	33

0301	Miscellaneous Administration	97	26	0
1015	Museum Curator	97	11	0
1101	General Business & Industry	97	10	1
0201	Personnel Management	96	2	0
0561	Budget Clerical & Assistance	94	8	0
0560	Budget Analyst	91	1	0
2005	Supply Clerical & Technician	79	5	2
4742	Utility Systems Repairing and Operating	78	6	11
4102	Painting	75	17	10
5803	Heavy Mobile Equipment Mechanic	75	1	1
0023	Outdoor Recreation Planning	72	30	0
0326	Office Automation	65	41	1
3603	Masonry	63	59	12
1010	Exhibits Specialist	62	4	3
1170	Realty	59	2	0
0802	Engineering Technician	57	28	1
0099	General Student Trainee	54	26	2
0525	Accounting Technician	54	0	0
4206	Plumbing	53	7	5
0305	Mail and Files	52	13	0
1106	Procurement Clerical & Assistance	51	7	0
0801	General Engineering	50	2	0
3566	Custodial Worker	49	57	6
0186	Social Service Aid & Assistant	48	3	1
0085	Security Guard	47	6	0
0408	Ecology	45	10	1
0212	Personnel Staffing	44	0	0
0335	Computer Clerk & Assistant	40	14	2
0028	Environmental Protection Specialist	40	2	0
0260	Equal Employment Opportunity	38	2	0
1001	General Arts and Information	37	17	3
5042	Tree Trimming	37	8	0
1084	Visual Information	37	4	0
0404	Biological Technician	35	213	11
0510	Accounting	35	0	0
0343	Management Analysis	34	2	0
0018	Safety and Occupational Health Management	33	0	0
0345	Program Analysis	32	4	0
5786	Small Craft Operating	30	12	7
0392	General Communications	29	6	2
0830	Mechanical Engineering	29	3	0
5408	Sewage Disposal Plant Operating	28	4	8
1082	Writing and Editing	28	3	0
1315	Hydrology	28	3	0

Appendix 8, continued

Code[a]	Occupation	Full-time Permanent	All Other	Seasonal[b]
4701	Miscellaneous General Maintenance and Operations Work	28	1	6
0462	Forestry Technician	27	85	10
4605	Wood Crafting	27	0	6
1035	Public Affairs	25	3	0
1350	Geology	24	3	5
5409	Water Treatment Plant Operating	24	1	1
0304	Information Receptionist	23	8	3
1371	Cartographic Technician	23	5	0
0486	Wildlife Biology	22	13	3
0230	Employee Relations	22	1	0
0856	Electronics Technician	22	0	0
5406	Ultility Systems Operating	21	3	3
2604	Electronics Mechanic	21	3	1
1171	Appraising and Assessing	21	1	0
0501	Financial Administration	20	0	0
0340	Program Management	19	2	0
4104	Sign Painting	19	1	2
6907	Warehouse Working	18	2	2
1071	Audio-Visual Production	18	2	0
1301	General Physical Science	18	1	0
0235	Employee Development	17	0	0
5201	Miscellaneous Occupations	16	14	10
0899	Engineering and Architecture Student Trainee	16	2	0
0544	Payroll	15	3	0
2001	General Supply	15	1	0
0850	Electrical Engineering	15	1	0
3703	Welding	15	0	1
0332	Computer Operation	14	5	0
4204	Pipefitting	14	0	0
0344	Management Clerical & Assistance	13	2	0
1712	Training Instruction	13	1	0
0221	Position Classification	13	1	0
1811	Criminal Investigating	13	0	0
0530	Cash Processing	12	13	0
1411	Library Technician	12	9	2
0817	Surveying Technician	12	5	0
0809	Construction Control	12	3	0

0188	Recreation Specialist	12	0	0
0437	Horticulture	12	0	0
5801	Miscellaneous Trans/Mobile Equipment Maintenance	11	3	0
1173	Housing Management	11	2	0
0819	Environmental Engineering	11	0	0
2810	Electrician (High Voltage)	11	0	0
0399	Administrative and Office Support Student Trainee	10	18	0
5701	Miscellaneous Trans/Mobile Equipment Operating	10	11	2
5001	Miscellaneous Plant and Animal Worker	10	8	4
0818	Engineering Drafting	10	7	0
1087	Editorial Assistant	10	4	0
0963	Legal Instruments Examining	10	0	0
1710	Education and Vocational Training	10	0	1
0391	Communications Management	10	0	0
5306	Air Conditioning	10	0	0
1083	Technical Writing	9	1	1
0342	Support Services Administrative	9	1	0
1410	Librarian	8	4	0
7404	Cooking	8	4	0
0190	General Anthropology	8	2	0
5048	Animal Caretaking	7	9	2
5788	Deckhand	7	5	0
0189	Recreation Aid and Assistant	7	3	3
5002	Farming	7	1	0
1370	Cartography	7	1	0
1715	Vocational Rehabilitation	6	13	0
5806	Mobile Equipment Servicing	6	7	1
1421	Archives Technician	6	7	0
0101	Social Science	6	4	0
1060	Photography	6	3	0
5334	Marine Machinery Mechanic	6	1	0
0430	Botany	6	1	0
2181	Aircraft Operation	6	1	0
3806	Sheet Metal Mechanic	6	0	0
5309	Heating/Boiler Plant Equipment Mechanic	6	0	0
0361	Equal Opportunity Assistance	6	0	0
0020	Community Planning	5	3	0
0688	Sanitarian	5	2	1
3910	Motion Picture Production	5	2	2
0007	Corrections Officer	5	2	0
5210	Rigging	5	1	0

Appendix 8, continued

Code[a]	Occupation	Full-time Permanent	All Other	Seasonal[b]
0482	Fishery Biology	5	1	0
0081	Fire Protection and Prevention	5	1	2
0499	Biological Science Student Trainee	5	1	0
1420	Archivist	5	1	0
1726	Secondary Teaching	5	0	0
5423	Sandblasting	5	0	1
5401	Miscellaneous Industrial Equipment Operating	5	0	0
0233	Labor Relations	5	0	0
5352	Industrial Equipment Mechanic	5	0	0
4737	General Equipment Mechanic	5	0	0
1740	Education Services	5	0	0
1311	Physical Science Technician	4	20	0
0540	Voucher Examining	4	3	0
5026	Pest Control	4	3	2
0610	Nurse	4	3	1
2151	Dispatching	4	1	0
0021	Community Planning Technician	4	1	0
0394	Communications Clerical	4	1	0
1054	Theater Specialist	4	0	0
4414	Offset Photography	4	0	0
4843	Navigation Aids Repairing	4	0	0
0880	Mining Engineering	4	0	0
1373	Land Surveying	4	0	0
0505	Financial Management	4	0	0
3830	Blacksmithing	4	0	0
1702	Education and Training Technician	3	7	0
0184	Sociology	3	5	0
1020	Illustrating	3	4	1
0150	Geography	3	4	0
0350	Equipment Operator	3	3	0
1412	Tech Information Services	3	2	0
0950	Paralegal Specialist	3	1	0
3801	Miscellaneous Metal Work	3	1	0
0312	Clerk-Senographer & Reporter	3	1	0
6904	Tools and Parts Attending	3	0	0
2003	Supply Program Management	3	0	0
1530	Statistician	3	0	0
8610	Small Engine Mechanic	3	0	1
0142	Manpower Development	3	0	0

0090	Guide	3	0	3
0460	Forestry	3	0	0
1670	Equipment Specialist	3	0	0
0698	Environmental Health Technician	3	0	1
0855	Electronics Engineering	3	0	0
0102	Social Science Aid & Technician	2	99	0
1316	Hydrologic Technician	2	8	0
1099	Information & Arts Student Trainee	2	2	0
0382	Telephone Operating	2	1	0
1199	Business & Industry Student Trainee	2	1	0
0454	Range Conservation	2	1	1
1360	Oceanography	2	1	0
0029	Environmental Protection Assistant	2	1	0
9924	Able Seaman	2	1	2
2101	Transportation Specialist	2	0	0
0457	Soil Conservation	2	0	0
0080	Security Administration	2	0	0
0803	Safety Engineering	2	0	0
0389	Radio Operating	2	0	0
1107	Property Disposal Clerical & Technician	2	0	0
1104	Property Disposal	2	0	0
1152	Production Control	2	0	0
0434	Plant Pathology	2	0	0
4417	Offset Press Operating	2	0	0
4401	Miscellaneous Printing and Reproduction	2	0	0
2601	Miscellaneous Electrical Equipment Installation and Maintenance	2	0	0
1340	Meteorology	2	0	0
3414	Machining	2	0	0
2010	Inventory Management	2	0	0
1810	General Investigating	2	0	0
4740	General Facility Management	2	0	0
1160	Financial Analysis	2	0	0
5415	Air Conditioning Equipment Operating	2	0	0
0360	Equal Opportunity Compliance	2	0	0
5313	Elevator Mechanic	2	0	0
5876	Electromotive Equipment Mechanic	2	0	0
2854	Electrical Equipment Repairing	2	0	0
0110	Economist	2	0	0
3653	Asphalt Work	2	0	0
0471	Agronomy	2	0	0
0470	Soil Science	1	2	0
0414	Entomology	1	2	0

Appendix 8, continued

Code[a]	Occupation	Full-time Permanent	All Other	Seasonal[b]
4754	Cemetery Caretaking	1	2	0
9961	Oiler Diesel	1	1	1
0393	Communications Specialist	1	1	0
9931	Chief Engineer	1	1	1
5402	Boiler Plant Operating	1	1	0
4402	Bindery Work	1	1	0
4604	Wood Working	1	0	0
2132	Travel	1	0	0
1140	Trade Specialist	1	0	0
2030	Distribution Facilities and Storage Management	1	0	0
1531	Statistical Assistant	1	0	0
3911	Sound Recording	1	0	0
6610	Small Arms Repairing	1	0	0
0019	Safety Technician	1	0	0
5706	Road Sweeper	1	0	0
1654	Printing Management	1	0	0
0351	Printing Clerical	1	0	0
0435	Plant Physiology	1	0	0
1310	Physics	1	0	0
0881	Petroleum Engineering	1	0	0
1515	Operations Research	1	0	0
1051	Music Specialist	1	0	0
4801	Miscellaneous General Equipment Maintenance	1	0	0
5301	Miscellaneous Industrial Equipment Maintenance	1	0	0
4601	Miscellaneous Woodwork	1	0	0
0302	Messenger	1	0	0
1520	Mathematics	1	0	0
9902	Master	1	0	1
4804	Locksmithing	1	0	0
5311	Locksmithing	1	0	0
9905	First Officer	1	0	1
5326	Drawbridge Repairing	1	0	0
5222	Diving	1	0	0
5725	Crane Operator	1	0	0
1802	Compliance Inspection & Support	1	0	0
0998	Claims Clerical Examining	1	0	0
1320	Chemistry	1	0	0

4606	Carpentry (Miscellaneous)	1	0	0
1176	Building Management	1	0	0
0511	Auditing	1	0	0
1056	Art Specialist	1	0	0
1801	General Inspection, Investigation, and Compliance	1	0	0
0699	Medical and Health Student Trainee	1	0	0
5737	Locomotive Engineering	0	8	0
3506	Summer Aid/Student Aid	0	6	0
5438	Elevator Operating	0	4	0
0199	Social Science Student Trainee	0	2	0
0410	Zoology	0	1	0
0701	Veterinary Medical Science	0	1	0
0299	Personnel Management Student Trainee	0	1	0
3606	Roofing	0	1	0
0455	Range Technician	0	1	0
0180	Psychology	0	1	0
3501	Miscellaneous General Service and Support Work	0	1	0
1750	Instructional Systems	0	1	0
0356	Data Transcriber	0	1	0
1550	Computer Science Student Trainee	0	1	0

Source: Computer printout from NPS PAY/PERS report system, Program-ID. PQP016, dated January 3, 1992.

a. Used governmentwide.
b. Included in other totals; all are subject to furlough.
c. The NPS ranger force having job titles of park ranger, superintendent, ranger (law enforcement), park manager, and so on.
d. U.S. Park Police. Located in the District of Columbia, Gateway NRA (N.Y., N.J.) and Golden Gate NRA (Calif.).

Bibliography

Albright, Horace M. *Origins of National Park Service Administration of Historic Sites.* Philadelphia: Eastern National Park and Monument Association, 1971.

———, as told to Robert Cahn. *The Birth of the National Park Service: The Founding Years, 1913–33.* Salt Lake City: Howe Brothers, 1985.

———, Russell E. Dickenson, and William Penn Mott, Jr. *The National Park Service: The Story behind the Scenery.* Las Vegas: KC Publications, 1987.

Brower, Kenneth. *Micronesia: Island Wilderness.* New York: Seabury Press, 1975.

Brown, William F. *Islands of Hope: Parks and Recreation in Environmental Crisis.* Washington, D.C.: National Recreation and Park Association, 1971.

Cahn, Robert. *Will Success Spoil the National Parks?* Boston: Christian Science Monitor, 1968.

Chase, Alston. *Playing God in Yellowstone: The Destruction of America's First National Park.* San Diego: Harcourt Brace Jovanovich, 1987.

DiIulio, John J., Jr., Gerald Garvey, and Donald F. Kettl. *Improving Government Performance: An Owner's Manual.* Washington, D.C.: Brookings Institution, 1993.

Everhart, William C. *The National Park Service.* Boulder, Colo.: Westview Press, 1983.

Foresta, Ronald. *America's National Parks and Their Keepers.* Washington, D.C.: Resources for the Future, 1985.

Galbraith, John Kenneth. *The Culture of Contentment.* New York: Houghton Mifflin, 1992.

Garrison, Lemuel A. *The Making of a Ranger: Forty Years with the National Parks.* Salt Lake City: Howe Brothers, 1983.

Gore, Al. *Earth in the Balance: Ecology and the Human Spirit.* New York: Houghton-Mifflin, 1992.

———. *From Red Tape to Results: Creating a Government That Works Better and Costs Less.* Report of the National Performance Review. Washington, D.C.: Government Printing Office, 1993.

Hamilton-Paterson, James. *The Great Deep: The Sea and Its Thresholds.* New York: Random House, 1992.

Hartzog, George B., Jr. *Battling for the National Parks.* Mt. Kisco, N.Y.: Moyer Bell, 1988.

Hogenauer, Alan K., "Gone but Not Forgotten: The Delisted Units of the National Park System," *George Wright Forum* vol. 8, no. 4 (1991).

Holland, F. Ross. *Idealists, Scoundrels, and the Lady: An Insider's View of the Statue of Liberty–Ellis Island Project.* Urbana: University of Illinois Press, 1993.

Hummel, Don. *Stealing the National Parks: The Destruction of Concessions and Park Access.* Bellevue, Wash.: Free Enterprise Press, 1987.

Investing in Park Futures: A Blueprint for Tomorrow. Washington, D.C.: National Parks and Conservation Association, 1988.

Kaufman, Herbert F. *The Forest Ranger: A Study in Administrative Behavior.* Baltimore: Johns Hopkins University Press, 1960.

Lee, Ronald F. *Family Tree of the National Park System.* Philadelphia: Eastern National Park and Monument Association, 1972.

Linenthal, Edward Tabor. *Sacred Ground: Americans and Their Battlefields.* 2d ed. Urbana: University of Illinois Press, 1993.

Maclean, Norman. *A River Runs through It and Other Stories.* New York: Pocket Books, 1976.

Mantell, Michael A., ed. *Managing National Park System Resources: A Handbook on Legal Duties, Opportunities, and Tools.* Washington, D.C.: Conservation Foundation, 1990.

National Parks for a New Generation: Visions, Realities, Prospects. Washington, D.C.: Conservation Foundation, 1985.

National Parks for the Future. Washington, D.C.: Conservation Foundation, 1972.

National Parks for the 21st Century: The Vail Agenda. Report and Recommendations to the Director of the National Park Service. Document no. D-726. Washington, D.C.: National Park Service, 1992.

Osborne, David, and Ted Gaebler. *Reinventing Government: How the Entrepreneurial Spirit Is Transforming the Public Sector from Schoolhouse to Statehouse, City Hall to the Pentagon.* Reading, Mass.: Addison-Wesley, 1992.

Rockefeller, Stephen C., and John C. Elder, eds. *Spirit and Nature: Why the Environment Is a Religious Issue.* Boston: Beacon Press, 1992.

Rothman, Hal. *Preserving Different Pasts: The American National Monuments.* Urbana: University of Illinois Press, 1989.

Runte, Alfred. *National Parks: The American Experience.* Lincoln: University of Nebraska Press, 1979.

Sax, Joseph L. *Mountains without Handrails: Reflections on the National Parks.* Ann Arbor: University of Michigan Press, 1980.

Sholly, Dan R., with Steven M. Newman. *Guardians of Yellowstone: An Intimate Look at the Challenges of Protecting America's Foremost Wilderness Park.* New York: William Morrow, 1991.

Simon, David J., ed. *Our Common Lands: Defending the National Parks.* Washington, D.C.: Island Press, 1988.

The National Parks: Index 1989. Office of Public Affairs and the Division of Publications, National Park Service. GPO:1990—262-098/00001. Washington, D.C.: Government Printing Office, 1990.

The National Parks: Shaping the System. Division of Publications and the Employee Development Division, National Park Service. GPO:1991—281-952/20004. Washington, D.C.: Government Printing Office, 1991.

Tilden, Freeman. *Interpreting Our Heritage.* Chapel Hill: University of North Carolina Press, 1967.

———. *The National Parks.* New York: Alfred A. Knopf, 1976.

Udall, Stewart L. *The Quiet Crisis and the Next Generation.* Layton, Utah: Gibbs-Smith, 1988.

U.S. Department of the Interior, *Budget Justifications, F.Y. 1995: National Park Service.* Washington, D.C.: National Park Service, 1994.

Wirth, Conrad L. *Parks, Politics, and the People.* Norman: University of Oklahoma Press, 1980.

Index

DWIGHT F. RETTIE joined the National Park Service in 1975 and retired from it in 1986, at which time he was chief of the policy development office in Washington, D.C. From 1971 to 1975 Rettie was executive director of the National Recreation and Park Association, and before that he directed a group of grant-in-aid programs in the U.S. Department of Housing and Urban Development to help local governments buy parks and open space and support local historic preservation. Before going to HUD, he was staff assistant to the under secretary of the Interior. Earlier, he worked for the U.S. Fish and Wildlife Service and the Bureau of Land Management. He began a federal career as a lookout-smokechaser and then fire dispatcher for the U.S. Forest Service in western Montana. A graduate of Yale University in political science, Rettie has a master's degree from the University of California at Berkeley.

STEWART L. UDALL is a former three-term congressman from Arizona and served as secretary of the Interior during the administrations of Presidents John F. Kennedy and Lyndon B. Johnson. A lawyer who lives in Santa Fe, New Mexico, he is the author of several books on conservation and has recently written a book relating to his work representing people injured by the nation's nuclear weapons program.